*Meditation for Therapists
and their Clients*

Meditation for Therapists

and their Clients

C. Alexander Simpkins

Annellen M. Simpkins

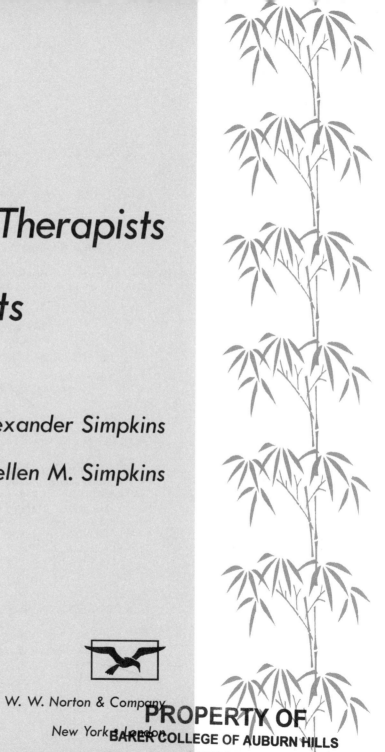

W. W. Norton & Company

New York • London

For information about permission to reproduce selections from this book, write to Permissions,
W. W. Norton & Company, Inc., 500 Fifth Avenue, New York, NY 10110

For information about special discounts for bulk purchases, please contact W. W. Norton Special Sales
at specialsales@wwnorton.com or 800-233-4830

Manufacturing by Malloy Printing
Book design by Jonathan Lippincott
Production manager: Leeann Graham

Library of Congress Cataloging-in-Publication Data

Simpkins, C. Alexander.
    Meditation for therapists and their clients / C. Alexander Simpkins,
Annellen M. Simpkins.—1st ed.
        p. ; cm.
    "Norton professional book."
    Includes bibliographical references and index.
    ISBN 978-0-393-70565-2 (pbk.)
    1. Meditation—Therapeutic use. I. Simpkins, Annellen M. II. Title.
    [DNLM: 1. Behavior Therapy—methods. 2. Meditation—psychology.
WM 425.5.R3 S612m 2009]
    RC489.M43S56 2009
    615.8'52—dc22   2008033343

W. W. Norton & Company, Inc., 500 Fifth Avenue, New York, NY 10110
www.wwnorton.com

W. W. Norton & Company, Ltd., Castle House, 75/76 Wells Street, London WIT 3QT

1 2 3 4 5 6 7 8 9 0

Dedication

We dedicate this book to our parents, Nat and Carmen Simpkins and Herb and Naomi Minkin; to our children, C. Alexander Simpkins Jr. and Alura and Anthony Aguilera; and to our clients who have been open to learning and growing with these methods.

About the Cover Artist

Carmen Z. Simpkins's abstract expressionist paintings suggest mood, movement, and mysticism. Simpkins painted for 80 years. Her first solo show took place in Camden, Maine in 1962, at the Broadlawn Gallery. She has exhibited throughout the world, and her works are in private collections in Europe and the United States. For more than 30 years, Simpkins sold her work through her studio/gallery. Currently she is retired, living in Camden, Maine.

Contents

Introduction   1

PART I: THE SOURCE: EAST AND WEST   9
1: Opening to Meditation   13
2: The Great Meditation Traditions   19
3: Scientific Efficacy and Neuroscience Research   42

PART II: THE ELEMENTS: TOOLS AND TECHNIQUES   61
4: Mobilizing Motivation   67
5: Developing the Tools   75
6: Breathing: Unifying Mind and Body   90
7: One-Pointed Awareness and Concentration   99
8: The Eightfold Path: The Method to Travel   108
9: Mindfulness: Of Body, Emotions, and Thoughts   121
10: Working with Qi: Activating and Centering   132
11: Engaging the Symbolic Through Mandalas and Mantras   149
12: Empty the Mind   161
13: Meditation Through Ritual and Art   169

PART III: BALANCE IN THE VOID: APPLYING MEDITATION   181
14: Transforming Through Emotions and Moods   188
15: The Way to Stress Reduction   212

16: Beyond Fear and Anxiety   232

17: Overcoming Addictions and Impulse Problems   251

18: Loving Relationships: Couples and Families   272

19: Enlightened Therapy: Facilitating the Meditative Process   290

References   301

Index   315

Introduction

Taking your own body and mind as the laboratory, see if you can use these different techniques: that is to say, engage in some thorough-going research on your own mental functioning, and examine the possibility of making some positive changes within yourself.

(Gyatso [The Dalai Lama] 1995, p. 4)

Meditation is widely accepted today as having many health benefits. An ever-growing body of research reveals that meditation can be a valuable therapeutic tool. Meditation has been tested for particular problems such as stress (Rausch, Gramling, & Auerbach, 2006) depression (Ma & Teasdale, 2004), and addictions (Bowen et al., 2006), to name just a few. Neuroscience research has provided further evidence by uncovering some of the neural correlates (Cahn & Polich, 2006; Newberg & Iversen, 2005; Siegel, 2007). With promising findings, psychotherapists can confidently incorporate meditation methods into their practice.

Meditation for Therapists and Their Clients offers an in-depth exploration of what meditation is, how to do it, and how to use it. This book, written for health care professionals, offers new methods that can be added into the treatment regime. Therapists will find meditation personally helpful to sharpen clinical acumen and for personal growth. The book also directly addresses the needs of clients, to help them learn these practices and make them their own.

Benefits of Meditation for Therapists

When the waves are choppy,

It is difficult for the moon to appear.

(Korean Zen master Chinul [1158–1210] quoted in Buswell, 1991, p. 27)

In modern times, as the world moves deeper into the digital age, we are influenced by its principles of linearity and sequential relationships. Rational thought is the most commonly used tool, and tends to follow linear patterns, organizing itself with beginnings and endings, and by first and last, biggest and smallest, and so forth. By contrast, psychological problems engage many levels at once. The emotional, cognitive, and behavioral aspects are just part of the problem. Deeper exploration often reveals that there are broader interconnections with cultural, economic, physical, and interpersonal levels. The psychotherapeutic process ultimately invokes a broader and more topological range. Successful treatment works on many levels at once, evoking whatever is needed for the problem at hand.

Therapists continue to search for better methods to expand and improve therapeutic effectiveness. Meditation offers a global, nonlinear topography. It works primarily with a nonrational, intuitive type of understanding that attempts to break out of the limitations brought about by rational thought and ethnocentric or ego-centered perspectives. It encompasses a long and well-developed history of techniques that are teachable and doable, open to anyone who would like to try. These methods can be seamlessly added into most therapeutic regimes, to offer new possibilities that access altered parts of consciousness to facilitate the process.

Successful psychotherapy reaches deep into the inner mind, altering life profoundly. But therapeutic methods sometimes become disconnected from the true essence if performed superficially. Meditation engages the "heart-mind," touching the human spirit as part of the greater universe. Through meditative experiencing, people can reconnect and become grounded in the natural humanity that is latent within us all.

Therapists are in a unique position to learn meditation. The psychological training combines harmoniously with the skills of meditation, drawing on the educated ability to observe mental processes objectively. Meditation's time-honored methods may enhance skills with attention and concentration. And meditation adds new techniques, such as working with breathing, symbols, sounds, and body positioning.

Therapists who meditate may improve their ability to think clearly. Senses become more acute, awareness is sharpened, and intuitive skills are honed. And therapists' emotions become more stable, so they may more accurately reflect the client's emotions (Nielsen & Kasznlak, 2006). Solutions to problems surface from the tranquil pools of insight found in meditation. Caregivers may find all of these skills especially helpful for psychotherapy.

Meditation can assist the therapeutic process from the very first session. Psychiatrist and hypnotherapist Milton Erickson often advised therapists to look for the real problem, which often is not what the client first presents. Moreover, sometimes the real problem is difficult to discern. Therapists who meditate develop clear, insightful understanding that improves discernment. This skill may help them to perceive beyond the presenting difficulty to discover the real problem, so that correct treatment can then follow.

The practice of meditation leads to greater sensitivity and use of the unconscious. Therapists need to know when to step in versus when to take no action and let nature take its course. Centered in the meditative moment, a balanced approach to problems is more likely to emerge, which is flexible, empathic, and compassionate.

Meditation also offers a worldview that differs from the typical Western psychological theories. Eastern paradigms add new dimensions and alternative interpretations. When the therapist can reframe the client's situation, potentials open up so that creative interventions spontaneously come to mind. Stubborn patterns may transform, problems resolve, and obstacles diminish.

Therapists may become stressed from the demands of their work, and this inner turmoil can interfere with their professional effectiveness. Research shows repeatedly that meditation reduces stress in health care professionals, so it may be helpful for the therapist's personal wellness (Oman, Hedberg, & Thoresen, 2006; Shapiro, Astin, Bishop, Cordova, 2005).

Benefits of Meditation for Clients

When you are sitting in the middle of your own problem, which is more real
to you: your problem or you yourself? The awareness that you are here, right
now, is the ultimate fact.

(S. Suzuki 1979, p. 40)

Research has shown that meditation can be successfully incorporated as part of the
therapy to help the process (Elkins, Marcus, Rajab, & Durgam, 2005). Meditation
may be performed between sessions, extending the influence of therapy into daily life.
Meditation can be done as little as a few minutes a day to set a process in motion.
Often, once people learn how to meditate, they naturally find themselves able to sustain it for longer periods of time.

Meditation helps to alter cognitive patterns. This is a valuable ability for therapies that work directly with attention, concentration, and perception. Skills learned
from meditation may help the therapist and client work successfully with a broad
range of mental functioning. Meditation tends to open perspectives and reduce rigidi-
ties. As a result, flexibility and receptivity to new possibilities usually develops. Meditating leads to better self-control, making it easier to incorporate the cognitive
restructuring the therapist presents in the sessions. Thus, therapeutic intervention
may be easier to give and receive, allowing it to have a more powerful impact.

One of meditation's most well-known and well-researched benefits is for calming
and centering. Regular meditators feel better and happier, getting greater satisfaction
from even the small things in their lives. Integrated with conventional forms of therapy, meditation will help clients progress faster and have greater comfort in the
process.

About this Book

The book is organized into three parts: Part I, The Source: East and West, Part II,
The Elements: Tools and Techniques, and Part III, Balance in the Void: Applying
Meditation.

Part I: The Source: East and West

From the roots come the essence (Zen saying), and so the first chapter offers a traditional doorway into the process. Chapter 2 gives a brief tour of the roots of meditation in the Eastern philosophies of Yoga, Buddhism, Zen, and Daoism. The conceptual frameworks from these philosophies gave rise to the forms of meditation practiced today. The roots are different from our Western foundations, so understanding these Eastern paradigms may extend the horizon of possibility with new potentials.

Chapter 3 presents some of the recent developments in research and neuroscience that have helped ground meditation in a scientific context as an efficacious method for treatment. Research supports the usefulness of meditation for facilitating mental health. Neuroscience has added a map for the territory that unlocks some of the mysteries of mind and brain.

Part II: The Elements: Tools and Techniques

First and foremost, meditation is an experience. Therapists in training often undergo their own therapy. Similarly, meditation is usually taught through personal practice. Thus, therapists and clients who plan to use meditation should experience it for themselves. There are many pathways into meditation, and people vary in which techniques work best for them. Chapters in Part II give step-by-step instructions in a varied sampling of some of the most important and therapeutically relevant, traditional meditation methods. One method will open the door to another, so that even though some methods may seem easier at first, with time and practice, more ways will become accessible.

Careful preparation will enhance early meditation experiences. Chapter 4 provides helpful guidance for readying oneself for meditation. Chapter 5 warms up the mental circuits with exercises to train the attention, concentration, visualization abilities, and the unconscious. Then in Chapters 6 to 13, readers are carefully taught how to meditate, with time-honored methods from the great Eastern traditions. Techniques are given, as is the rationale behind each, to give a deeper understanding that will lead to individualizing for therapeutic purposes. This section offers a variety of techniques and encourages experimentation for successful learning and application.

Part III: Balance in the Void: Applying Meditation

Meditational therapy is a field theory with all the parts coming together in their own unique pattern. Each chapter in Part III is part of the field, to be explored and developed fully in the context of a typical therapeutic problem. Therefore, we describe and discuss a range of theories and approaches so that therapists and clients will be able to broaden their approach as they naturally integrate the meditational theory into what they know and do. Specific meditation scripts are given along with case studies from the successful use of these meditation methods. Applications to common problems draw upon the varied meditation paradigms presented in Part I and meditation methods in Part II.

The book addresses problems that are commonly brought to the therapist's office: emotion and mood issues, stress, fears and anxiety, addictions and impulse control problems, and relationship concerns. The final chapter offers a meditative therapeutic approach to take the client through a transformation using these methods. Meditation includes methods to foster lasting change and a happy life, and instructions for integration are given throughout. With these templates in mind, readers will be able to adapt meditative methods for working with their clients' problems.

How to Use this Book

Some meditation traditions steer away from concepts, preferring to begin with experience as the foundation. Others utilize the study of the literature in the belief that concepts assist the process. We provide both experience and concepts in this book so that readers can gain a deeper, more complete understanding. Some people will want to read the theoretical sections before trying to meditate. But others may prefer to begin by trying to do it, and then fill out the experience afterwards with theoretical understanding. This is a matter of personal preference.

Our modern scientific orientation teaches us to test hypotheses without bias by putting assumptions in parentheses and letting the facts come into view. Similarly, when meditating, approach the concepts and the exercises with an open-minded attitude. Set judgments and preconceptions aside and allow new perspectives to emerge.

This book offers guidance to therapists on how to integrate meditation into treatment. We also offer meditation instructions that address the client directly. Therapists can apply these instructions with the client. We assume that they will use their therapeutic sensitivities to the client's reaction and needs just as they would when applying any therapeutic method. The instructions can be a basis for improvising as well. In this way, therapists can learn how and when to use meditation, and also be guided toward what to say. Therapists may also find the instructions personally helpful for incorporating meditation in to their own lives.

Whenever exercises are offered, we encourage you to do them. Read an exercise over twice and then set the book down to try it. Give yourself time and space to experience. Like any new skill, meditation responds to practice, so please be patient. As you come to understand the principles behind the methods, other applications may suggest themselves. Trust yourself and enjoy the process!

The Source: East and West

Inside and outside, they need each other
No black without white, no sister without brother.
We have no tomorrow, without today
Speech is not possible, without something to say
There are no wise ones without the fools
The nature of life is expressed in the dual.

(C. Alexander Simpkins)

Part I introduces meditation from two directions: East and West. Traditionally, meditation is taught in the context of particular philosophical belief systems with a spiritual intent to uplift and transform. The sources of meditation in the Eastern traditions include rich and thought-provoking conceptions that are very different from Western views. These underlying backgrounds will supplement the understanding of meditation and foster a better grasp of the concepts.

The West has made contributions to what is known about meditation; it is not exclusively an Eastern tradition. The West's understanding of meditation has developed over several centuries. Many studies have been done to elucidate the active factors that are taking place, what meditation does, and to speculate how it may work. There is now a large body of evidence pointing to meditation's therapeutic potential. Modern therapists, being aware of the importance of therapeutic efficacy, want to ensure that the therapeutic methods they employ have been empirically verified. Researchers have studied how meditation affects the brain, emotions, cognitions, and behaviors. Selections from these studies are given in Part I.

Nonspecific Factors

Thoughtful therapists can integrate findings from psychotherapeutic research with their own understandings, both learned and intuitive, to maximize the effectiveness of treatment. Early research showed that nonspecific factors such as hope, faith, trust, expectancy, therapeutic rationale, and experiences of mastery have an effect on therapeutic outcome (Frank, Hoehn-Saric, Imber, Liberman, & Stone, 1978). Later research showed that specific factors, such as cognitive-behavioral therapy for depression, affect therapeutic outcomes as well (Lambert, Shapiro, & Bergin, 1986). Thus, the 21st century therapist should be aware of and utilize both specific and nonspecific factors for best results.

Meditational therapy activates many of the nonspecific factors. Meditation and the theories that surround it offer hope, a rationale, and positive expectancies. Meditation has been applied to help people for more than 2,500 years. The long history of meditation along with contemporary research findings provide evidence for placing trust in these methods. Thus, the client can expect that it may be helpful now.

Meditation provides specific methods for the client to practice. These can be performed outside the office, between sessions, as well as during therapy. As clients become proficient with the skills, they develop mastery that can have a more general effect. Confidence from this mastery can engender an overall feeling of confidence.

One general result that meditation research shows across all types is that meditation brings about a feeling of well-being. This generalized effect could be considered a nonspecific factor of meditation.

An important question is whether all meditation methods are the same or are there important differences? Research has supported both positions, as Chapter 3 reveals. We believe that both specific and nonspecific factors are in play. This is similar to psychotherapy in general: nonspecific factors when combined with specific factors from methods can work well together for the best results. The philosophical background of the forms of meditation may activate specific factors. Research supports various positions.

Opening to Meditation

The great path has no gates,
Thousands of roads enter it.
When one passes through this gateless gate
He walks freely between heaven and earth.

(Mumon quoted in Reps, 1980, p. 114)

He had trained in the ultimate techniques of therapy. He knew the latest research findings. But he was always looking for the most recent methods to fill out his repertoire. He had read about the new research on meditation and had heard that there was a renowned Zen master with unusual healing abilities living quietly on the outskirts of the city. He could not rest until he met this Zen master.

He arrived at the master's doorstep and greeted him with his request to learn: You are famous for your powerful healing methods. Would you be willing to teach me? I know a lot about therapy. I have studied the classics, Freud, Jung, and Adler, and have added many modern methods as well. I am well versed in behavior therapy, NLP, cognitive approaches, and person-centered nondirective therapy. I have also been trained to hypnotize and guide clients into progressive relaxation. I am greatly experienced in all the latest therapeutic approaches but I am eager to learn your techniques.

The master smiled gently and answered quietly, "Ah yes, of course. Come in and have some tea!"

The student thought the master's invitation sounded promising, and so he said, "Well thank you. I would enjoy a cup of tea." He followed the master into a sparsely furnished room. He noticed the worn wooden floor covered by several small straw mats. A single, perfect flower sat in an earthenware vase on a simple, hand-hewn wood shelf. As he stooped down to enter the low doorway, unaware that the low door was intended to level people of all rank to enter the tearoom humbly, he said, "I know a lot about tea. I've sampled many kinds of tea, oolong tea, green tea, black tea, fermented tea, but my favorite tea is peppermint tea because it doesn't have any caffeine and its good for you. In fact, I like all kinds of herbal teas like chamomile, rosehips, and then there are healing teas like echinacea and goldenseal, burdock...."

When the student paused for a moment, he realized the master was already seated and had motioned him to sit down too. The student sat, and the master quietly began preparing the tea. As the master worked, the student looked down at the teacups and said, "Oh that's nice pottery. What dynasty? I collect pottery as a hobby. I like Tang Dynasty pottery, but I also think that porcelain Raku is very beautiful. Do you know that it is fired at a very high temperature, which makes it exceptionally hard? Korean Yi dynasty pottery is distinctive and individualized, but of course, modern styles can be very striking. Some of the new materials are interesting as well, and they don't break or wear out. I see that this teacup is not quite symmetrical. It seems a little imperfect."

He knew nothing of imperfect perfection.

As the student continued talking, the master began to pour tea into the student's cup. The student maintained a steady flow of conversation. "I wanted to ask what your philosophical beliefs are concerning psychology. Are you a materialist or a functionalist? And do you think that behavior is determined by genetics or do you believe environmental influences are stronger? I have given these matters quite a bit of thought and believe...." As he half-watched the tea fill the cup to the top and spill over the sides, he suddenly realized what was happening and shouted, "Master! Master! My cup is overflowing!"

"Yes," answered the Master softly. "As is your mind! First, empty your cup. Then it can be filled."

This traditional story (with modern characters and updating) is one of the classic introductions to Eastern meditation. Meditation was often taught through stories, and

Figure 1.1. The Empty Cup:
Empty your cup so that it
may be filled.
(Artists: C. Alexander & Annellen
Simpkins, San Diego, CA, 2007;
walnut burl and maple burl,
wood on wood)

this story illustrates the mindset for entry into meditation, one of the world's oldest and most well-respected traditions.

During a typical day filled with back-to-back therapy sessions, many thoughts with related connections fill the precious space granted us for attention to our work with clients. In the same way, attention jumps from one set of associations to another. Clear thinking is lost in a sea of associated ideas, rushing around. Even during less scheduled moments, when the mind could take some time to reflect, most people don't use the opportunity to stop and notice.

This situation can be changed through meditation, which goes to quiet depths, steering through the flood of conscious thought, navigating into calm seas, and revealing reality in its crystal-clear reflection. Here we find the ideal mindset for psychotherapy.

What is Meditation?

Who can find repose in a muddy world?
By lying still, it becomes clear.

(Dao De Jing quoted in Grigg, 1995, p. 35)

Meditation is a time for sitting quietly, seemingly doing nothing. In the empty moment, meditation can be discovered. To Westerners, sitting quietly and doing nothing is often seen as a waste of time. How can anything significant be accomplished by doing nothing? Or is it really doing nothing? The answers to these questions require a shift in perspective. When people are willing to experiment with this shift, a new world of possibility may open up. Meditation is a tool for experiencing clearly, resulting in a direct and immediate link between thought and action. What seems at first to be a nonactivity is in fact its own kind of activity.

People who do not know much about meditation often think of it in a limited sense, as deep thought or contemplation. *Webster's Dictionary* (1998) defines meditation similarly: "To reflect on; ponder. To engage in contemplation." From its long and rich early history, to its widespread and diverse practice today, meditation includes thinking, but it is a much broader endeavor. No standard definition includes all types of meditation. Attempting to confine it to a simple definition is like trying to summarize a play by Shakespeare in one sentence. Each of the major Eastern philosophies has its individual approach. There are many paths to choose from, and this book does not prescribe one approach over all others, but rather explores useful methods of meditation that can be applied to therapy.

A master of meditation will deny that meditation has a particular approach or even any techniques. Such statements may seem baffling, but the teacher is attempting to communicate the real meaning of meditation. Meditation must be experienced.

Therapists may be able to relate to this idea by recalling their beginner mind when they were first introduced to the field of psychotherapy. Perhaps it was a psychology course in college, where the different forms of therapy were described, or maybe an inspirational mentor. Later, after years of training and probably a period of time undergoing personal therapy, the therapist attained an experiential understanding. The concepts and theories may be helpful, but they cannot replace the transformational experience of the therapeutic process. The process is similar with meditation: The methods and techniques presented in this book are a pathway into meditation, but not the meditative experience itself. So, don't get lost in technique for technique's sake. Use the technique like a boat to cross the river. Once having arrived on the other shore, explore the territory.

Types of Meditation: Empty the Mind and Fill the Mind

Broadly considered, meditation methods fall into two categories: one method is intended to empty the mind of all thoughts, the other is intended to fill it with chosen thoughts (Simpkins & Simpkins, 1996). We use the term *mind* to represent mental processing, recognizing the close relation to brain activity, as modern neuroscience has revealed. Philosophical questions about the validity of mind as a real entity outside of its identity with brain (Churchland, 1988; Place, 1956) are debated by contemporary philosophers, cognitive scientists, and psychologists, but these issues are very old, having been tackled by the ancients as part of the rich philosophical theories of the East. Readers familiar with the issues may recognize these modern themes, recast in creative ways that offer helpful perspectives.

Daoist practitioners believe that through calm mental processing, empty of specific thought content, the spirit of the Dao—the creative principle that orders the universe—can be followed. On the other hand, certain Yoga and Buddhist meditation sects believe that filling the mind with wonderful, pure thoughts will raise practitioners to a more enlightened plane. There are appropriate situations for both approaches.

Some meditation styles teach meditators to withdraw from the external world. The rationale may vary; perhaps it stems from a belief that the world of humankind and its activities is transitory, imperfect, or even unreal. Therefore, to withdraw in some way from the world of events is a step toward a more fundamental reality. Taken to the extreme, people who hold this position may choose to withdraw into monasteries or live as hermits on mountains or in caves, to live a life that is pure and free from worldly concerns.

An opposite belief is that we live our lives alienated from ourselves and that filling the mind by fully immersing ourselves in our being will lead to an integrated wholeness, a revelation. The meditation style of Zen Buddhism teaches practitioners to give up the concept of a separation between thought and action, to unify and thereby live fully in the moment so that even mundane tasks can be used for profound meditation.

Meditation sometimes specifies what meditators should attend to. For some, the object of meditation is to direct attention to the inner realm. Thus, eyes are closed and meditators imagine or think about something within. Others focus on the outer realm, with instructions such as, "Think of a tree. Meditate on all aspects of it."

These qualities of meditation fall into the yin-yang pattern, the union of opposites, encompassing both, to bring about a higher consciousness. Meditation brings about this union, a balance among many factors. The ancient yin-yang symbol depicts this union of opposites: within the white there is black, and within the black there is white. The two sides intertwine, one with the other. When we explore the mind, the body is affected. When we work with the conscious mind, the unconscious mind becomes involved. As skill develops in meditation, the balance is found.

First and foremost, meditation is an experience. The experience is so highly valued that it is considered an inward "art." Though the meditator returns to the center within the self, paradoxically he or she may transcend the limitations imposed on the self. So we invite you to empty your cup and enter into the experience of meditation. There may you make new discoveries that will carry you through the therapeutic seas to a life of happiness and fulfillment.

2

The Great Meditation Traditions

It is good to know that the ancient thinkers required of us to realize the possibilities of the soul in solitude and silence, and to transform the flashing and fading moments of vision into a steady light, which could illumine the long years of life.

(Radhakrishnan, Vol. 2, 1923, p. 373)

Yoga, Daoism, Buddhism, and Zen are some of the great traditions from the East in which meditation methods are central. As religions and philosophies, these traditions succeed best when practiced with commitment to ethical action. Traditionally they were practiced together along with Confucianism in China, Japan, and Korea, to offer a path for every aspect of living. Similarly, open-minded Westerners can find creative ways to integrate these traditions within their own paradigms.

Each of these traditions is complex, with a long history of scholarly achievements that reaches beyond the scope of this book. Yoga centers, Daoist temples, and Buddhist or Zen monasteries offer lectures, classes, and retreats for those who might be interested in delving deeper into any of these traditions.

Yoga

Yoga is restraining the mind-stuff from taking various forms.

(Patanjali, *Yoga Sutras* quoted in Yutang, 1942, p. 121)

Yoga, originating in ancient India, is often associated in people's minds with the postures of Hatha Yoga. But Yoga is a larger set of meditative practices that may or may not include the use of physical postures. The word *Yoga* means to yoke or link the individual mind to the larger universe. It also means discipline. All forms of Yoga incorporate meditation, and all forms of meditation incorporate Yoga.

Yoga is a very ancient discipline, beginning before recorded history. Its root themes began to be referred to more clearly in the four *Vedas* (*Rig, Yajur, Sama,* and *Atharva*), or ancient Hindu texts (Panikkar, 2001). The Vedas are among the earliest surviving writings of Indian thought, believed to have been composed between 5000 and 2000 BC. *Rig Veda,* the best known, expresses spiritual knowledge in 1,028 lyrical hymns. Important Yoga themes are mentioned such as sacrifice, discipline, and praise for virtue and beauty as personified in nature.

Yoga was more explicitly referred to in the *Upanishads,* written between 800 and 600 BC. For example, the *Yoga Sattva,* included in the *Upanishads,* specifically refers to some aspects of Yoga such as posture, breathing exercise, and mental training (Simpkins & Simpkins, 2003a).

The best known systematic description of Yoga is the *Bhagavad-Gita,* a part of the larger Indian epic, the *Mahabharata.* Although its exact date is unknown, the *Bhagavad-Gita* (Deutsch, 1968) was composed later than the *Upanishads,* between the fifth and second centuries BC. Written as a dialogue between a warrior, Arjuna, and his charioteer, the God Krishna, this work shows the application of Yoga philosophy. Krishna's teachings define and explain the different branches of Yoga. Though the original context of the *Bhagavad-Gita* was a war between families for power, Yoga relates to all aspects of life. The *Bhagavad-Gita* shows how people can use Yoga discipline to take control of their lives in their own circumstances, to become what they want to be.

Modern Yoga philosophy also draws on the *Vedanta,* the later classical literature of India. The word *veda* means knowledge and *anta* refers to end or conclusion. Thus, the *Vedanta* is often translated as the culmination of knowledge. This most recent of the ancient texts contains interpretations of the earlier texts along with theoretical

Figure 2.1. *Dialogue between Krishna and Arjuna on the battlefield of Kurukshetra.* (from the Bhagavad Gita). Opaque watercolor and gold on paper, ca. 1820; 5–5/16" x 7–5/16." Pahari school, India, Himachal Pradesh, Guler. Edwin Binney III Collection, 1990: 1251. San Diego Museum of Art.

chapters about themes of the *Vedas.* These writings also contain clear references to Yoga and its practices (Simpkins & Simpkins, 2003a). *Vedanta* texts were added over the centuries. Vivekananda, one of the first to introduce the Eastern religions to the West, authored a modern *Vedanta* (Vivekananda, 1953; see Chapter 3).

The Eight Limbs

Patanjali was the first to formally gather the practices of Yoga into an ordered, consistent system, in his famous *Yoga Sutras*, compiled around AD 200. Yoga, as Patanjali explained, is not just for attaining a specific purpose but also is a method for living a healthy and fulfilling life. His concepts and general descriptions, originally of Raja Yoga, in one form or another are now part of Yoga systems today. His outline of the eight stages or limbs of Yoga set a pattern that all Yoga systems use. The system offers guidelines for leading a practitioner to establish a firm foundation and then climb step-by-step to enlightenment. The method provides eight groups of healthy and wholesome practices.

The first limb, known as the *yamas*, includes outlines for renouncing five types of negative actions: not to harm, lie, overindulge, steal, or be greedy. The second limb, the *niyamas*, includes five types of positive actions to perform: be pure and clean in mind, body, and spirit; cultivate self-awareness; practice a disciplined lifestyle; keep learning and developing; and incorporate faith into your life.

The third limb, *asanas*, consists of ways of moving and placing the body into specified positions to foster a process of relaxation, strength, and health. The fourth limb, breathing or *pranayama*, is the practice of breath control to be integrated with the postures as well as in everyday life. This limb begins the process of turning attention inwards and linking mind and body together.

The fifth limb is *pratyahara,* withdrawal of attention from the external world to turn attention to the spiritual realm within. This level teaches skills needed for meditation. The sixth limb, *dharana*, is one-pointed, focused concentration, an important meditative tool. Contemplation, *dhyana*, is the seventh limb, and the eighth limb is *samadhi*, happiness through oneness with the universe, enlightenment (Simpkins & Simpkins, 2003a).

Prana

Prana is a very real energy that helps to link the individual with the universal. Like the Chinese *Qi*, Prana is a vital energy that permeates everything and everyone. With each breath we take, we partake in universal energy. Breathing in tune with visualization plays a central part in some Yoga methods. Better control of the breath leads to good health and mastery over body and mind. Yoga practitioners can learn to control involuntary processes such as the heartbeat and body temperature, and perform feats of unusual strength and mind control that are impossible for people who do not practice Yoga. Meditation can have far-reaching and measurable effects, as yogis have shown through the ages.

Forms of Yoga

There are many types of Yoga. Each has developed into its own form, with some unique and some shared methods and philosophy. Hatha Yoga, widely practiced in the

West, combines postures with breath control and concentration. In Raja Yoga, higher consciousness is sought through directly training the mind with the will. Bhakti Yoga, the way of altruistic love, practices charitable, self-sacrificing, religious devotion. Personal limitations are transcended as the individual unselfishly helps others. Karma Yoga, the way of work, teaches ethics and values that can transform the meaning of everyday work. Then work offers happiness through service and fulfillment of one's destiny. Mantra Yoga, now incorporated into modern methods such as Transcendental Meditation (TM) and in Amida or Shin Buddhism, uses the repeated chanting of a mantra to help focus the mind and energy. Chanting "Om," Sanskrit for "Oneness," is the way to gain knowledge and destroy obstacles. Gnani Yoga uses philosophical concepts to transcend mundane consciousness through logic. Practitioners study philosophy and then meditate on the insights, transcending self to become part of the "Allness." By means of these and other methods, Yogis seek to unite with the greater whole, the true self.

Modern Yoga schools often offer varieties of traditional Yoga practices, some of which are being applied to therapy. For example, a form of Kundalini Yoga has recently been applied to psychiatry, couples therapy, and medicine (Shannahoff-Khalsa, 2006).

Yoga Meditation

Yoga meditation develops disciplined control of breath and movement, thought and action, tension and relaxation, leading to mastery of the mind. According to the Yoga teachings, as people learn to control their mind and body, they can take control of their life to direct it in positive ways. Through Yoga meditation people can make changes to bring about a healthy, ethical, and well-disciplined life. Techniques similar to Yoga are found in Tibetan Buddhism, Daoism, and Zen, through their practice of meditation, the cornerstone of Eastern philosophies.

Daoism

"One who knows Dao will surely penetrate the principle of things," said the spirit of the North Sea, "and one who penetrates the principle of things will surely understand their application in various situations."

(Chan, 1963, p. 307)

Daoism is an ancient philosophy from China. Over many centuries, Daoism evolved into a philosophy with practical applications to medicine and health as well as art, politics, architecture, and martial arts.

Daoism Evolves

Laozi (b. 604 BC) is the legendary founder of Daoism. The Chinese historian Ssu Ma Ch'ien wrote that Laozi's actual identity and personal history was mysterious, like the Dao itself. Laozi worked in the capital city as the Keeper of the Archives for the royal court of Chou (Ssu-Ma, 1994, pp. 145–186). This position gave him access to the classic texts that were kept in the archives. Laozi never opened a formal school, but true to Daoist philosophy, even though he did not form a school, students came to him. As time passed, Laozi became frustrated by the moral decay of the society around him, so he decided to leave the city for the unsettled west to become a hermit. He began his trip through the west city gate. The gatekeeper recognized him and begged him to leave some record of his wisdom. Laozi sat down and composed the 5,000-character book now known as the *Dao De Jing* (Legge, 1962). This small book of Eastern wisdom is the most translated book, next to the Bible. The gatekeeper was so moved by its content that he decided to leave with Laozi. The two disappeared together, never to be seen again.

Others carried forth Daoist philosophy. Zhuangzi and Leihzi both wrote about the Daoist approach to wisdom through a calm mind, attuned to the natural way of things

Figure 2.2. *Two people, one step. Laozi and the gatekeeper leave the city.*
(Artist: Kasumi, 1995; ink on paper; www.kasumifilms.com)

(Simpkins & Simpkins, 1999a, 2002). Daoism continued to grow in popularity through the centuries.

Daoist Alchemy

Alchemy emerged gradually in China, and joined seamlessly with Daoism. Based in the ancient Five Element theory, alchemy envisioned the universe as comprised of five fundamental elements: earth, wind, metal, fire, and water. Each element restrains or overcomes another element, while each element also promotes or stimulates a different element. Thus, the interaction among elements is continual transformation and change. This diagram has been used as a basis for diagnosis and treatment in Eastern medicine.

Daoist theory led naturally to practical alchemical applications for transforming one thing into another. The Daoist alchemists experimented with compounds and elements, such as cinnabar, to transform mortal human beings into immortal beings.

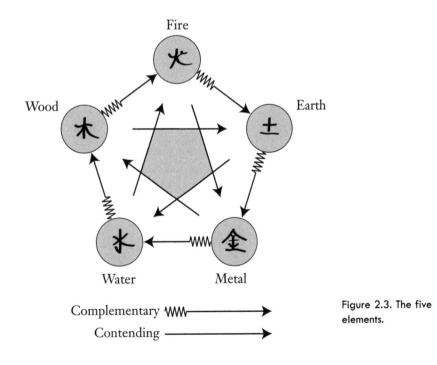

Figure 2.3. The five elements.

They incorporated a system of symbols and formulas to foster long life, good health, amazing memory, happiness, and personal powers. Gradually the Daoist alchemists began to recognize the real dangers of ingesting the deadly concoctions of mercury and other poisons. Daoist alchemy with real materials fell into disuse due to its dangers. However, some useful substances were studied and catalogued, such as gunpowder for firearms and cinnabar for red paint pigment. The science of chemistry evolved from these roots.

A new trend called Symbolic Alchemy began to develop as a substitute for physical alchemy. This shift has contributed to many Daoist practices continuing to this day. Analogical symbols were substituted for the use of actual toxic substances, keeping the formulae and methods as a metaphor for processes of transformation. Thus the cauldron that heated the potions referred to the fire within, a vital force located in energy centers of the body. Breathing techniques were developed to stimulate and increase body heat (Qi energy). Different elements contained in the elixirs translated as symbols of mental processes, compounded by means of visualization and the slow movements of Qi Gong and Tai Chi, to induce self-transformation (Simpkins & Simpkins, 1999a, 2002; Wong, 1997).

Religious Daoism

Daoism also developed into a religion that traced its inspiration back to Laozi and the *Dao De Jing.* Religious themes were implied in the early philosophical Daoist writings, but were made explicit around the first century AD. Laozi was elevated in spiritual status from a mortal man to a deity, merging him with earlier mythologies and occult sciences of the Yellow Emperor, considered the first doctor as well as a great leader. Eastern medicine grew out of this merging of Daoist philosophy with religious Daoism (Cleary, 1991, 2000).

Daoism gathered many followers during the Han dynasty (200 BC–AD 221). Charismatic healers created Daoist health sects, promising a better life through the healthy, moral living fostered by these groups. Members were taught meditation methods combined with diet regulations and exercise techniques. Eastern medicine has its roots in these ancient Daoist sects.

From its humble beginnings in small rural communities, the Daoist sects grew larger in number and size, evolving into a religion. By AD 184 most of China practiced Daoist religion, and by the time of the Tang Dynasty (AD 618–907), Daoism had become an integral part of Chinese life (Bokenkam, 1999). The Daoist religious institution was powerful and influential, advising kings and eventually gathering its own armies. Daoist sages were well respected at every level of society. A lineage of Daoist religious leaders was passed down along family lines. Buddhism and Confucianism contended with Daoism for power and royal favor. Eventually, the three religions were practiced in conjunction with each other. However, the Daoist religious institution has also endured as an organization to this day, with followers in many places around the world (Simpkins & Simpkins, 1999a).

The Dao

The thread that runs through all of Daoism's long history is the Dao, a mystical source for all things. The word *Dao* can translate as *way* or *road.* When Eastern philosophies speak of the Way, they are referring to Dao. Dao is emptiness, before creation, the essence of all things. Emptiness, according to Daoism, is not just a state of lacking, or a vacuum needing to be filled. Instead, emptiness is a resource filled with potential, the source of life. "Dao is empty (like a bowl). It may be used but its capacity is never exhausted" (*Dao De Jing*, quoted in Chan, 1963, p. 141) Life or *De* follows Dao. Returning to nothingness restores the natural balance. In restoring the balance, Dao can become manifest.

Meditation brings people closer to Dao. When silent and quiet, there is space for Dao to appear. "Attain complete vacuity; Maintain steadfast quietude" (*Dao De Jing*, quoted in Chan, 1963, p. 147).

Yin and Yang

The [Yellow] Emperor said: "The *yin* and *yang* are the law of the heaven and earth, the rule of everything, the parents of variations, the root of life and death, and the locus of power of the universe."

(Ming, 2001, p. 6)

Figure 2.4. *The Yin-Yang.*
(Artists: C. Alexander &
Annellen Simpkins, San Diego,
CA, 2000; walnut and birch,
wood on wood)

From the Dao comes the One, and from the One comes two, yin and yang. Yin-yang theory is older than Daoism and permeates Chinese thought (Wilhelm & Wilhelm, 1995). Its doctrine is simple, yet its influence is profound. Almost everyone has seen the yin-yang symbol: a circle, half black and half white, with a dot of white on the black and a dot of black on the white. Yin symbolizes the passive, receptive, weak, and destructive. Yang is positive, active, strong, and constructive. Within the whole, there are always opposites in dynamic balance, always in relation to each other. The contrast and difference of opposites, yin and yang, is fundamental to human understanding and experience of the world. For example, how can one understand "up" without a sense of "down"? Darkness cannot be known without the experience of light. Each needs the other for context. Human beings know the world by contrast and difference. These ideas are reminiscent of contemporary relational theories.

The applications of these principles are primary for healing. Eastern medicine, for example, analyzes body and mind in terms of yin and yang. Problems occur when yin and yang are out of balance. Treatment restores the balance. Excess dryness is moistened, heat or inflammation is cooled, and rest balances strain. In tune with central harmony, yin and yang dissolve back into Dao (Kaptchuk, 1983).

The Nature of Change

One of the classic references for Daoism and Confucianism is an ancient text, *I Jing (I Ching)*, *The Book of Changes* (Wilhelm & Wilhelm, 1995). Thousands of years ago, the Chinese people recognized that life is continually undergoing transformation. Therapists are concerned with bringing about change, and these ancient insights may stimulate new ideas.

The inroad to understanding the transitory nature of existence is an idea central to Daoism: simplicity. This conception is reminiscent of our modern scientific valuing of parsimony. "The good that lies in the easy and the simple makes it correspond to the highest kind of existence" (Wilhelm & Wilhelm, 1995, p. 24).

Observe the simple qualities of experience: one cannot help but notice that everything is perpetually changing. Through the process of conceptualizing people step away from the simple and fabricate a solid world of enduring reality. The *I Jing*, like Daoism, encourages people to turn back to natural, simple perception and look at what is always there: constant change.

The *I Jing* distinguishes three kinds of change. The first is cyclical transformation: one thing changes into another, but eventually is restored back to the original. An example of cyclical change is the seasons, in which summer inevitably becomes fall, then winter, spring, and back to summer again: a cycle.

A second form of change is progressive development. Transformation takes place a little at a time. Each contains the previous, always moving forward. A life span is a good example of progressive development. People are born, live, grow older and older, and then they die. Change is not just linear. Each stage of development is linked to the former one, but more in the spirit of the development of an oak tree from an acorn than walking on a path of stepping-stones.

The immutable law that works through the other transformations is the third type of change. Change begins small, almost unnoticeably, but as things go through their transformations, changes multiply exponentially, with enormous results. For example, clients may not report much change from one session to the next. But many years later, a client who has successfully gone through the therapeutic process will often report many large changes in lifestyle, emotions, and thoughts. The *I Jing* points out that even heaven and earth began small and evolved over eons of time to become the complex universe of today. The Wu Chi Tai Chi (Wuji Taiji) Diagram shows the transformations on a universal scale.

Nonaction

Another premise of Daoism is nonaction, *wu-wei.* Problems arise from too much effort, too much doing, contending and pushing.

Figure 2.5. The Wu Chi
Tai Chi diagram shows
transformations on a
universal scale.

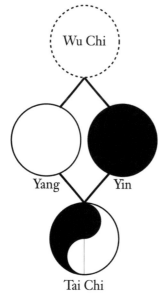

Wu Chi

Yang   Yin

Tai Chi

According to Daoism, noninterference is often the best action to take. Don't fight upstream against the current. Instead, get in tune with the direction of the stream. Align with the stream of events, flow with the river of life itself. Then maneuver and proceed without effort, comfortably carried along by the natural currents of the Way. Daoism offers a path to follow, to get in touch with the natural tendencies that are already there and stay close to them, close to Dao. "Dao invariably takes no action; and yet there is nothing left undone" (*Dao De Jing*, quoted in Chan, 1963, p. 138).

Qi Energy

The interplay of yin and yang in continuous change generates a dynamic flow of energy, called Qi. Disruption of normal energy patterns can be observed in many disorders. The way to a healthy, happy, and wise life is to allow Qi to flow unhampered. Qi can be worked with in a number of sophisticated ways, found in acupuncture, massage, feng shui, herbal medicine, and Qi Gong (Mann, 1973). For example, acupuncture is based on the theory that Qi travels freely through the body along 12 meridians. Illnesses come about from imbalances and blockages in the natural flow of Qi. By stimulating the meridians using thin needles, heat, and massage, imbalances and blockages are corrected. The natural flow of Qi resumes and health returns naturally. Feng Shui operates according to a similar theory. By manipulating the flow of Qi occurring externally, such as in a home or office, blocked Qi can be freed to create a healthier environment.

Qi Defined: Matter and Energy

Daoists don't make a clear distinction between matter and energy or between the material and the nonmaterial, which is reflected in how Qi is defined, as both solid matter and energy. Modern physicists might agree to an extent, because on the molecular level all matter in our universe is comprised of subatomic particles: positive, negative, and neutral energy interacting together.

Qi manifests itself in many ways in our world. From the Eastern perspective it serves as a good example of how the nonmaterial and material are actually two sides of the same coin. Qi is energy, somewhat like electricity that cannot be seen under a microscope, yet without it, material things would not be what they are. Qi is manifested throughout the material world, giving living things the vitality and spirit that make them alive. In the sense that everything and everyone partakes of Qi, we all share in a universal unity.

French philosopher Henri Bergson conceived of the material and spiritual as an intimately intertwined unity, similar to Daoism. He called the nonmaterial life force the "elan vital," the process of existence. This life force is not static or material. Bergson offered a way of thinking about the relationship that is helpful for understanding Qi's quality of being both energy and material at the same time:

> A very small element of a curve is very near to being a straight line. In the limit, it may be termed a part of the straight line, as you please, for in each of its points a curve coincides with its tangent. So likewise, "vitality" is tangent at any and every point to physical and chemical forces, but such points are, in fact, only views taken by a mind, which imagines stops at various moments of movement that generates the curve. In reality, life is no more made up of physico-chemical elements than a curve is composed of straight lines.
>
> (Bergson quoted in Durant, 1968, p. 455)

Whether one subscribes to a materialist or nonmaterialist view, one can utilize the ancient Chinese meditation methods. Materialists may prefer to view Dao as a metaphor to stimulate physiological processes, while nonmaterialists may ascribe a reality to the ancient belief. When Daoist principles are correctly incorporated into technique, results follow, regardless of rationale.

Daoists attune meditatively to the nature of things as they are. Daoist meditation restores balance. Do less to accomplish more. Let the Qi flow. This is the Way of Dao.

Buddhism

Those whose mind is well grounded in the seven elements of knowledge who without clinging to anything, rejoice in freedom from attachment, whose appetites have been conquered, and who are full of light, they are free even in this world.

(*Dhammapada* quoted in Yutang, 1942, p. 333)

Buddha: The Awakened One

Buddhism is another important philosophy that uses meditation. It can be traced back to one man as founder, Siddhartha Gautama (563–483 BC). He was born a prince of a small kingdom in northern India, and enjoyed many luxuries and comforts. But he must have had the heart of a therapist, because he felt disturbed when he saw others suffering and felt compelled to find a solution. He left the luxury of the palace and lived for years in the forest. Tirelessly, he searched for answers among the ascetics, wise men of the time who lived outdoors in nature and practiced austere forms of self-denial. But as he neared death from starvation, Siddhartha realized he was no closer to finding a solution. Finally, one night, he sat under a bodhi tree and meditated, vowing to reach understanding, searching within, deep in thought. As the sun rose over the horizon, he suddenly became enlightened. Thereafter, he was known as the Buddha, the Awakened One, and Buddhism was born.

Figure 2.6. Bodhisattva. (Stone, ca. 565. 38–1/2" x 29" x 16." China, Xiangtang Shan Region, Northern Qi Dynasty. Bequest of Mrs. Cora Timken Burnett, 1957: 469. San Diego Museum of Art.)

The Four Noble Truths and the Eightfold Path

The eightfold path is that path which opens the eyes, and bestows understanding, which leads to peace of mind, to the higher wisdom, to full Enlightenment, to Nirvana.

(Buddha's Sermon at Benares, quoted in Yutang, 1942, p. 360)

Buddha's enlightenment showed him a solution to human suffering, the doctrine of the Four Noble Truths, a Middle Way between extremes, the cornerstone for all Buddhists. Many of these ideas, although couched in an unfamiliar lexicon, are not so foreign to the therapeutic process.

The First Truth is to recognize that life includes suffering. Although this may seem pessimistic, Buddha believed it was optimistic, because facing the problem is the first step to solving it. As the Dalai Lama said, "If you directly confront your suffering, you will be in a better position to appreciate the depth and nature of the problem" (Dalai Lama & Cutler, 1998, p. 136).

The Second Truth is that the root of suffering is self-centered desires. This is a paradox. Why wouldn't satisfaction of desires and wishes bring lasting pleasure? Buddha's answer for this paradox was that even the happiest times inevitably come to an end. So, we cannot help but be disappointed when we long for permanent happiness. Impermanence is the other side of existence. Our world as we know it is altering continuously. In this way, it is empty of any fixed existence.

The Third Truth, to stop creating suffering, is to refrain from doing the things that cause suffering. Buddha taught a Middle Way, the way of moderation. The Middle Way means more than just avoiding extremes. On an existential level, the Middle Way also means not to become entangled in the duality of pleasure and pain. The way to overcome suffering is to let go of craving for pleasure and hating to suffer. This acceptant attitude leads to freedom from the vicissitudes of life that are often experienced as so disturbing. Life becomes just what it is, moment-to-moment.

The Fourth Truth offers eight different forms of awareness training to bring a stop to suffering. They are known as the Eightfold Path: Right Views, Right Intent, Right Speech, Right Action, Right Livelihood, Right Effort, Right Mindfulness, and Right Meditation. The Eightfold Path is a meditative journey that enhances development with every step along the path (Simpkins & Simpkins, 2000, 2003c).

Buddha taught, "All that we are is the result of what we have thought: It is founded on our thoughts, it is made up of our thoughts" (*Dhammapada* quoted in

Yutang, 1942, p. 327). As good therapists, we know that if the mind creates a world of suffering, then the mind can also bring freedom from it.

Buddhism Evolves

Disciples gathered around Buddha and eventually became teachers themselves. Through meditation, which helped them recognize impermanence and give up desires, the monks sought to find enlightenment. They became known as *arhats*, followers of the saintly, noble way. In deep meditation on the Eightfold Path, they lived in seclusion to foster and develop their enlightenment. Buddhism spread throughout India and to other lands. Eventually Buddha's teachings were given written form as sutras, and the writings helped to spread the philosophy even further (Mizuno, 1995).

Gradually, a new, more liberal form of Buddhism, known as Mahayana, split away from the traditional Buddhism of the Elders, known as Theravada (Dube, 1980). The new doctrine gave Buddha a supernatural role. He was recast as all Being, the meaning within all phenomena, beyond time, space, and words. According to the Mahayana doctrine, wisdom is virtue, and thus being compassionate, kindly, and patient was the correct interpretation of the Buddha's teaching, not becoming wise and dispassionate. So the bodhisattva replaced the arhat as the ideal role model. Bodhisattvas did not withdraw from society to find Nirvana. Altruistic ethics encouraged good works in the interest of the whole world. This opened Buddhist philosophy to all people. With rituals and traditions to follow, Buddhism became one of the world's great religions.

A third iteration of Buddhism evolved in Tibet, known as Vajrayana. Tibetan Buddhism blended with Yoga to incorporate auditory mantras, visual mandalas, and body positioning mudras. The Dalai Lama and a number of Tibetan Buddhist teachers have helped to make this form of Buddhism accessible.

Empty World, Empty Ego

Thus shall ye think of all this fleeting world:

A star at dawn, a bubble in a stream;

A flash of lightning in a summer cloud,

A flickering lamp, a phantom, and a dream.

(*The Diamond Sutra*, quoted in Price & Mou-lam, 1990, p. 53)

Similar to Daoism, Buddhist philosophy is based in emptiness as the ultimate reference point. Objects have a dependent existence, moment to moment, a temporary existence. But no timeless essence in the material world of reality actually exists. As therapists, we see examples of this in our clients who are following successful therapy: longtime real life problems dissolve, obstacles disappear. Buddhists would predict this because objects change, moment to moment. The relationship between an object's elements and its use is all that is there, with no timeless essence apart from the interdependency.

The world is impermanent and so is the self: impermanent, ever changing, and without substance (de Silva, 1975). This understanding has great potential to free us from the fetters of a limited self-concept and narrow self-concern.

> Realization of egolessness is not something negative like losing one's self-identity, but rather is positive in that through this realization one overcomes one's ego-centeredness and awakens to Reality.
>
> (Abe, 1985, p. 213)

Buddhism's specific concept of an empty self-nature is an extension of emptiness in general. We all share in the same inner empty nature. So, the loss of belief in our ego-centered existence lets us discover our deeper true nature, at one with the greater universe, what the Buddhists call, the Buddha Mind (Simpkins & Simpkins, 2000, 2003c).

Meditation as the Way

Buddhism emphasizes meditation as the only effective pathway to wisdom. Many of the sutras teach people how to meditate. For example, the *Diamond Sutra* gives this instruction for meditation: "The mind should be kept independent of any thoughts that arise within it" (Price & Mou-lam, 1990, p. 33). Truth is within the mind, detached from the problems of everyday life, and even detached from the self.

Buddhism confounds logic further by explaining that to attain enlightenment is not really to attain anything. Everyone already has the capacity within to achieve enlightenment, but few come to realize it. Wisdom is accessible to all who sincerely turn attention inward and meditate.

By facing things as they really are, people can overcome suffering. The miseries of life come from ignorance. Life isn't what it seems. Our concepts of the self and the world are illusions. The happiness we seek trying to fulfill our desires will never last. We are always bound to be disappointed. Buddha's words, "Rouse thyself by thyself, examine thyself by thyself; thus self-protected and attentive, wilt thou live happily!" (Yutang, 1942, p. 322) encourage us to truly understand ourselves. Becoming aware lets us break the chains of desire and frees us to discover the deeper, empty nature of reality. When we are able to replace ignorance with awareness through meditation, as Buddha did, we can become enlightened.

Zen Buddhism

Buddha is Sanskrit for what you call aware, miraculously aware. Responding, perceiving, arching your brows, blinking your eyes, moving your hands and feet, it is all your miraculously aware nature. And this nature is the mind.

(Bodhidharma quoted in Pine, 1989, p. 25)

Figure 2.7. *Daruma (Bodhidharma).*
(Artist: Hakuin Ekaku, 18th century, Los Angeles County Museum of Art, Gift of Murray Smith; hanging scroll; ink on paper; 44?" x 19?")

Zen was a new form of Buddhism that arose in China during the fifth century. Buddhism had become steeped in elaborate rituals and practices, and some felt that it had lost the pure meditative roots. The legendary founder of Zen was Bodhidharma (AD 440–528), an Indian Buddhist monk who had a strong commitment to meditation. He was a powerful man, often pictured with large, penetrating eyes. Bodhidharma took the message of meditative awareness to China. There he not only inspired a whole new generation of Buddhists with his pure form of meditation, but also founded martial arts (Simpkins & Simpkins, 2006).

Living on Chinese soil, Bodhidharma's meditational Buddhism took on a new character. The Chinese blended India's metaphysical Buddhism with the indigenous philosophies of Daoism and Confucianism to form Zen Buddhism. During the Tang dynasty (AD 618–907), Zen branched out further, cultivated by generations of charismatic masters. This helped Zen to flower in the later Sung periods (960–1279), when it would be transmitted to Japan and then westward (Simpkins & Simpkins, 1997b). The consistent message was to be awake and aware. As the Fourth Patriarch Dao-hsin said, "The mind is awake and never ceasing; the awakened mind is always present" (Dumoulin, 1988, p. 100). Zen taught people to use meditation to wake up.

Meditation as the Path to Enlightenment

The word *zen* means "meditation," and Zen emphasizes the practice of meditation over the study of doctrine in bringing about enlightenment. Zen wisdom is beyond words, an intuitive insight. All concepts, practices, and rituals are like a finger pointing to the moon, not the moon itself. A famous Zen monk named Chao-chou was said to have had his enlightenment after this exchange with his teacher, which is paraphrased from Sekida (1977, p. 73).

Chao-chou asked, "What is Dao?"
The master answered, "Your ordinary mind is Dao."
"Then, how can I live completely in the Dao?" asked Chao-chou.
"As soon as you intend to live in the Dao, you lose it."
"But without intending to do it, how can I succeed?"
"The Dao," answered the Master, " doesn't belong to either knowing or not knowing. Knowing is false understanding and not knowing is blind ignorance. To really understand the Dao is like a clear sky. Why drag in right and wrong?"

With focused attention and clear awareness, typical ways of experiencing through the rational mind are bypassed to discover a deeper nature. We are all born with an enlightened mind. We just don't know how to access it. Meditation shows the way.

Everyday Life is Enlightening

Enlightened awareness does not come from somewhere beyond where you are. Meditation is not passively sitting alone in a darkened room, nor is it a deliberate effort.

Enlightenment is here and now, actively involved in ordinary life. Just do what you ordinarily do, wholeheartedly, awake and aware. Then everyday work, gardening, cleaning, and cooking can be meditative: You can discover meditation at every moment in your life now. The path begins with mindful awareness.

Deconstructing

Part of the process of transformation involves deconstruction. In other words, take away whatever interferes with direct, clear perception. Zen master Bankei (1622–1693) told the many people who came to hear him speak, "Basically, there's not a thing wrong with you; it is only that you let slight, inadvertent mistakes change the Buddha-mind into thought" (Bankei quoted in Waddell, 1994, p. 81). Many of the distinctions we make between what we should and should not do or feel lead to problems. Judgments can reveal or hide reality. Thus, Zen offers a solution to psychological conflicts. As Zen master Huang-Po said, "Give up erroneous thoughts leading to false distinctions. There is no "self' and no "other." There is no "wrong desire," no "anger . . ." (Blofeld, 1994, p. 154).

When clients can let go of troubled conceptual thinking, they see things as they are. Then where is the disturbance? Meditation opens up the possibility of being awake and aware without adding anything extra. Correct perception is desirable and possible.

Sudden Enlightenment: Gradual Cultivation

The Sixth Patriarch Hui-neng (AD 638–713), added a new idea: Sudden Enlightenment (Price & Mou-lam, 1990). The awake and aware state of Zen could happen in a sudden flash of insight. Anyone could experience it, no matter what his or her background or education. Hui-neng's enlightenment occurred while he was selling firewood in the marketplace. As he listened to a man reciting the *Diamond Sutra* (Hanh, 1992), he was so moved by the words that he suddenly became enlightened. This suggests a paradigm that applies by analogy to nonreligious therapeutic situations.

Often clients experience sudden insight during a session. And although the insight may be pivotal, the implications and consequences need to be thought through and applied to the client's life. Zen masters also recognize this need for working through, which they call gradual cultivation. True, one can have a sudden, immediate awakening, but sustaining the resulting awareness in everyday life takes time. Eventually, Zen practice can become part of everyday routines in a natural, effortless manner. The link between thought and action becomes spontaneous and direct. "In walking just walk. In sitting just sit. Above all, don't wobble" (Watts, 1957, p. 135).

Japanese Zen

Zen was brought from China to Japan sometime around the 12th century. Dogen (1200–1253), was considered one of the greatest Japanese Zen monks of all time. His devotion to Zen and only Zen reminds us of Bodhidharma. He gave up all worldly possessions and pursued meditation single-mindedly. He introduced the practice of *zazen*, or meditative sitting. He believed that by our sitting regularly in meditation, problems could be solved. Through zazen the mind becomes clear and there is unity between mind and body (LaFleur, 1985).

Dogen often told his students that the practice of meditation *is* enlightenment. Some advanced psychotherapists may experience analogous moments in their own practice. Becoming a skilled therapist is not found outside yourself. Day-to-day practice of therapy is often where you find wisdom to pass on to clients. When you can truly appreciate each moment, and stay fully aware, you know yourself and are truly in touch with clients. Dogen's teachings became the foundation for Soto Zen, one of the major worldwide sects of Zen today.

Zen Arts

Zen arts are a Way, a path to enlightenment. Some traditional Zen arts are haiku poetry (Henderson, 1977; Shiki, 1998; Simpkins & Simpkins, 1999b, 2007; Suzuki, 1973), archery (Kushner, 2000), calligraphy (Fontein & Hickman, 1970), martial arts (Simpkins & Simpkins, 1999b, 2006) flower arranging (Herrigel, 1958), and tea (Sadler 1963; Sasaki, 2002). What all Zen arts share in common is how they train the mind, to unify with deeper nature and higher wisdom. The external product is secondary to the inner attitude. The creations that flow from applying Zen are

Figure 2.8. *Twenty-four warriors of Koyo (close up).* (Tosa Mitsunori, Japanese, 1583–1638. Ink on silk, undated. 59–1/2" x 30–1-/8." Museum purchase with funds provided by the Asian Arts Council, 1967: 139. San Diego Museum of Art.)

outer reflections of the inner spirit, enriching the artist and the viewer. Zen arts have traditionally been used for meditation, to help guide the practitioner to deeper insight.

> To the degree that the pupil can summon up courage for the necessary self-discipline and this keeps pace with his artistic ability, he will find, not only as an artist but also as a human being, a special relationship to his performance, to this quiet, unswerving creation out of inner harmony.
>
> (Herrigel, 1958, p. 23)

Koans

Hakuin (1685–1768) was one of the most dynamic, prolific, and influential monks of Rinzai, the other major Zen sect in Japan. He codified koans as a way to teach Zen.

The famous koan, "What is the sound of one hand clapping?" was created by Hakuin to help students begin the process (Yampolsky, 1971).

Koans offer a puzzling question that does not have a rational answer. When students enter into enlightened perception they are able to give an acceptable response. Because rational thought does not help, students are forced to turn away from their typical use of the mind (Loori, 1994; Muira & Sasaki, 1965; Simpkins & Simpkins, 1999b, 2003b). The koan, if taken seriously, inevitably leads to a great doubt that takes precedence over all else. As Hakuin said, "At the bottom of great doubt lies great awakening. If you doubt fully you will awaken fully" (Dumoulin, 1990, p. 381). In Zen, the koan helps focus attention and facilitates the discovery of insight, which leads to an awakening: enlightenment (Batchelor, 1990).

Zen is an experiential path to wisdom. The main vehicle, meditation, can be applied through koans, arts, sitting or moving, work or play, eating and sleeping. No matter what you do or where you are, you can always be practicing Zen.

Conclusion

These meditation traditions present interesting perspectives and new paradigms for philosophy and psychology. We hope the ideas have inspired novel paradigms, creative associations, and new insights for the therapeutic process. The meditation methods in Part II will fill out the experiential understanding of these ideas. Meditation includes varied methods and techniques that can help you and your clients to find the way to health and well-being.

Scientific Efficacy and Neuroscience Research

In summary, it appears that meditation is a useful manipulation or intervention in the treatment of a variety of psychologically related problems.

(Wallace & Fisher, 2003, p. 149)

From ancient times, meditation has been thought to produce amazing mental and physical abilities. Yoga masters claimed to be able to stop and start their hearts at will. Tibetan Buddhist monks alleged that they could dry wet towels placed on their exposed backs in frigid temperatures. Daoist sages avowed that they could heal illness. They all believed that these amazing achievements derived from intuitive wisdom acquired by regularly practicing meditation. To the scientifically minded Westerner, just claiming something does not necessarily prove that it is true. So, researchers began to investigate some of the claims about meditation, and the past few decades have seen a surge in Western scientific research on this topic. The findings from these studies have been promising. A growing number of studies indicate that many of the claims do seem to be substantiated with experienced meditators. And at the very least, meditation is proving to be an effective therapeutic tool. With these positive findings, more therapists are becoming interested in learning about meditation so that they can integrate it into their practice.

Beginnings of Scientific Interest in Meditation

Meditation was known only obliquely until our modern era. As late as the 1800s, few Westerners had any acquaintance with Eastern philosophy. Those individuals who studied Eastern ideas tended to be philosophers. In the tradition of one of the earliest philosopher/scientists, Aristotle, philosophers of the 17th, 18th, and 19th centuries were also scientists. These philosopher/scientists integrated Eastern philosophy into the very fabric of their scientific thought as well as their philosophies.

One of the most famous philosopher/scientists was Gottfried Wilhelm Leibniz (1646–1716). He was a primary founder of modern calculus and was deeply involved in Chinese studies. He expressed its importance to him in a letter to a Jesuit friend, who was on a mission to China:

> For this is a commerce of light which could give to us at once their work of thousands of years and render ours to them, and to double, so to speak, our true wealth for one and the other. This is something greater than one thinks.
>
> (Leibniz quoted in Perkins, 2004, p. 42)

Leibniz incorporated Eastern principles into his thought. The cornerstone of his philosophy was an idea that was also primary to the Chinese: the unity of all things. "I do not conceive of any reality at all as without genuine unity" (Leibniz quoted in Perkins, 2004, p. 70).

Similar to the conception of substance in the *I Jing, The Book of Changes*, Leibniz believed that the essence of all substance was interrelationship. "I maintain also that substances, whether material or immaterial, cannot be conceived in their bare essence without any activity, activity being of the essence of substance in general (Leibniz quoted in Perkins, 2004, p. 92). Perhaps his interest and understanding of the highly developed Eastern theories of mind and change affected his formulations of calculus, the mathematical characterization of change. He believed that each part of the universe includes and mirrors the others, coexisting in preestablished harmony. This conception resonates with Buddhist thought.

Ralph Waldo Emerson (1803–1882) was another Western philosopher who was actively involved in Eastern thought. Emerson cast Eastern ideas into his transcendental philosophy. For Emerson, the universe had a divine, ordered nature, similar in many ways to the Eastern view of the Dao. The Daoist sage would agree with Emerson's statement that, "These laws execute themselves. They are out of time, out of space, and not subject to circumstance" (Emerson quoted in James, 1918, p. 43).

A few Westerners worked in the Far East. For example, the Englishman L. Austine Waddell was stationed in India with the Indian Medical Service and took an active interest in meditation. When his work sent him to Tibet, he seized the opportunity to delve into the then little-known Buddhism of Tibet, known as Lamaism. He learned the language and conversed directly with the lamas and other Tibetans. His book, *The Buddhism of Tibet or Lamaism* (Waddell, 1894) was a product of these years of study. This book portrayed Tibetan Buddhism as a mysterious and magical religion. Although he often found the practices to be strange and bizarre, meditation also fascinated him. His book is filled with detailed descriptions of what he saw and experienced. He had no precedents to follow, and so his understandings were sometimes limited and tinged with prejudice. However, he did a great service in bringing the tradition to the attention of the West.

First Formal Introduction to the West

Meditation was brought onto Western soil for the first time at the World Parliament of Religions, a conference held in Chicago in 1893. It offered a forum for great leaders of religion, East and West, to meet and interact for the first time. Many great leaders from the East attended the conference, opening the first East–West dialogue on religion.

VIVEKANANDA

The keynote speaker, Vivekananda (1863–1902) was a famous yogi who helped to demystify the practices of the East and opened the way for Western scientific inquiry. Vivekananda believed people become isolated in their own cultural traditions. It was his sincere belief that these ethnocentricities could be transcended. In one of his addresses at the Parliament, "Why We Disagree," he said, "I have to thank you of America for the great attempt you are making to break down the barriers of this little world of ours, and I hope that in the future the Lord will help you to accomplish your purpose."

He was optimistic about scientific study of Eastern practices. In another paper read at the parliament he said, ". . . The Hindu is only glad that what he has been cherishing in his bosom for ages is going to be taught in more forcible language, and with further light, from the latest conclusions of science" (Vivekananda, 1953, p. 190). Following the Chicago parliament, Vivekananda made many appearances in Western countries. His teachings embodied a synthesis of science and religion, which did much to open the way for scientific inquiry into meditation.

RADHAKRISHNAN

Sarvepalli Radhakrishnan (1888–1975) was another important bridge builder between Eastern and Western philosophy. He was an accomplished scholar in both traditions, and thus was able to clearly express one in terms of the other, to make Eastern thought accessible to Westerners and vice versa. His books on Indian philosophies, including Hinduism, Yoga, and Buddhism, still speak to English language readers, with their clear histories and accounts of the philosophical ideas, along with his own insightful analysis. His philosophical writings looked for interfaces between East and West. He wrote cogent commentaries on many of the most important Eastern classics such as the Bhagavadgita, the Upanishads, and the Brahma Sutra. First he was an accomplished university professor at the University of Calcutta and a professor of Eastern Religions and Ethics at Oxford University (1936–1939). Then, like Plato's ideal, he became a philosopher-ruler. He served as the first Vice President of India from 1952 to 1962 and then as President from 1962 to 1967. Radhakrishnan helped to open an intelligent dialogue between East and West. Plato would have approved.

D. T. SUZUKI

Daisetsu Teitaro Suzuki (1870–1966) was another scholar-teacher who made Eastern traditions accessible to the West. He first came to the West as a young attendee at the 1893 Chicago conference who served as the translator for the Zen representative, Shaku Soen. Through the conference, Suzuki met the American publisher Paul Carus (1852–1919), founder of the Carus Publishing House. Suzuki remained in America, living at Carus's home in Illinois for 10 years (1897–1908) while he wrote and translated books on Zen and Daoism, beginning with the *Dao De Jing*. Suzuki returned to Japan to teach Buddhist philosophy at Gakushu-in University in 1910, but he soon met and married an American woman, Beatrice Erskine Lane (d. 1939) returning with her to the West. Suzuki made an extensive lecture tour across the United States and taught at Columbia University.

Suzuki was a mystic. He believed that there is a way of perceiving through "prajna intuition," a different way of perceiving that is much more accurate and closer to truth than logic and reason. The mystical aspect of Zen enlightenment draws upon intuitive insight, not unlike the mystical experiences pointed to by William James in his *Varieties of Religious Experience* (James, 1902), a book Suzuki studied and admired.

During his long and productive life, Suzuki wrote over 125 books and articles in English and 18 books in Japanese. His wife wrote about Buddhism as well (Suzuki, 1969). At home in both Eastern and Western cultures, Suzuki was able to communicate the ideas of Zen so that Westerners could not only understand them conceptually but also identify with and embrace them. He inspired a lasting interest in Zen, with its promise for wisdom and spiritual fulfillment.

THE DALAI LAMA

Perhaps one of the best known spokesmen for Eastern meditation is the current Dalai Lama, Tenzin Gyatso (b. 1935). A likeable individual with a broad vision for Tibetan Buddhism and for the world, the Dalai Lama often surprises people with his sense of humor, humility, and openness. He has taken an active interest in science, in the belief that science and spirituality are more compatible than is often assumed. He has actively engaged in a number of dialogues with researchers in the areas of physics, neuroscience, and cognitive psychology (Haywood & Francisco, 1992). In discussions on the relationship between mind and brain, the Dalai Lama has pointed to an inter-relationship between inner patterns and outer form. In Tibetan Buddhism, form is content and content is form: the two coexist without duality in a circular relationship. Similarly, modern identity theories of mind (Place, 1956) recognize an integral, non-dual interrelationship between the material physiology of the brain and conscious experience. Today there is a growing sense of a unity between mind and brain, bringing Western theories much closer to Eastern views.

Western Spokesmen for Eastern Traditions

Vivekananda, Radhakrishnan, Suzuki, the Dalai Lama, and many other wise teachers have inspired Westerners to learn about meditation. During the 20th century, more and more Westerners became personally involved in meditation. They wrote informative books that described the practices sympathetically, broadening the West's exposure to Eastern approaches.

Walter Y. Evans-Wentz (1878–1965) was one of the first Americans to popularize Tibetan Buddhism in the West. Evans-Wentz had a spiritual nature from childhood.

He attended Stanford and then Jesus College, Oxford. Continually in search of deeper insights, he traveled extensively, eventually finding his way to Tibet, where he studied with a Tibetan lama, Kazi Dawa-Samdup. He collaborated with Lama Samdup to produce the first English-language translations of Tibetan Buddhist sacred texts (1954, 1960, 1967), including the *Tibetan Book of the Dead*. Unlike Waddell's (1894) earlier book on Tibetan Buddhism, which he had written as an interested outsider, Evans-Wentz wrote with an insiders insight and the practitioner's knowledge as well as being a scholar, which allowed him to render the texts and his explanations with clarity and sympathy.

R. H. Blyth was another Westerner who contributed to the introduction of Buddhism to the West in the 1950s and 1960s, with his many volumes devoted to Zen, the Zen classics, and haiku. He felt that one threat of our modern age was the growing trend toward mechanistic, unpoetical lifestyles. He firmly believed that the study of Zen would help people rekindle a deeper, spiritual, and poetic sense of life. Zen could be compatible with Western ideas. As he said, "'Man is the measure of all things' has its parallel in the Buddhist idea that without man there is no Buddha" (Blyth, 1960, p. 122). He hoped to make it possible to find integration between them.

Eugene Herrigel and his wife both learned to practice Zen meditation by engaging in a Zen art—archery for Eugene and flower arrangement for his wife. They observed their experiences and wrote books that carefully chronicled their learning (E. Herrigel, 1960, 1971; G. Herrigel, 1958). Herrigel's book on Zen archery sold widely, with its inviting first-person account of entering into Zen. As educated and intelligent observer/practitioners, the Herrigels did a great deal to point to important aspects of meditation though their rigorous and highly focused accounts. But they were not scientific researchers and did not perform any experimental studies.

First Research on Meditation: Physiological Studies

Many (Murphey & Donovan, 1997; Shapiro & Walsh, 1984) consider the first truly scientific study of meditation to have been performed in 1931 by an Indian psychology graduate student at Yale, Kovoor Behanan. Behanan measured the physiological effects of Yoga (pranayama) breathing on oxygen consumption (Behanan, 1937) and found significant changes in oxygen levels.

Another early researcher was French cardiologist Thérèse Brosse. She performed EKG measurements on yogis in India who claimed to be able to stop their heart. Brosse found that their heart potentials and pulse rates did approach zero and remained very low for several seconds (Brosse, 1946).

The researchers M.A. Wenger and B.K. Bagchi traveled through India with an eight-channel EEG machine, measuring yogis' physiological responses (Wenger, Bagchi, & Anand, 1961; Wenger & Bagchi, 1961). They found that the yogis could control physiological processes such as temperature, respiration rates, breathing rates, and sweating of the palms. They concluded that meditation was an active process, and made conservative claims about the physiological changes they observed (Wenger & Bagchi, 1961). These careful, quantitative measurements showed that meditation could be examined scientifically and objectively.

Another group of studies was performed at the Menninger Foundation in Topeka, Kansas with the well-known yogi Swami Rama. Rama underwent an intensive set of studies on yogic control of involuntary processes. In one experiment, researchers observed and measured Swami Rama's ability to control his heartbeat. While sitting perfectly still he produced an abnormality: an atrial flutter of 306 beats per minute that lasted for 16 seconds. Ordinarily, during a fibrillation of this kind, a section of the heart oscillates rapidly while the chambers do not fill and the valves do not work properly. Measurements revealed that Swami Rama experienced no pain and showed no damage to his heart (Green, Green, & Walters, 1970). These are but a few examples of the early scientific experiments on meditation that attempted to measure physiological changes in experienced meditators.

Scientific Investigations of the Properties of Meditation

During the 1960s, there was an enormous increase in interest in altered states of consciousness, among both scientists and the general public. Western scientists became interested in studying meditation as a possible type of altered state. Early experiments compared meditation to other kinds of consciousness-altering methods such as hypnosis, biofeedback, and progressive relaxation, noting the similarities and differences (Shapiro, 1980a). As time went on, researchers studied meditation for its own innate properties.

An early study by Deikman (1963) attempted to understand meditation as a method to produce a mystical experience by "deautomatizing psychic structures." In other words, Deikman thought that in everyday life, people behave automatically, without thought or consciousness. Meditation helps to break out of this automatic functioning, and as a result, people may have a mystical experience. His experiments helped to establish meditation as an empirically demonstrable phenomenon. The way was opened for further study in the laboratory.

Some experimenters attempted to categorize factors of meditation. They used regular meditators as subjects who were given questionnaires following a meditation session. Osis, Bokert, and Carlson (1973) identified six factors, each with subfactors that correlated with what the ancient traditions taught. For example, one of the factors involved self-transcendence, openness, a feeling of merging with others, and a unified feeling of oneness with the eternal. Another factor was an intensification and change of consciousness that included feelings of love and joy, perceptual enrichment, and depth of insight. The factors were analyzed statistically using factor analysis.

Some experimenters attempted to take measurements during meditation. While meditating, people were asked to push a button whenever they had an intruding thought. These results were later compared with what the subjects reported after meditating (Van Nuys, 1973). This method was developed further with more complex feedback buttons. Kubose (1976) used this method along with a questionnaire to compare meditating to not meditating. He found that meditators tended to have thoughts more in the present moment than nonmeditating control subjects. Also, meditators had less intruding thoughts than nonmeditators.

A different set of studies (Kohr, 1977) gave questionnaires before and after meditation. These studies confirmed Osis et al.'s factors (1973). Furthermore, they found that the mood subjects felt before they started to meditate did not alter the meditation session. This led experimenters to theorize that meditation is not affected by transitory moods or circumstances. Instead, meditation might be an altered state of consciousness (Shapiro, 1983; Shapiro & Giber, 1978; Tart, 1975; Walsh 1980).

The altered state view continues to be debated by current researchers as they uncover the neurological activity that accompanies meditation and compare it to other mental activities.

By the second half of the 20th century, a number of scientists became interested in meditation as both practitioners and researchers (Walsh, 1978). They helped to improve the quality of scientific studies through their first-person knowledge as practitioners. Charles Tart, for example, practiced meditation and wrote about his experiences. He cautioned researchers to be careful not to lose their scientific objectivity, but suggested that in order for researchers to truly understand the phenomenon they were studying, they should have special training in it (Tart, 1975).

Cognitive Neuroscience Research on Meditation and the Brain

New imaging equipment such as EEG, PET scans, and fMRI has made it possible for researchers to learn more about meditation. Now it is possible to observe the brain activity of a person during meditation and to measure the long-term effects of meditation on the brain.

The Dual Action of Meditation: Relaxation and Activation

Meditation has been shown to produce deep relaxation. A comprehensive meta-analysis (Dillbeck & Orme-Johnson, 1987) confirmed these findings by gathering 31 physiological studies that compared meditation to resting with eyes closed. The study evaluated three key indicators of relaxation and found that meditation provided a deeper state of relaxation than simple eyes-closed rest.

Early research had established that meditation produced relaxation and calm, but it was not immediately evident that meditation would also produce activation. A number of studies found this interesting dual effect. Not only were the meditating subjects more relaxed, but their brains were also activated. Usually when people are attentive they are correspondingly stimulated, but in meditation, people seem to be able to remain calm while at the same time remaining highly aware. Staying alert and relaxed at the same time might improve performance in varied situations. Further research will undoubtedly explore the potentials and limits.

A dual pattern of physiological activity and relaxation was first observed in the 1950s in studies of seven experienced yogis. A combination of brain waves, including recurrent beta rhythms of 18 to 20 hertz, generalized fast activity of small amplitude as high as 40 to 45 hertz, and slow alpha rhythms were all seen at various stages of the yogic meditation (Das & Gastaut, 1955). A later study found similar results; Yoga meditators had an increase in beta band activity as measured by EEG. Increased beta activity is associated with wakefulness and alertness (Schneider & Tarshis, 1986). Along with the beta activity, the meditators also showed more relaxation than non-meditators. This was indicated by an increase in the slower alpha and theta activity, associated with relaxation (Bhatia et al., 2003). These studies indicate that meditation entails both relaxation and alertness.

Brain Wave Coherence

Another observation was that EEG coherence increased between and within the cerebral hemispheres during meditation. EEG coherence is a quantitative index of the degree of long-range spatial ordering of brain waves. Higher coherence means that more of the brain is being used and is associated with improved quality of attention. For meditators with two years of meditation experience, coherence began to spread before the meditation session. Halfway through the meditation period, coherence spread to high and lower frequencies. High coherence continued into the eyes-opened period after meditation. During meditation, even new meditators showed an increase in EEG coherence (Badawi, Wallace, Orme-Johnson, & Rouzere, 1984).

A comparative study of advanced Tibetan Buddhist and Vedic meditators also found increased brain coherence (Hankey, 2006). Hankey speculated that by activating larger areas of the brain, meditators are moving toward higher development of the brain's potential. This activation could lead to better mental development in general.

Another study of long-time Tibetan Buddhist meditators (Lutz, Gretschas, Rawlings, Ricard, & Davidson, 2004) compared them to people exposed to a short course in meditation. The experienced meditators had a higher gamma baseline synchronized across both hemispheres of the brain. Higher gamma indicates that attentive processes were integrated among many parts of the brain. Gamma is associated with attention and working memory, which may seem surprising for objectless meditation. This study also showed the dual action effect of a corresponding relaxation with increased alpha waves. The researchers interpreted this as a decoupling of attention from arousal during meditation. In the normal waking state, attention and arousal occur together: With focused attention usually comes higher arousal. But meditation has consistently shown that meditators are highly attentive while remaining deeply relaxed.

Meditation and Aging

CORTICAL THICKENING

Meditation may actually help to lessen the negative effects of aging. One recent study performed by a large group of investigators (Lazar et al., 2005), showed that people who meditate over many years develop increased thickness of certain important parts of the cerebral cortex. This study compared typical Western meditation practitioners who were skilled in insight meditation with a control group of people with no meditation or Yoga experience. The meditators had a daily routine that included career, family, friends, and hobbies along with daily meditation. The researchers found distinctive differences in cortical thickness. Although the average cortical thickness did not differ, areas involved with sustained attention, sensing of inner experiencing, increased spontaneity, and visual and auditory sensing were thicker. Normally, the frontal region of the cortex gets thinner as people age. But even older meditators had thicker frontal cortexes. For example, in one of the frontal areas (BA 9/10) the average cortical thickness of the 40- to 50-year-old meditators was similar to the average thickness of 20- to 30-year-old meditators. Nonmeditators of all ages had less thickness of the brain areas. The investigators concluded that regular practice of meditation may slow the rate of degeneration of this important area of the brain.

SLOWING OF AGING PROCESS

Some studies have compared benchmarks of aging in meditators to nonmeditating controls, discovering that meditation seems to slow down the aging process in many respects. One study found that after five years of regular meditation, subjects were physiologically 12 years younger than their chronological age, as measured by reduction of blood pressure, better near-point vision, and improved auditory discrimination. Short-term meditators were physiologically five years younger than their chronological age for these factors. The study controlled for the effects of diet and exercise (Wallace, Dillbecic, Jacobe, & Harrington, 1982).

Another meditation study compared the sleep patterns of people aged 20 to 30 to those of people aged 31 to 55. Each age group had meditators who used either Sudarshan Kriya Yoga (SKY) or Vipassana meditation compared with nonmeditating controls. Whole night polysomnographic recordings were carried out in 78 healthy male subjects belonging to control and meditation groups. Sleep patterns were comparable among the younger controls and the two meditation groups. Slow wave sleep showed a 3.7% decline in the older group of controls, but no such decline appeared in the older group of meditators. The authors concluded that meditation practices help to retain slow wave sleep and enhance the REM sleep state in the 31- to 55-year-old group; meditators appear to retain a younger biological age so far as sleep is concerned, showing the benefits of meditation for antiaging (Sulekha, Thennarasu, Vedamurthachar, Raju, & Kutty, 2006).

Of course, further studies will need to be done, but all of these studies are promising for what they demonstrate about real physiologically based changes that can combat the effects of aging.

Psychological Studies

The regular practice of meditation can improve psychological functioning in many measurable ways, both specific and general. Here are a few samplings from the many studies that have been done on the psychological effects of meditation.

Increased Perceptual Acuity

Mental acuity has been claimed to be one of the positive effects of practice, and many of these claims have been tested. Brown, Forte, and Dysart (1984) found that mindfulness practice enabled practitioners to become aware of some of the usually preattentive processes involved in visual detection (Brown et al., 1984a). The authors believed their results supported the claims that meditation changes perception. One study tested the relationship between meditation and visual sensitivity. Practitioners of mindfulness meditation were tested for visual sensitivity before and immediately after a three-month meditation retreat. Subjects practiced mindfulness meditation for 16 hours each day and the staff, who did not meditate, served as the control group. Visual sensitivity was defined by (1) a detection threshold based on the duration of simple light flashes and (2) discrimination threshold based on the interval between successive simple light flashes. All light flashes were presented tachistoscopically and were of fixed luminance. After the retreat, practitioners could detect shorter single-light flashes and required a shorter interval to correctly differentiate between successive flashes. The control group did not change on either measure. Another study also reported enhanced perceptual sensitivity (Shapiro & Giber, 1978).

Improved Memory and Intelligence

Studies have been performed to test memory. For example, college students instructed in meditation displayed significant improvements in performance over a two-week period on a perceptual and short-term memory test involving the identification of familiar letter sequences that were presented rapidly. They were compared with subjects randomly assigned to a routine of twice-daily rest with eyes closed, and with subjects who made no change in their daily routine (Dillbeck, 1982). In several studies, regular university student meditators showed significant improvement on intelligence measures over a two-year period, compared to control subjects (Cranson, et al., 1991; Dillbeck, Assimakis, Raïmondi, & Orme-Johnson, 1986).

Global Improvement

A meta-analysis of 42 independent studies considered the effects of meditation on a general increase in self-actualization. They found that meditators had markedly higher levels of self-actualization as compared with other forms of relaxation. The analysis controlled for length of treatment and quality of research design (Alexander, Rainforth, & Gelderloos, 1991).

Researchers have found that meditation has a positive effect on health in general. In two companies that introduced meditation, managers and employees who regularly practiced meditation improved significantly in overall physical health, mental well-being, and vitality when compared to control subjects with similar jobs in the same companies. Meditation practitioners also reported significant reductions in health problems such as headaches and backaches, improved quality of sleep, and a significant reduction in the use of alcohol and cigarettes, compared to personnel in the control groups (Alexander, Swanson, Rainforth, & Carlisle, 1993).

Another study performed a decade later with healthy employees measured the effects of brain and immune function following an eight-week mindfulness meditation program (Davidson et al., 2003). They measured brain electrical activity before meditation and immediately after, and again four months later. They found significant increases in left-sided anterior activation, a pattern previously associated with positive affect in the meditators as compared with the nonmeditators. They also found significant increases in antibodies to an influenza vaccine as compared with controls. The researchers conclude that meditation may change brain and immune function in positive ways.

A large set of studies measured a reduction in weekly fatalities due to automobile accidents, suicides, and homicides in the United States during periods when large-scale Transcendental Meditation groups were holding regular meditation sessions. Measurements were taken in the United States between the years of 1982 and 1985. During periods when the size of the groups of meditators was smaller than the square root of 1% of the U.S. population, fatality rates were higher, but when group size was greater than 1% fatality rates dropped. Time series methodology was used to ensure that these effects could not be due to random variation, seasonal cycle, or long-term trends (Dillbeck, 1980).

Reduction of Violence

Meditation is known to produce a feeling of inner peace and well-being. A number of large-scale studies seem to bear out these time-honored claims. One experiment reduced violence in a community (Hagelin et al., 1999). Four thousand practitioners of Transcendental Meditation assembled in Washington, DC from June 7 to June 30, 1993. The local police monitored the crime rate for the district. Statistics revealed that crime decreased 15% during this period of time and stayed lower for some time after the 21-day event.

Another large group meditation study revealed a distinct improvement in the quality of life in Rhode Island. Crime rates dropped, auto accidents decreased, and there were less deaths due to cigarette smoking and alcohol consumption (Dillbeck, Cavanaugh, Glenn, Orme-Johnson, & Mittlefehldt, 1987).

Meditation has even been shown to help in a wartime situation. There was a reported decrease in hostilities during a wartime period in Lebanon from collective meditation sessions (Abou Nader, Alexander, & Davies, 1992, Davies & Alexander, 1989).

Research on Differences Between Forms of Meditation

This book describes some different meditation traditions within Yoga, Buddhism, Zen, and Daoism. Each of these teaches certain mental skills. For example, Yoga develops the ability to withdraw attention from the outer world and focus it inwardly. This ability allows meditators to maintain a deeply concentrated state even in the midst of distractions. Anand and Chhina (1961a) researched the effects of this form of meditation. They measured four experienced yogis and found that they exhibited persistent alpha activity with increased amplitude during trance. When the yogis were exposed to loud noise and bright lights, they exhibited no alpha-wave blocking. They also maintained persistent alpha activity while holding their hands in ice-cold water for 45 to 55 minutes (Anand & Chhina, 1961b). These results indicate how the intense inward focus, withdrawn from the external environment, led these long-time meditators to be able to maintain their intense attentional focus even in the midst of environmental disturbances (Cahn & Polich, 2006).

By contrast, Zen trains practitioners to be alert and aware of each moment, mindful of everything that is happening. An interesting group of EEG research projects showed an effect of these different skills. Kasamatsu and Hirai (1966, 1969) presented seasoned Zen monks with a clicking sound. Each time the click occurred, their brain waves registered a response as if the sound was heard for the first time. By contrast, control subjects eventually stopped hearing the click due to the natural tendency to habituate. Zen teaches its practitioners to always be alert and aware, so habituation does not occur. Each moment, every click, can be experienced anew, as if for the first time.

These experiments offer us one possible way to understand the different mental skills that are developed by various forms of meditation. Later results of such comparisons have been mixed, leading researchers to debate the differences between forms of meditation (Cahn & Polich, 2006). There seem to be many overlaps in the end results brought by years of regular meditation. It remains to be seen whether experienced meditators from different traditions would share more in common than have differences. However, there are unique types of skills that each form of meditation develops. Therapists will benefit from understanding the cognitive differences so that they can incorporate the appropriate method to fill the need of the individual client. The informed therapist who has an understanding of the varied tools of meditation and their uses can sensitively attune to the client's personality and cognitive style; and provide a meditative method that will be most compatible and accessible. See the introduction to Part II for further discussion of these issues.

Research on Specific Forms of Meditation for Treatments

Many forms of meditation have been tested and shown to be therapeutically helpful. For this reason, therapists can have confidence in choosing from the broad range of techniques and methods that are presented in this book. The later sections of this book will describe these different meditation methods and provide guidance in how and when to use them.

The Daoist meditation method of Qi Gong has been studied scientifically. For example, one study compared 80 Qi Gong meditators with 74 nonmeditators using the Eysenck Personality Inventory (EPI) and found that the meditators were significantly less neurotic than nonmeditators, even after controlling for age, gender, and education (Leung & Singhal, 2004). The researchers concluded that Qi Gong meditation had a significant correlation with mental health and could provide a viable treatment option for long-term wellness.

Mindfulness is another form of meditation that has recently received a great deal of attention from researchers. As a result, mindfulness is now accepted as an effective clinical application. Research has shown that mindfulness can be applied to a wide range of difficulties with significant success (Siegel, 2007). Research has shown that mindfulness improves immune response and reaction to stress, while also giving a general feeling of well-being (Davidson et al., 2003). Another researcher has investigated mindful learning (Langer, 1989). She found that mindful awareness helps learners to be more open to new material so that they can remain alert to distinctions and understand new perspectives. Witkiewitz, Marlatt, and Walker (2005) found support for mindfulness meditation as a treatment for preventing relapses for alcohol and substance abuse.

A German investigator indicated that practicing Zen meditation by psychotherapists made a difference in therapeutic effectiveness. Therapists direct their attention in some manner during psychotherapy and this project found that directing attention using a Zen mindfulness approach improved therapeutic effectiveness (Grepmair et al., 2007). A program was proposed for training psychotherapists in core principles of Zen, such as emptiness, impermanence, and paradox (Twemlow, 2001). An earlier study found that Zen meditation helped to develop empathy in counselors (Lesh, 1970).

The Yoga meditation approach has been applied successfully to treat many psychiatric problems such as obsessive-compulsive disorder, depression, addictions, sleep disorders, and attention deficit hyperactivity (Shannahoff-Khalsa, 2006). Shanahoff-Khalsa has also used Kundalini Yoga in a novel approach to working with couples. Yoga has been shown to help people who suffer from many other problems; for example, epilepsy (Panjwani et al., 2000).

Many varied forms of meditation can help with a wide variety of difficulties to bring about a therapeutic change. We have offered a few selections from the many studies in this ever-growing area of research.

Conclusion

Scientific understanding of meditation is just beginning. Interest grows as meditation is integrated into varying forms of psychotherapy. Only a sampling of the numerous studies has been presented here. Interested readers will find many more studies on the Internet and in compendiums of meditation research such as Murphey and Donovan (1997) or Shapiro and Walsh (1984). Certainly, therapists and clients can have confidence that regular meditation will have positive effects at many levels.

PART II

The Elements: Tools and Techniques

Before I started to study Zen, mountains were mountains and rivers were rivers. Then, when I was in the midst of learning Zen, mountains were no longer mountains and rivers were no longer rivers. Now after years of studying Zen, mountains are once again mountains and rivers are once again rivers.

(Traditional Zen Story)

Therapists know that a single therapeutic method may not be helpful for all clients. Therefore, therapists are careful to pick the methods that will be most effective in working with each client's needs, problems, and reactions. This insight holds true for meditation as well: One form of meditation may not be as useful for a particular client or problem area as another form might be. The varied meditation traditions presented in Part I offered four major approaches: Yoga, Buddhism, Zen, and Daoism. Each has the potential to bring about different therapeutic effects by developing helpful skills. The therapist can apply the varied methods thoughtfully to meet the unique needs of each client. Then the nonspecific effects of meditation common to all forms will be activated, along with the specific individual benefits. This is best accomplished by matching the client's tendencies and talents to a particular form of meditation for the most natural pathway into the experience. Built upon this foundation, other forms of meditation can be learned as well.

The practices of meditational approaches also have an indirect effect. The meditative techniques allow the client an experience to react to and learn from. The therapist can study these reactions and help the client to work with them in other contexts as well. As skills build, the process generalizes, helping the client to cope more effectively with life.

Different Methods for Different Needs

The chapters in Part II offer meditation methods with specific techniques. Each chapter develops different types of skills. This section will help the therapist to discern the specific forms of meditation. Knowledge concerning when to use each technique develops as the therapist becomes more personally familiar with meditation, so we encourage the therapist to practice these meditation methods to enhance his or her personal understanding. Experiencing meditation will facilitate knowing how and when to apply these methods with others. There are some guidelines for choosing, but keep in mind that personally experiencing the methods is essential for truly understanding and using them. Some therapists may want to receive further training from a meditation master.

Sometimes these skills are used in therapy just as they are in meditation. Symbols and rituals can facilitate the process. For example, mandalas, mantras, and ritual, as in tea ceremonies, can help promote a calm experience as well. Art is another way, such as in writing haiku.

In summary, some meditation methods give strategies of concentration and detachment, others offer techniques of mindful engagement, while others show how to release and be free of problematic constraints. These methods overlap. Distinctions are made to help map the way through the territory. As therapists become more familiar with the different methods of meditation by doing them, they will be able to adapt them well to the individualized needs of the client. Part III will describe this process more fully.

Knowing Where to Begin

Some methods will seem easier than others. Try the different types of meditations to discover which ones seem most natural, to find the most accessible doorway into the experience. But remember that individuals differ in what comes naturally at first. For example, some will find it easier to begin by filling the mind with an experience, such as focusing on a mandala or breathing. Others may be more at ease with clearing or emptying the mind, without a narrow object of focus. Some will be more body oriented, gravitating naturally toward attention to breathing and Qi Gong, while others may prefer to work with cognitive processes. Notice what feels easy and what feels like a struggle. Build upon the seemingly easier skills to develop and deepen the process. Eventually, skills generalize to even include the methods that seemed difficult at first.

Making Distinctions without Distinctions

Another common difficulty sometimes encountered by beginners is not being able to notice differences. Even though some of the specific meditations occasionally seem to resemble others, such as focus on breathing in Chapter 6 and concentration with breathing as the object of focus in Chapter 8, each involves a different cognitive process. As readers become familiar with meditation, they will become aware of subtle distinctions that are commonly encountered in the terrain of the mind.

One typical Western way to make clear distinctions is by careful use of language. For example, the Alaskan Inuit native language was believed to have four words for snow: *aput* ("snow on the ground") *qana* ("falling snow"), *piqsirpoq* ("drifting snow"), and *qimuqsuq* ("snowdrift"). By contrast, as first pointed out by anthropologist Franz Boaz (1911), English has only one noun ("snow"), although there are numerous adjectives to describe it, as evidenced by our attempts to translate the Inuit words. Later, in a popular 1940 article on the subject, the famous linguist B. L. Whorf (1956) noted that he had learned three additional Inuit words for snow, making a total of seven. He proposed that the Inuit language sensitizes and helps its speakers to recognize the many types of snow that they typically encounter in their northern environment. They perceive subtle distinctions in the actual experience of the substance and can recognize snow in ways we do not. Language precedes experience.

Conversely, meditation practice sensitizes and attunes the practitioner to notice distinctions of experience that can then be expressed with words. According to meditational theory, experience precedes language. These wordless sensitivities and attunements are useful when applied for therapeutic purposes.

These meditation techniques are practiced on a level where they interconnect with each other beyond the linguistic distinctions used to describe them. In other words, use the fine distinctions between meditative techniques as a map to help navigate through the territory, but don't mistake the map for the territory. Meditation is not just a technique; it is an experience, beyond the words used to describe it. Whorf seemed to intuit the nature of direct experience when he said (1956):

We are constantly reading into nature fictional acting entities, simply to say, "It flashed," or "A light flashed," setting up an actor, "it" or "light," to perform what we call an action, "to flash." Yet, the flashing and the light are one and the same! (Whorf, 1956, p. 243).

So let the distinctions be beacons, to light the way through a sometimes hidden territory. Although the map is not the territory, the map can be a guide through the terrain. The instantaneous flash reveals an undiscovered country to be added to your therapeutic insights.

4

Mobilizing Motivation

Readying for Meditation

If you never wholly give yourself up to the chair you sit in, but always keep your leg-and-body-muscles half contracted for a rise; if you breathe eighteen or nineteen instead of sixteen times a minute, and never quite breathe out at that—what mental mood *can* you be in but one of inner panting and expectancy, and how can the future and its worries possibly forsake your mind? On the other hand, how can they gain admission to your mind if your brow be unruffled, your respiration calm and complete, and your muscles all relaxed?

(James, 1918, p. 29)

Meditation is an experience, but the experience can be made easier to achieve by creating the proper foundations. You can guide circumstances to be most conducive for success. This chapter shows how to ready yourself for meditation beginning with practical considerations. Next, methods are given for preparing the faculties of attention, visualization, and the unconscious that will be utilized during meditation.

Practical Considerations

Just as important as the techniques for experiencing medition, the setting is part of the total meditation experience. Eventually, the inner state of meditation is capable of becoming independent of the outer circumstances.

A PLACE TO MEDITATE

At first, the client will learn meditation in the office. But meditation should also be performed between sessions. Encourage the client to find a quiet place to meditate. It may be a quiet room or even a certain corner in the house. The atmosphere of the place for meditation can be very helpful especially when first beginning: Quiet surroundings help to foster a quiet mind. Eventually, meditators learn how to find inner quiet in varied environments. But in the early phases of practice, some settings will prove more conducive to the experience than others.

For example, Zen tearooms have served as a refuge from the stresses of everyday life for centuries. Unpretentious and simple, these carefully constructed environments create an atmosphere of sanctuary: Quiet surroundings point to inner calm. Walls and floors are empty of decoration. Diffused light softly illuminates a lone calligraphic scroll hanging on a wall or a flower in perfect bloom resting in a simple stoneware vase on the floor. Seating is a simple cushion placed on a woven mat. Participants in the tea ceremony find the surroundings help guide them gently into the meditative experience.

Therapists can create a meditative atmosphere in a corner of the office. Make the lighting subdued, not too dark or too bright. Keep decorations simple, but try to add an aesthetic touch to provide a beautiful point of interest. Engaging the sense of smell with a subtle incense or fragrant plant may also be helpful. Place a pillow on the floor for sitting or a mat to lie down on.

Some people will feel that they cannot meditate at home. Open other options. Traditionally, nature has been an inspiration for meditation. Meditation done outdoors, at a park, in the woods, or perhaps in a tranquil garden can help to bring about a feeling of communion with nature. Water can also have a calming effect. The beach, the shore of a lake, the edge of a pond, or the banks of a stream can all serve as sites for a meditation session. Some of the meditations included in this book are readily adapted to being done outdoors. For those who prefer to be indoors, a library or religious institution may provide another alternative where people may find sanctuary.

Frequently people find it easier to meditate with a group. The commitment and momentum of a group embarking on meditation together will carry the individual along. The therapist might want to provide this opportunity as part of a regular group therapy session, or even by offering group meditation sessions. Another alternative is to direct the client to the many meditation groups that are available through

Buddhist, Daoist, and Yoga centers. These institutions offer both brief hour-long meditation classes and weekend retreats.

Whether the client prefers to meditate with others or alone is a matter of personal preference. The most important consideration in choosing the meditative environment is that the meditator feels at ease there. Consider these decisions with an open attitude. There are no prerequisite conditions, but one: meditate!

Return to the same place each time for meditation. Habit and consistency help to set the mood, and like a conditioned response, a meditative response will become easier to bring about.

A TIME TO MEDITATE

The amount of time to devote to meditation depends on the needs and the situation. People often complain that their lives are so hectic and busy that they could not imagine finding any time to meditate. They are surprised to discover that meditation can be done in as short a period as one minute and still bring positive results. Everyone has otherwise wasted moments that can be used. Beginners might start with as little as one or two minutes a day. Clients suffering from attentional disorders may need to begin with only 30 seconds. But with practice, most people can increase the amount of time they devote to meditation at one sitting. Typically, 30 minutes to an hour is an effective length of time for one sitting, but even a few minutes a day can set a process in motion. Activation of inner processing does not rely upon clock time the way conscious cognition does. Sometimes the deepest meditative experience occurs in a flash. Then again, an insight may evolve over many months of practice.

Meditate at least one time nearly every day. When working on something, as described in subsequent chapters, meditate several times during the day. Start with a duration of time that can be done comfortably and will fit with the client's schedule and lifestyle. But above all, meditate regularly.

Body Positioning for Meditation

What we call "body" cannot be considered apart from the rest of the human being. Without the body, we could not move or think or create. What we call "body" is ourselves.

(Keene, 1979, p. 10)

The mind and body are linked, each having influence upon the other. Therefore, how the body is positioned is an important element in the meditative experience. Some people are naturally more aware of their bodies than others. The exercises that follow offer guidance for those who are dissociated from body sensations to enhance mind–body links. This training will also assist in finding some optimal body positions for meditation.

FINDING MEDITATIVE POSITIONS

Meditation has traditionally been done in a sitting position on a pillow placed on the floor, but many body positions can be used. Positioning should not interfere with the experience. If body positioning is approached with awareness, the process of discovering a suitable posture can help to deepen the meditation.

Meditation is not prohibitive for people who are unable to sit in traditional cross-legged postures, since the experience is not reliant on any single position or place. If you are unable to sit down on the floor, feel confident in using a chair. Finding a comfortable, natural way to sit provides an excellent starting point. This series of exercises turns the focus on body balance in standing and then sitting to assist in finding your best postures for meditation.

We all live under the influence of gravity. When aligned with gravity, standing, walking, and running become easier, and so does meditation. But how can one become more aligned? Simply standing or sitting upright is not the answer. Turn attention toward the body to find the answers. In the process, you may develop new sensitivities. This series of exercises will assist in finding balance and positioning that is most aligned and comfortable.

DISCOVERING BALANCE

Stand with legs shoulder-width apart, at a comfortable distance, with feet flat on the ground, hands at the sides, head upright, and eyes looking ahead, at ease. Now, rock gently back-and-forth, forward-and-back, on the balls of the feet, then on the heels, back-and-forth, forward-and-back. Concentrate on the sensations. With each swaying motion, there is a point in the middle where muscles are less tense and the body is most at ease. Slowly reduce the sway, to arrive at this balance point, at ease, aligned, and still.

Next, move the same way from side-to-side; gently rocking slowly so that weight shifts first to one foot, then to the other. Gradually reduce the motion until a point in the center is found, where muscles are most relaxed and weight is evenly distributed on both feet. This is the exact balance point, where the body is optimally aligned with gravity. Repeat the exercise several times to ensure that the best center point has been found. If possible, let go of any unnecessary tensions. Enjoy the relaxation for a few moments, and then move on to the next exercise.

ATTUNING TO STANDING

Stand upright with the feet approximately shoulder-width apart and eyes closed. Pay attention to how the feet relate to the floor surface. Do they seem to be pressing down on the floor, or does the floor seem to be pressing up on the feet? Does it feel hard, soft, warm, or cool? Is the whole foot making contact or is the most weight on the heels, or is weight forward on the toes? There are many possibilities. Now focus attention on standing and nothing else. Do not label the experience with words. Instead, try to feel the sensations of standing.

FINDING THE SITTING POSITION

This exercise guides in discovering alignment with gravity for the most comfortable sitting position. The sitting position is the most common meditative posture. Sit cross-legged on the floor or on a small cushion. If floor sitting is uncomfortable, sit upright in a straight-backed chair. Let the arms rest comfortably extended over the knees, and close the eyes. Rock back and forth gently and feel the bones located at the base of the pelvis. Experiment with swaying forward and back and then side to side as in the standing exercise, to find the aligned center. From this centered position, sit upright without being rigid, to allow breathing passages to be open and air to flow freely in and out. Align the head upright in relation to the body, keeping the neck and shoulders as relaxed as possible. Maintain the position with back straight and shoulders open without hunching forward. Sitting upright with the head straight allows the breathing passages to remain clear. Sometimes people will slouch forward as they focus. Keep the spine comfortably upright throughout meditation.

EYE POSITIONS

Meditation traditions vary on eye closure. One way is to keep the eyes fully closed. Sometimes eyes are kept half-open, half-closed. Another method is to fix the gaze on

Figure 4.1. Meditation
sitting position.

one point with eyes open. Experiment with these different approaches. We will advise using one method or another at times, but for therapeutic purposes, work with whatever feels most natural for the particular meditation. When a client has difficulty focusing, closing the eyes may help to lessen distractions. Clients with a less stable reality sense or a tendency to withdraw should meditate with eyes open.

HAND POSITIONS

The hands can be placed in a number of different meditative positions. Figures 4.2a, 4.2b, and 4.2c demonstrate these positions.

Once a comfortable position is found, sit still for several minutes. Quiet sitting provides excellent preparation for meditation.

Figure 4.2a. Meditation hand position. Extend the arms so that the backs of the hands are over the knees. Clasp the forefinger and thumb in a circle, with the other three fingers extended.

Figure 4.2b. Place the hands one on top of the other, palms up, with thumbs touching.

Figure 4.2c. Fold the two hands together. Fingertips can be either together or with a rounded space between them.

5

Developing the Tools

The mind's capacity is limitless, and its manifestations are inexhaustible.

(Bodhidharma quoted in Pine, 1989, p. 23)

Attention, visualization, and the use of the unconscious are primary cognitive tools for meditation. People sometimes feel ill equipped to meditate because they have not been trained in these skills. Clients undergoing psychotherapy may be grappling with problems that make these abilities even less accessible to them. This section encourages the development of skills to strengthen the faculties that will be most useful. In the process, what is gained may be applied to other areas of therapy as well.

Attention

. . . Each of us literally chooses, by his ways of attending to things, what sort of a universe he shall appear to himself to inhabit.

(James, 1896, p. 424)

Honing the Tool of Attention with Better Seeing

Paying attention frequently involves seeing, but people are dissociated from their experience of seeing, such as when they look at one thing and think about something else. Furthermore, the senses may become exhausted by the demands placed on the eyes in both work and play. Many jobs require long hours looking at a computer screen. People often strain to read small print, sometimes in poor light conditions. But we rarely think about our eyes unless they become a problem. Eyes, just like other parts of the body, can be relaxed and freed from rigid patterns. Ancient Yoga methods for training and improving vision are still used today. These exercises will help the practitioner to become more relaxed in the eyes, a preliminary step to enhance attention and visualization skills.

EYE SWING EXERCISE

Stand comfortably, weight balanced evenly on the two feet with hands extended downwards at the sides. If any back trouble is present, check with a physician before proceeding. Begin to gently and loosely swing the arms around from one side of the body to the other. Bend the knee of the trailing leg slightly and lift the heel of the foot a little, to permit adjustments for flexibility. Keep the body aligned, upright; in balance. Allow the body to twist naturally with the arms, pivoting the feet as well. Keep the head upright, turning in synchrony with the body. Breathe comfortably, as needed. With each swing, keep the eyes directed straight ahead and relaxed, so that the field of vision rotates with the body movement. The surroundings will seem to rush past. Let the eyes focus spontaneously, without effort, turning naturally with the movement. After several minutes of pivoting, back and forth, the eyes will begin to relax. Alternatively, let the shoulders turn, but do not swing the arms; perhaps, place the hands on the hips during the action.

Figure 5.1. Palming.

PALMING

The eyes can become tired from excessive use, and this tension carries through the whole body. Palming can relieve and relax the eyes. First, wash the hands and dry them. Sit or lie down comfortably. Cup the hands. Close the eyes. Place palms lightly over the eyelids. The fingertips can rest on the top of the forehead. Do not press. Rest for several minutes. Allow the eyes to relax beneath the warm palms. Let go of any unnecessary tension in the eyes or face.

Observation

Concentration of attention is one of the most essential tools for meditation. Many clients suffer from an inability to focus their attention well. The exercises that follow will begin to gently guide the faculty of attention so that it can be developed more fully for use with meditation.

OBSERVATION EXERCISES

Observation is an important component of attention. Attend to seeing and the experience will lead to development of cognitive skills in many areas. One natural way to train the attention through observation can be drawn from an everyday task: Going to the store. For example, grocery store observations are readily accessible. Most people visit such stores frequently for the practical purpose of purchasing food. However, grocery stores also present many varied objects with intense colors, shapes, and smells that provide an accessible place to practice observational skills. Other stores, such as hardware, auto parts, or clothing stores can be equally used with slight adaptations of the instructions.

Make a visit to a local grocery store without the intention of making any purchases. Disregard brands, labels, or even what things are. Instead, notice the colors, patterns, and shapes. Note how the bright colors of containers, the lettering sizes and colors, and packaging shapes catch the attention. Display groupings offer opportunities to exercise observational skills. Perhaps other qualities or properties will also emerge.

Each aisle has characteristic odors. Observe how the sense of smell helps to orient attention. For example, experiment with finding the aisle with detergents and soaps simply using the sense of smell. Extend this to other categories of items. Turn the attention to other senses, such as the sense of sound and touch, and orient with that instead. Note how directing attention to different senses affects the experience of what is noticed.

A task or project helps to focus attention. An interesting variation of this exercise is to study how attention is affected when action is goal-directed. Visit the supermarket with a particular item in mind to buy. Make note of any differences between the trips to the grocery store with and without a goal. Vary this by substituting other places that may be of interest. Often the spotlight of attention is narrowed when a goal is involved. Westerners are often very skilled at goal-directed behaviors. However, goalless awareness has benefits too.

TESTING OBSERVATION SKILLS

Walk into a room; pause briefly for one minute, then leave. Now from outside the room, attempt to describe everything in the room: the objects, the room itself, the atmosphere, the lighting. If doing this exercise alone, it can be helpful to write down what is remembered. Then, return and compare the actual experience to the remembered one. Again, observe carefully, and spend a bit more time, perhaps five minutes, observing. Then leave and describe the room and its contents. Try grouping similar items into categories. And once again, return. Look around, to compare. How many things are noticed this time? There are many possible variations of this exercise. For those who are more intrigued by auditory experience, try this experiment with an auditory impression. Find a place where a variety of sounds are available and record the sounds for one minute. Then try to recall all that was heard. Play back the recording and compare it to what was recalled.

Another way to test auditory observation is to listen to a favorite CD or album, paying careful attention to the details of the rhythm, the bass, the beat, the harmony, the melody, the theme, and so on. Then pause the recording and recall as clearly as possible what was heard. Once again, listen to the actual music and compare it to the memory image. These exercises can improve observational skills, while enhancing memory.

INNER AND OUTER ATTENTION

Attention can be directed to inner or to outer objects of consciousness. Some clients may have difficulty recognizing the distinction between these two dimensions of experience. Learning how to deliberately direct attention may prove helpful with various psychological problems. Sensations, feelings, thoughts, or beliefs are attention turned inward, whereas observing things in the environment, such as house, friends, family, nature, or art, is attention turned outwards. The following exercises practiced in succession will help the practitioner to gain an experiential understanding and to improve skills in directing the focus of attention.

INNER ATTENTION EXERCISE

Sit comfortably with eyes closed. Pay attention to the skin. Does it feel warm, cool, or right in between? Keep attention focused on the skin temperature. Does the sensation of temperature alter with the focus of attention? Now, turn attention to the temperature of a specific part of the body such as the face. Then note the temperature of another area such as the hands. Are there any temperature differences between the face and hands? For a variation of this exercise, focus on different parts of the body. Other points of focus can be used such as lightness and heaviness, comfort and discomfort, or tension and relaxation. When finished, open the eyes.

OUTER ATTENTION EXERCISE

Attention may be trained using other objects as well. Direct the client's attention to the office. Look around the office. Then stand up and walk around the room. Observe the wall decorations, the flooring, and the furniture. Notice the lines, the colors, the size and shapes, and the themes of the décor. The intention to observe is an important component of this exercise. How is the quality of attention different from when the focus was placed on an inner object of experiencing?

SPONTANEOUS VS. DELIBERATE USE OF ATTENTION

> All objects are not apprehended on equal terms. Under instantaneous illumination, several words can be clearly read; if, however, one is intent upon the precise form of a single letter, all the other letters become less clear; while with repetition the range of the attentive "point of regard" may increase. . . . Under attention, apprehension of disparate objects is unitary.
>
> (Wundt, 1932, p. 616)

Interest and attention are linked. It is easier for people to pay attention to what they are interested in. The pioneers of psychology such as William James and Wilhelm Wundt spelled out varieties of attention (James, 1896; Wundt, 1932). Two important distinctions were immediate or derived attention and deliberate or voluntary attention. Immediate attention occurs when the attention is grabbed by something that draws the interest right away, whether willed or not. For example, imagine driving calmly down the road not thinking about anything in particular. Then a fire engine comes racing down the street, siren blasting, approaching rapidly. Immediately, paying very close attention to it, the driver pulls over and gets out of the way. This illustrates spontaneous attention: sharp, effortless, and immediate.

Most have experienced the effort needed to stay awake or focused on a boring class or work assignment. This is an example of the use of deliberate attention. Willpower is developed, in part, through the discipline of deliberately attending to something that might not capture the interest spontaneously. To some, willpower is a virtue. With practice, it becomes easier to focus attention deliberately. Stilling the mind requires focus.

Attention can also be free flowing and spontaneous. Ericksonian hypnosis is a clinical example of utilizing the natural free flow of attention without deliberate direction (Rossi, Erickson-Klein, & Rossi, 2006). Daoist meditation also relies on allowing attention to be free to wander.

Both deliberate and spontaneous attention can be useful, depending on the circumstances. Try working with deliberate and then spontaneous use of attention in the two exercises that follow. Adapt the exercises creatively as appropriate.

EXERCISE IN SPONTANEOUS VS. DELIBERATE ATTENTION

This exercise can be assigned as "homework" to be done between sessions in order to explore spontaneous vs. deliberate attention. Discuss the selection of a place that the client would enjoy visiting, such as an art gallery, a sporting event, or a walk in the woods. Encourage exploration in that setting, first of inner experiencing and then of outer experiencing as performed in the previous exercises. Attention will tend to be spontaneously engaged because the environment is one that is naturally interesting. People tend to find that their attention is spontaneously drawn to the situation, seemingly without effort.

For contrast, go to a place that is not interesting, a place that the client typically finds dull, tedious, or dry. For example, ask the art lover to attend a sporting event, the athlete to go to an art gallery. The nature lover might visit a downtown metropolitan area. Notice how deliberate effort is required to attend to a situation where spontaneous interest is absent. This form of attention may feel forced and tiring, much like struggling to stay engaged in boring homework. These exercises help to illustrate differences in the use of attention. Skilled meditation takes advantage of all these natural capacities and more.

Visualization and Imagination

> When people's eyes are open, they see landscapes in the outer world. When people's eyes are closed, they see landscapes with their mind's eye. People spend hours looking at outer landscapes, but there is just as much to see in the inner landscapes. The landscapes are different, but they are equally valid.
>
> (Samuels & Samuels, 1973, p. 34)

Meditators develop the ability to visualize. Visualization is a fundamental skill for many healing systems both in the East and in the West. For example, guided daydream methods are used in psychotherapy. Hypnosis incorporates visualization approaches both for trance induction and for suggestion. Tantric Yoga methods are based in visualization as well. Visualization has been widely used because it is powerful and effective.

Some people are naturally able to visualize. If asked to imagine a beautiful scene in nature, a vivid image appears instantly. For many others, however, nothing comes to mind. For those who have difficulty with visualization, the following exercise will give the experience of an automatic visualization. Based on a natural tendency of perception, everyone will have an afterimage that can form a bridge to visualizing more readily.

PRELIMINARY VISUALIZATION EXERCISE

Tape a six-inch square piece of red colored paper to a well-lit, white or nearly white wall. Stand several feet away from the wall and look fixedly at it for two to three minutes. As an alternative, using a computer, create a six-inch red square placed on a white background. Observe closely and do not let the eyes wander from the colored square. After the allotted time, close the eyes. An image of a green square will appear. This afterimage is similar to an imagined image.

AUDITORY VISUALIZATION EXERCISE

The sense of hearing can also leave a sort of afterimage of sound, much like the colored shape on the wall or computer. In this exercise, listen to a piece of music. Turn the volume up a bit and listen intently. Then, midway through the piece, stop the music. With eyes closed, listen to the silence. The music will be heard like an afterimage.

The more senses that are used to visualize, the easier and more natural visualizations will become. People vary in how they orient themselves. For some people, vision best helps them take stock of where or how they are. For others, it is the sense of touch. Still others are most aware of sounds. For this reason, the client may find one sensory modality easier to use than another. By experimenting with all of these modalities, mental tools are honed for meditation.

SENSORY VISUALIZATION EXERCISE

Here is another way to call forth a visual image, using the motor responses. Draw an imaginary simple figure with the index finger on the other hand—such as a circle, square, or line. Then close the eyes and imagine the simple figure that was drawn. For a more active approach, crawl a letter on the floor. Then stop, and with eyes closed, imagine the letter. Try this with a circle or a square as well. Rather than moving the entire body, substitute an arm movement, or a foot movement. Try it on the beach, on a rug, in the grass. Even a partner's back can serve as a "blackboard." Draw a letter or shape on the blackboard by touch with the index finger. Index finger motions in the air can be used as well. Draw a simple shape in the air with the finger.

FROM ENVISION TO INVISION

Active, alert seeing is an important component of visualization, to move from an external seeing to internal vision, from *envisioning* to *invisioning*. As the process develops, intuitions of the outer world take a new, inner form, revealing essential features and a deeper nature. The word *invision* refers to the special kind of visualizing that occurs in certain forms of meditation, such as the use of mandalas, where outer becomes inner. Creative variations arise spontaneously. These exercises are the first steps in a process that is developed extensively in meditation.

OBJECT INVISIONING

Choose a simple, ordinary object used in daily life, such as a cup, a vase, a ball, or a flower. Place it on the floor and sit down next to it. Look at it for two to three minutes. Notice everything about how it looks. Next, move to the opposite side and look from another perspective. Move closer to the object and inspect the details. Notice colors, textures, and how the light strikes it. After spending several minutes envisioning this object thoroughly, close the eyes and *invision* it. Usually an image of it will appear. It may be very vague, just a glimmer, or extremely clear and distinct. If nothing appears, open the eyes and look at the object again. Repeat the process several times until an image appears in the mind's eye. Remember, visualization is a natural capacity. Discovering how to experience and direct it may take some practice.

CREATIVE INVISIONING

The next step is to imagine things that are not exact replicas of the environment. Children do this all the time in their play. With eyes closed, imagine a two-dimensional shape such as a triangle, circle, or square. Try to *invision* it, with a definite size and color. Allow it to become larger and larger until it appears huge. Next, let it become smaller and smaller until it is seen as a single dot. For a variation, change the shape, for example, from circle to square. When finished, open the eyes.

PASSIVE IMAGERY EXERCISE

The visualization exercises above are samples of active visualization, with a deliberate image to actively produce inwardly. Next, experiment with passive visualization and tap into unconscious perception. To work with the mind in this way, take a more wait-and-see attitude. Be curious about what will occur; curiosity and wonder open the perception to receive new data.

In the early 1900s, the German psychiatrist Hans Silberer (1909) found he could solve complex problems by using an altered state. He performed experiments when he was in what he called the "Twilight State": the drowsy state between sleeping and waking that is now known as hypnagogic. The attention is free to drift while in this state, and the body is relaxed. He discovered that if he presented himself with a problem to solve and then waited, patiently and attentively, a meaningful image that symbolized the solution would emerge. Many famous scientists, artists, and writers have drawn from the wellsprings of inner imagery for creative inspiration. One famous example is the German organic chemist F. August Kekule (1829–1896), a founding father of chemical structure theory. He claimed to have recognized the structure of benzene as a ring through a dream he had of a snake chasing its tail.

Inner symbolic imagery comes to mind spontaneously and later can be consciously contemplated to determine its meaning. This form of imagery is known as hypnagogic imagery because it takes shape just below the threshold of the conscious mind. Often, since hypnagogic images reach deep into the psyche, such imagery can be personally meaningful.

Hypnagogic images are often deeply symbolic; that is, they put together and communicate many aspects into one meaningful, unified picture. This capacity of the mind to find understanding symbolically has been known and used for millennia. For example, Tibetan Buddhists have created elaborate mandalas, rich with symbols, in order to understand a higher reality. The capacity to visualize and symbolize can be developed for creative use to solve problems. The exercises that follow are a guide to developing these skills.

EXERCISE IN HYPNOGOGIC IMAGERY

Close the eyes. Invite an image to appear. Do not be specific as to what image; rather, remain open and wait patiently. The key to passive visualization is to invite the image generally, in an invitational sense. Do not push or dictate with a definite set of instructions, but rather, allow an image of significance to come in an open-ended manner. Hypnagogic imagery is easiest to access in certain situations such as in the evening, when tired, just before sleep, while listening to music late at night, while sitting in a car while someone else is driving on a long trip, or when first awakening from sleep in the morning.

DA VINCI'S DEVICE

Visual thinking is natural and can be helpful for problem solving. Video games use this concept for entertainment. The capacity to reason intuitively using imagination and visualization can be developed through meditation. Leonardo da Vinci created this exercise to teach creative invention though imaginative seeing. In allowing his mind to wander creatively, he stimulated his visual imagery. This may be adapted to other senses.

Look at a wall that has cracks, chips, and paint stains. Let the imagination wander. Notice resemblances to shapes of animals, landscapes, or whatever comes to mind.

UNLOCK PATTERNED VISUALIZATIONS

Architecture students train to see their world more creatively by using specific exercises for pattern reorganization. Take an ordinary object, such as a fan, box, bowl, book—anything. Imagine slicing it into a number of parts and then put the parts back together in a totally new way. Do not worry about the function of the new object. Play with the ideas. Some people may enjoy drawing the new object as well.

The Unconscious

It really doesn't matter what your conscious mind does because your unconscious automatically will do just what it needs to.

(Erickson, 1978)

Attending to the Unconscious Mind

People are accustomed to attending to what they are aware of, to what they can visualize and imagine, but many do not consider learning to attend to what they are unaware of. Most of the exercises presented up to this point have involved conscious awareness. But another part of the mind can provide positive resources through meditation: Processes outside of conscious awareness; or in other words, unconscious.

Learning how to attend to the unconscious is somewhat paradoxical, because once one becomes aware of unconscious processing, its character changes. One can learn how to develop an accepting and open, free-floating kind of attention. Then the range of mental processing broadens, giving new options, emerging from the dark unknown.

The following exercise is designed to help recognize unconscious processes by analogy. Images and symbols become meaningful when allowed into awareness.

CONSCIOUS VS. UNCONSCIOUS

Imagine sitting in a car in front of some train tracks at a crossing, waiting for the signal, watching. A train slowly approaches from the distance. It grows closer and closer and then begins to pass. It is very long. The wheels make a sound: *clack, clack,* on the track. At first attention is drawn to the cars as they pass. Each one is different; some are passenger cars, others carry cargo. But then the spaces between the cars become interesting. At first the background behind the cars is barely visible. It is a flicker, a view that appears for a split second and then is gone, yet it is still there again to be perceived, between the next cars. But as attention is focused on that space between cars, awareness of the scenery behind becomes the foreground while the passing cars in front are seen as a blurred background.

This background behind the cars, with the capacity to be glimpsed, is like the unconscious. Think of the cars as the conscious sensations, feelings, and thoughts stretching across the horizon. The view glimpsed between the rhythmically spaced boxcars as they pass is the content of the unconscious. For example, while reading this book, you probably are not noticing your foot. But as soon as the foot is mentioned, attention turns to the foot with its sensations. These and other thoughts and experiences remain unconscious until attention is turned to them. These unconscious experiences can be used for meditative states. Hypnosis is another altered states method that has developed the use of the unconscious to help with clinical problems (Simpkins & Simpkins, 2005).

When attention is withdrawn from the conscious level of mental processing, it does not merely become inattention. Freed to look between the cars, the mind can wander and make connections. To explore inwardly, attention is released from linearly focused conscious awareness. Unconscious attention, as a free-floating searchlight, can move randomly, until an interesting association or impression appears in the light. Then unconscious attention spontaneously focuses, lighting up, like a spotlight, what is there in the background but rarely revealed. In this way, new discoveries become possible. Poised, free-floating, creative—these are also qualities of attention used in meditation. People are often pleasantly surprised that new discoveries may occur.

Here is another exercise that will help develop skill with unconscious processing. Later, in the meditation sections, this skill will be developed more fully.

EXERCISE IN UNCONSCIOUS RESPONSE

Sit in a supportive chair, with your hands resting either on your lap or on the arms of the chair. Close the eyes and relax for a moment. Then notice the hands. Attend to the sensations in the hands. Do they seem to be cool or warm, light or heavy? Wait for the experience to occur. Some people might find that one hand becomes heavier than the other, warmer, or even tingly. Any of these sensations are communications from the unconscious. Consciously, one does not know what the hands will feel like while waiting, until the spontaneous response occurs. These surprises come from the unconscious.

UNCONSCIOUS SUGGESTION USING VISUALIZATION AND IMAGINATION

From earliest recorded times, meditation has utilized unconscious visualizations in the form of positive suggestion. Self-hypnosis also uses suggestion to evoke unconscious visual imagery for many fascinating experiences (Simpkins & Simpkins, 2004).

Visualizations held vividly in mind tend to engage the ideomotor and ideosensory sensibilities, where the idea (*ideo*) tends to find expression in the action (*motor*) or the senses (*sensory*) systems of the body. The link is made through a fundamental phenomenon: suggestion. Suggestion is the process through which an idea, image, thought, or feeling can activate other processes without effort. Suggestion can be used to get in touch with normally involuntary abilities and activate new possibilities. Suggestion works through the unconscious because its mechanisms often occur automatically, without conscious, rational thought. It is valuable for meditation, where it has been utilized for centuries. The exercises included here will help to recognize and work with suggestion through linking visualization with motoric sensations.

EXERCISE IN SUGGESTION USING VISUALIZATION

Find a comfortable place to sit, and then close the eyes. Imagine a very pleasant experience, a memory of being very relaxed. Now think about a tart lemon. Imagine the taste, the smell of lemon, and its yellow color. Picture it as clearly as possible, especially remembering the tart taste. Wait. Do you find the mouth producing extra saliva? The body produces this automatic response in reaction to the visualization of the lemon: an experience of how an idea, suggested by the mind, gets translated to the body.

THE CHEVREUL PENDULUM

Ideomotor theory draws upon the kind of experience developed in the previous exercise, the ability of the mind to suggest an experience to which the body responds automatically. An idea when fully accepted by the mind can be automatically translated into a motoric, body response. The classic exercise to develop ideomotor phenomena is called the Chevreul Pendulum, after the prominent chemist who wrote about it.

EXERCISE IN IDEOMOTOR RESPONSE

Get a plumb bob or metal ring. Attach a thin string to it. Hold the string from the top and let the object dangle freely. Support the elbow on a table so that you are comfort-

Figure 5.2. Chevreul pendulum.

able holding the string, but leave the arm and wrist free. Now close the eyes. Imagine that the pendulum begins to swing back and forth. Picture it vividly. Do not deliberately move or interfere with the hand that holds the string. Instead, focus on the imaginative image of swinging. Visualize the rhythmic sweep of the swing becoming longer. After a few minutes, open the eyes and look at the pendulum. Most people will find that it is swinging back and forth. Some will find this easy, some difficult, to do.

Now close the eyes again. Imagine that the object begins to swing in the other direction.

Exaggerate the image so that the arc becomes larger and larger in the new direction. Picture it as vividly as possible. Once again, do not disturb the hand that holds the string. Simply focus on the visualization. After a time, open the eyes. Is the pendulum swinging in the new direction?

Close the eyes one last time. Imagine that the pendulum swings in a circle. Allow the circular orbit to become larger and larger. Open the eyes to check.

Some people can do these exercises almost immediately. Others expand their abilities over time. Regular daily practice will help build skill quickly. The relationship to the unconscious that is developed by doing these exercises will be applied often in the meditation chapters. Meanwhile, enjoy the fun of these experiments. The unconscious mind is a reservoir of potential. Meditation can help to tap this resource.

6

Breathing: Unifying Mind and Body

Pranayama is the conscious, deliberate regulation of the breath replacing unconscious patterns of breathing. . . . The regular practice of pranayama reduces the obstacles that inhibit clear perception.

(*The Yoga Sutra of Patanjali* quoted in Desikachar, 1995, pp. 181–182)

The breath is a gateway to inner being, a bridge between mind and body. When someone is emotionally agitated, breathing becomes more rapid. Similarly, when relaxed, breathing slows and the mind becomes calm. In the course of a therapy session, the client's breathing patterns may alter dramatically. These patterns can reveal subtleties of experiencing that may be helpful for getting in touch with inner experiencing. And learning to work with the breath can become a valuable tool to enhance and promote emotional balance.

Breathing has profound meaning. Each breath we take puts us in touch with the universe. Breathing gives and sustains life, from the first breath taken at the moment of birth until the last breath taken at the end of life. Breathing patterns have the potential to promote health just as they can play a role in sickness. We are always breathing, and so it becomes an ever-present resource, ready to be tapped into when needed.

All of the Eastern philosophies in this book incorporate breathing theory. In Yoga, the meaning of *pranayama*, the word for breath control, reveals its far-reaching significance: *Ayama* means to stretch or extend and *prana* refers to "that which is infinitely everywhere" (Desikachar, 1995, p. 54). Pranayama is a gateway that links inner vitality to the energy that surrounds us in the universe. Daoism has a similar conception: Breath is linked to vitality as *Qi*, translated as air, breath, or energy flow. Qi is the life force that exists in every living thing. Its correct regulation holds the key to health and the cure for illness. Daoist healing incorporates breathing as a way to move the internal energy and help it flow through the whole body. Buddhism and Zen also turn attention to breathing as a direct pathway to an awake, aware mind. Zazen, a primary Zen meditation method, is centered in the breath. Through deliberate modifications and methods, breathing can be brought under conscious control. In all these philosophies, conscious breathing patterns direct the flow of energy into and out of the body for health and vitality.

> Pranayama really means controlling the motion of the lungs, and this motion is associated with the breath. . . . Prana is not breathing, but controlling that muscular power which moves the lungs. . . . When this prana has become controlled, then we shall immediately find that all the other actions of prana in the body will slowly come under control.
>
> (Vivekananda, 1953, p. 595)

Anatomy of the Breath: Direct and Indirect Methods

Yoga has analyzed breathing in order to develop its fullest potential. Breathing can be divided into four parts. The first is inhalation (*puraka*), when the air is brought into the body. The second is a pause, with held-in breath, *kumbhaka*, a moment between breathing in and out. The third is exhalation, *rechaka.* Air is let out. Finally, the fourth part is followed by a pause, or held-out breath: *shunyaka.* Then the pattern can repeat again.

After years of disciplined pranayama practice, accomplished yogis can vary their breathing rhythms at will. The process starts with gradual, gentle changes to normal breathing and builds from there. By changing the pattern, timing, and force of different parts of the cycle of breathing, practitioners can gain voluntary control over what usually seems to be an involuntary process. This control can generalize to other processes.

The discipline of Qi Gong has developed the control of the breath in Daoist meditations. Some use control methods similar to Yoga, developing voluntary control over involuntary processes. But there are also indirect methods where breathing is allowed to flow naturally, leading to a gentle movement of energy that circulates seemingly in and of itself.

These direct and indirect breathing methods are analogous to direct and indirect methods of therapeutic intervention. Direct forms of therapy offer clear interventions to follow, such as cognitive-behavioral therapy's assignment of homework for observing, analyzing, and altering thinking patterns. Indirect forms of therapy work more implicitly by providing an open-ended framework for therapeutic experience, such as a hypnotic trance, during which clients explore inwardly and allow change to occur. Of course, therapists and clients discover that directive methods of therapy involve indirect and nonspecific therapeutic learning and that indirect therapies include specific learning as well. Similarly, both forms of breathing meditations engage both direct and indirect work with breathing, as will become clear in the practice. So we recommend the practice of both forms, individualizing the application for the greatest benefit, using the form most appropriate to the client's needs.

Begin with Awareness

Breathing is usually an unconscious process that takes care of itself. But in leaving the breathing process to chance, we may get into poor habits of tension and restriction that use only a small portion of the potential for self-control and health. Awareness can help to gently promote better breathing habits, for greater vitality, and calm, deeper relaxation. The first step is awareness. Begin by turning the attention to breathing.

Control of breathing must always be done carefully and gradually. Ultimately, the breath happens of itself naturally. You just help it along. The art lies in being able to deliberately enhance the natural potentials of the body with corrective techniques for optimal functioning without forcing anything. The body will respond best to gentle, gradual extension of its capacities.

Developing Awareness of Breathing

Begin by turning attention to the act of each breath. One time-honored method of breath awareness is counting. The other is listening. Both methods help to link breathing to attention. Experiment with both of these exercises to see which seems more natural. Either exercise can teach concentration on breathing, an important stepping-stone to successful meditative breathing. A more general improvement in concentration is also developed by attending to breathing, an ability that will prove useful in many forms of meditation.

If new to meditation, try doing each of these exercises for a brief time. Set a timer for one minute and then begin. As you become comfortable with a short time, increase the duration of concentration for longer periods of time. Don't force it, but be persistent. You will be pleasantly surprised at how the powers of concentration can be developed with practice.

Focus on Breathing: Counting the Breaths

This ancient Yoga exercise can help the beginner keep attention on breathing by counting the breaths. Meditation instructions in the *Mahamudra*, an ancient Tibetan Buddhist text, instructed meditators to count up to 21,600 breaths (Evans-Wentz, 1967) Although we intend much more modest goals in this exercise, this ancient text indicates the potential of monks to maintain focus for extended periods of time.

Sit cross-legged on a pillow on the floor or upright on a chair if sitting on the floor is uncomfortable (see Chapter 4 for instructions on sitting positions). Close the eyes and begin inwardly counting each breath. Each number refers to the entire breath, from inhalation to exhalation. Count up to 10 and then begin again. If attention wanders away from the count to other thoughts, gently bring it back as soon as possible. Over time, you will be able to stay focused on the breathing at will.

Listening to Breathing

Some people find listening to breathing comes easier than counting the breaths. Sit comfortably and close the eyes. Pay close attention to the sound of the air as it enters the nose. Keep the attention focused on the sound as it exits again. Keep focusing attention on the sound of breathing. If distracted, gently bring the attention back to the sound of the breathing.

Hear the breathing more easily by placing the hands lightly over the ears. Notice how the sound becomes more pronounced. Listening for a short time tends to bring about sensitizing to the breathing sounds, thereby making it easier to stay attuned.

The Complete Breath

The complete breath is one of the cornerstones of Yoga, used in conjunction with most of the postures. A form of the complete breath is also referred to in the Daoist writings of Zhuangzi, who encourages breathing down to the toes (Watson, 1968).

Without realizing it, people often get into the poor habit of holding their chest, ribcage, diaphragm, and abdomen rigid while breathing. Such inflexibility prevents a full breath from happening. As a result, energy becomes blocked or even stuck, resulting in discomfort and even illness. The complete breath initiates a process to free breathing as it frees the body. It naturally brings about movement of the chest, ribcage, diaphragm, and abdomen. When done correctly, the complete breath expands the lungs forward, sideways, and backward and uses all the respiratory muscles optimally. By involving the breathing processes in this way, people learn to let go of unnecessary tensions, releasing energy to flow naturally and fully.

Instructions for the Complete Breath: Standing and Sitting

The complete breath can be performed standing up, lying down, or sitting. For the first attempt, stand with the feet together and hands down at the sides, palms facing in toward the body. Let the head sag forward slightly and exhale. Slowly begin inhaling while raising the arms out from the sides, arms straight with palms up. Synchronize the timing so that the lungs become completely filled with air just as the hands meet up above the head. Hold for a moment and then slowly begin exhaling while lowering the arms. All the air should be expelled when the arms are back down at the sides.

The complete breath can also be done while sitting. Find a comfortable seated posture. Begin by inhaling. When first learning, place the hands on the upper abdomen to feel the motion of the breath. The hands should move out and the fingers should move slightly apart as the lungs fill with air. Exhale and let the abdomen deflate, bringing the fingers together again.

Expanding the abdomen is just part of the complete breath. The diaphragm, ribcage, and chest are also involved. Place the hands on the diaphragm/rib area to feel this part of the breath. While inhaling, notice how the diaphragm naturally expands downward as the ribs spread outward. The chest also expands and the shoulders rise slightly. The complete inhale, done correctly, will bring about movement in the abdomen, diaphragm, ribs, chest, and shoulders.

Exhaling is just the opposite. Begin by relaxing the chest first, then the ribcage, and finally, lightly tighten the stomach muscles to help push the last bit of air out. The chest and ribcage contract, and the shoulders drop with exhalation. One complete inhale and exhale, with one following the other, make up a complete breath.

TIPS

Inhalation and exhalation should be evenly timed, with a slight pause. One way to synchronize is to count to four with the inhalation and then four with the exhalation. Breathe for up to six counts. Do what feels comfortable.

Beginners often find it easier to do a longer exhalation, but it is better to keep the length of time the same for inhaling and exhaling. This probably means shortening the exhalation rather than lengthening the inhalation. Do not force breathing to be longer or shorter. Be sensitive to inner rhythms.

Even though the complete breath is performed deliberately in a certain way, keep the breaths as relaxed and natural as possible. Breathing should not be strained, hard, or sudden. Relaxation and calm follows naturally from balanced and comfortable breathing.

Timing the Breath

Sit comfortably and breathe naturally for a few moments, paying attention to breathing. When ready, inhale for a count of three with a complete breath in. Then hold the air for a comfortable count of one or two. Exhale for four counts with a complete breath out, and then hold for one or two counts. Practice this gently and softly, making breathing as relaxed as possible. Increase the length of each part of the breath as long as it is comfortable to do so, but keep the ratios the same. Controlling the timing of breathing comfortably is an advanced skill that develops very slowly with practice. Be patient; these skills take time to develop.

Alternate Nostril Breath for Balance

This exercise balances the energy currents on both sides of the body. It can also enhance concentration. Curl the first two fingers of the right hand and rest the thumb against the curled fingers, pointing up. Extend the fourth and fifth fingers out straight. Cover the right nostril with the thumb and inhale through the left nostril, allowing the air to flow fully as in the complete breath exercise. Then shift the hand to block the left nostril with the extended fingers and exhale through the right nostril, performing a complete exhale. Inhale fully through the right nostril and then block it while exhaling with the other. Alternate back and forth in this way for 5 to 10 breath cycles.

Visualization and Breathing Meditations

Yoga and Daoist philosophy encourage people to increase internal energy to help revitalize. Each of these traditions includes methods known as cleansing breaths. These techniques facilitate air circulation by clearing out impurities and replacing them with fresh, clean air. If possible, perform this exercise outdoors when there is a breeze, such as at the beach, in the woods, or in a park.

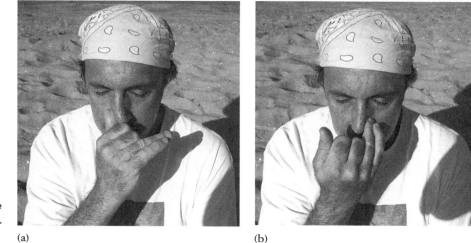

Figure 6.1a, b. Alternate nostril breathing.

(a)   (b)

Visualize the breath, soft as a spring breeze, gentle and cleansing. With each breath in, allow the aroma of fresh air to circulate naturally within. Then with each breath out, imagine feeling refreshed and renewed. Continue to breathe softly and quietly.

Indirect Methods: Allowing Breathing

Many of the traditional breathing meditations involve deliberately controlling the breath in one way or another. But in this exercise, use body awareness to permit breathing to find a natural rhythm. Then relax by letting go of tension, without forcing it.

Lie down comfortably so that the breathing passages are free and open. Place the hands gently on the lower ribcage at the solar plexus, palms down. Some may want to raise the knees and place the feet flat on the floor so that the lower back can relax. Close the eyes and allow breathing to be comfortable. Pay attention to the movement of the ribcage, noticing how each breath feels with the palms. Shift attention to feel the temperature of the hands on the ribcage. After a while, a slight warmth may develop. Allow each breath to be as it is, without altering it. After some time has passed, remove the hands from the ribcage and continue gently breathing. Then replace the hands again and notice any difference in sensation. Eventually, does the breath find its own natural rhythm of itself? If not at this moment, perhaps, with patience, the breathing will find a comfortable rhythm at another moment. Return to this meditation at different times.

Zen Breathing

The Zen approach to meditative breathing enhances attention to breathing while allowing the breath to be natural. Sit cross-legged or just comfortably relaxed. Attend to breathing. While inhaling, pay attention, allowing the air in as needed. When ready to exhale, keep attention focused, letting air out comfortably. Keep attention on each breath, in and then out, allowing the process to happen without interference. Do not try to breathe deeper or shallower, just breathe. If thoughts intrude, gently bring the attention back to breathing. Experience each breath anew, as it comes. Continue to let breathing be, moment-by-moment, staying sensitive to the needs of the body. This can be applied to other situations, sensitively finding the best rhythm and depth of breathing for the activity, without interfering by deliberately taking breaths in a rhythm.

Integrating Breathing with Postures

Careful use of the breath is always incorporated into Yoga postures and Daoist movements. Martial arts are another example of integrated breathing and movement. This exercise integrates breathing patterns with movement while also limbering the spine.

Stand with feet shoulder-width apart, and arms down at the sides, hands open. Breathe in through the nose while raising the arms horizontally out to the sides, hands extended. Arch the back slightly with the inhalation. Let the ribcage expand, giving a gentle stretch to the spine. Then exhale while allowing the arms to lower in relaxed manner down to the sides, with hands still extended. Round the back very slightly in the opposite direction from the exhalation and tuck the chin down slightly. Repeat the gentle movements coordinated with breathing for three to five repetitions, focusing attention on the process. Remember not to force the movements or increase the volume of breathing. Keep relaxed, slow, and gradual. Coordinating breathing with motion helps to limber the muscles and calm the mind.

Integrating Attention to Breathing

Specific breathing exercises can be performed at various times during daily activities. The first step involves making a decision to pay attention to breathing by taking a few relaxed, aware breaths randomly throughout the day. Without realizing, many people tighten the ribcage unnecessarily during breathing, or even forget to breathe at times during concentrated effort. The opportunity to gently let go of tensions comes with the willingness to deliberately notice breathing. Be willing to take an inward glance from time to time, a moment of self-awareness for developing better habits. Relaxed breathing enhances overall relaxation and optimizes energy for more vitality.

7

One-Pointed Awareness and Concentration

He who has faith, who is intent on knowledge and who has controlled his senses, obtains knowledge and having obtained it, goes quickly to the highest peace.

(Bhagavad Gita, translated by Deutsch, 1968, p. 65)

Archery was offered to the youth of the warrior class in India to train their focus and acuity. Arjuna was a young warrior in training, later to become the main character in the *Bhagavad Gita.* Arjuna's class was instructed to draw their bows and aim for a bird perched in a distant tree to see who was the best. While the students held their bows taut, the teacher asked, "What do you see?"

The first student answered, "I see a field, some trees, and a bird in one of the trees."

The second student said, "I only see the tree that has the bird in it."

Arjuna's response was, "All I see is the eye of the bird." The teacher declared Arjuna the winner.

Begin by Withdrawing

In everyday life, awareness is diffuse, due to responding to a broad range of stimuli coming in from the environment and from internal reactions. Attending to these stimuli often takes precedence, keeping us from attending to important spiritual realities and higher consciousness.

Patanjali's fifth limb of Yoga, Pratyahara, is the art of withdrawing attention from outer, less important concerns. By disengaging attention from habitual involvements, it becomes available for meditation. Freed of such involvements, attention can be turned inward toward deeper, profound concerns. Traditionally, pratyahara was interpreted more narrowly as withdrawing from the outer world of illusion to the truer reality within. Today it has taken on the broader interpretation of withdrawing attention from less important concerns to focus on more important ones. When working with clients who have a tendency to withdraw or lose contact with their environment, use the broader interpretation of pratyahara, and perform it with eyes open if that suits the client's needs.

Pratyahara can be understood by considering it from two dimensions: not-doing and doing. The not-doing side is not attending to distracting and unnecessary thought. By withdrawing from involvement with what might interfere with meditation, energy is conserved and attention is freed for positive use for the path to concentrated attention.

The doing side of pratyahara involves the next step, actively focusing attention to direct awareness at will, pinpointing it precisely so that it is placed where intended. Concentration, or Dharana, naturally follows. Practicing both sides clears away what interferes with meditation while training useful skills. Flowing contemplation follows naturally.

Not-doing Meditation

Take a few minutes of the day for this meditation. The classic Yoga way to perform pratyahara is lying down in savasana pose. Savasana is a prone position, on the back, with arms out from the sides and legs slightly apart. Many may find this a comfortable way to begin.

The place to perform this meditation should be calm, peaceful, and somewhat quiet, a place where distractions are minimal. Turn up the temperature slightly or have a blanket handy to prevent getting cold, because the body temperature may drop a bit when lying still. Lie quietly and relax. At first thoughts may wander around and little things might be distracting. Be patient and wait for thoughts to gradually quiet down.

Figure 7.1. Savasana pose.

Begin narrowing the field by not-doing: Turn attention away from the outer world. To accomplish this, don't, for example, listen to the sound of traffic outside and instead do turn attention to the immediate surroundings: the air, the temperature, the texture of the floor or bed. Next, don't pay attention to the immediate surroundings and instead do notice inner body sensations, area by area. Begin at the head. Pay attention to the face or neck. Notice the holding of muscles. Is there any unnecessary tightening? If possible, relax any tensions that can be relaxed. Then don't attend to the face and neck but do direct attention down toward the shoulders. Pay close attention to them. Mentally trace out the distance between the shoulders. Notice any tension in the shoulder muscles and let go if possible.

Continue down through the body, first withdrawing attention from the previous area and then paying close attention to the next area. If the attention wanders away to anything other than the area of focus, gently bring it back. But do not force it. Simply notice where the attention is, encourage it to return to the area of focus, and wait for it to do so.

Next, withdraw attention from body sensations to focus on thoughts. Maintain attention to thinking by applying the method used for the body. Similarly to turning attention away from one body area and toward another, turn away from thoughts about outer matters and turn attention toward inner focus. Consider any thoughts such as those that anticipate what might need to be done later or something that happened earlier, to be outer concerns. Keep attention fixed on this quiet moment. Don't think about anything else. If thoughts wander away, gently bring them back to inner focus as soon as possible. Pinpoint thoughts on inner focus for 5 minutes up to 30 minutes. With practice a deep sense of quiet well-being will develop.

Dealing with Resistance

Sometimes people have difficulty withdrawing. If so, think about any habitual ways of attending to the outer world. For example, some people are constantly mentally rehearsing what they will do next. Others dwell on what happened earlier, comparing this moment with past ones. Sometimes people have beliefs from hidden assumptions, such as a belief that they must be busy to be happy or that relaxation is just laziness. Delve deeply and question these beliefs that are taken for granted. If these or other mental patterns are revealed, question whether such thoughts can be temporarily set aside right now. Everyone has individual habits of attending that are not necessarily the best, so don't judge or chastise, just observe. By adopting a nonjudgmental attitude, attention may be easier to enlist in the effort.

Now try again to focus attention on inner experience right now. If the habitual tendency or belief emerges, make a small change during pratyahara practice. For example, if thoughts wander to planning what to do after the pratyahara session, stop planning and bring the attention back to the moment. Or if recalling an earlier event, let go of the memories, for now. Whenever thoughts wander away from the practice, gently bring them back, and eventually, extraneous thinking will stop.

It can be renewing to take some time out from busy routines and the concerns of everyday life to practice pratyahara. These inwardly focused, quiet meditative moments can add a new dimension to life, for greater self-control and peace of mind.

Focused Concentration

The skills of focus developed in pratyahara are used for working with meditative concentration. When the concentrated mind is focused on something, the inner meaning of that thing is revealed. Like an fMRI that can reveal inner brain activations, focused concentration can reveal deeper truths that are usually missed. Great scientists who make important discoveries probably unconsciously tap into these powers of concentration without realizing it. Clear perception is possible when we set aside the interference from distractions. The process involves taming the wandering attention, narrowing it down into a single point focus.

Correctly directing the focus of attention is the beginning of concentration. Attention can then be concentrated, to a single point and kept there. Deliberately cultivating perception by staying focused helps gain control of attention. Then attention can be directed at will. The focus developed by this practice becomes a great resource.

Method acting is a highly regarded classical application of intense focus of attention. The influence continues in present times. The founder, Constantin Stanislavski (Stanislavski, 1961, 1983) searched deeply for techniques and concepts that would help actors evolve. He believed that when actors learn to concentrate their attention on the circle of the stage they occupy, awareness of the audience lessens, reducing distraction; and thereby, development of the craft results. So he designed exercises that combined concentration, breathing, and imagination to enhance mental skills. Then, the method actor could delve deeply into the unconscious and feel memories and experiences intensely, from which a character and role would creatively emerge and take form on the stage.

Concentration on One Thing

Any object, picture, or piece of art can be used as the object of concentration. Pick an object that is personally interesting, such as a painting or sculpture. Or focus on the picture provided here. Place it in clear view. Sit upright cross-legged on the floor, on a small pillow, or sit on a straight-backed chair, and look at the object. Keep the attention focused on it and notice as many aspects of the picture that can be thought of: color, shade, texture, shape, size, function, and meaning.

Now focus on the process of concentration itself. Notice the quality of attention required. If the attention is focused, intense, and fully engaged, continue to use it to explore the object. If the attention is unfocused, vague, and undifferentiated, notice this quality of attention. For example, when attending to the picture: are there any

Figure 7.2. *Focus.*
(C. Alexander and Annellen
Simpkins. Wood on wood,
macassar ebony and mahogany,
satinwood. San Diego, CA,
2006)

points of interest? Is there difficulty thinking about the picture? If attention wanders away, where does it wander? Then, retrace the links back to the object of focus. If distracted by unselected objects of attention, gently bring attention back to the object originally selected, noticing the process of doing so. Begin with just two or three minutes of concentration. Gradually increase the time as you become able to maintain focus. Skills in concentrating improve with practice.

Concentration on an Inner Image

After focusing on the object with eyes open, close the eyes and picture the object. People who are naturally able to form visual pictures will see a vivid image of the object. For others the picture may be vague. Keep the attention focused on the image even if the imagined image is vague. Notice all the details that were seen when looking at the object such as texture, color, and patterns. Stay relaxed in the sitting position with the eyes lightly closed. Some people might notice the eyes tightening up as they concentrate. Try to relax them. If the eyes continue to be tight or feel tired, return to Chapter 5 and perform the Eye Swing Exercise and Palming Exercise. Keep focused for several minutes and then go back to focus on the inner image using the same methods as in the previous exercise.

Concentration on Sound

Concentration can be placed on any object. Sound is accessible and enjoyable as an object of focus. Sounds such as mantras and chanting are long-standing meditative traditions to use. In the exercise, focus attention on a sound and concentrate on it.

Begin with a simple sound, although there are groups of sounds and complex chants that may be learned over time (see Chapter 11). Om is a simple and universal symbol, a syllable with profound significance in many traditions. In Yoga philosophy, Om is a primary mantra. Mantra sound can be used to vibrate the body and activate energy centers, as well as clear the mind by listening.

To pronounce the sound *Om*, begin with the sound, "oh," then say "uh," and then close the lips and finish with "mmm," slightly humming it. Glide the sounds together as one combined syllable. While making the sound Om, focus all the attention on it: Listen to it and feel the physical vibrations in the body. Do this for several minutes, increasing the time gradually. Focus attention with the intense quality of concentration that is developed, as with a visual object. When finished, wait for a moment to allow and deepen experience of the effects.

Concentration on Breathing

A traditional object of focus is breathing. Any of the breathing exercises in Chapter 6 can be used to prepare the breathing for one-pointed focus of attention.

For this exercise, sit cross-legged on a pillow, sit on a chair, or lie down on the floor on the back. As in any breathing exercise, allow the breathing passages to be relatively relaxed. Close the eyes and turn attention to breathing. Breathe through the nose, not the mouth. Notice the air as it comes in through your nose, then flows down into your lungs and out again. Pay close attention to how your chest, diaphragm, stomach, and back feel when they move as you breathe. Don't interfere with the natural pattern of breathing. Just relax and breathe normally while keeping the attention focused on the feeling of breathing. If your attention wanders, gently bring it back to focus on breathing.

Once attention is focused on breathing, notice the quality of this attention. Apply the same concentration on the process of concentrating as in the previous exercises. How intense is the quality of focus? Try to intensify by narrowing the focus to one part of the breath and then another, such as the sounds of breathing or the flow of air in each breath. When finished, sit quietly to experience any aftereffects.

Concentration on Motion

Apply this concentration meditation with an everyday action such as walking or standing. One classic exercise often performed in Zen practice is meditative walking. Set aside some free time during the day, 10 minutes or more, and go out for a walk in nature. But if for some reason you can't walk outdoors, simply walk around in a room at home. Focus your attention fully on walking. Walk slowly and carefully, breathing gently, noticing space around you, while attending sensitively to nuances of sensation, balance, motion, and other awareness that emerges.

As in the previous exercises, notice how movement affects concentration. Then pick a particular quality of walking for the focus. For example, concentrate more fully on breathing. Pay close attention to each breath while continuing to walk. Be sure to breathe naturally, neither deeper nor shallower. Due to intense concentration, people sometimes forget to breathe naturally.

Next, shift concentration to another aspect of walking, such as the process of stepping. Pay attention to the shift in weight from one foot to another. Notice how the muscles in the foot react to the floor. When finished, lie or sit down with your eyes closed. Breathe comfortably and relax completely for a few minutes.

Concentration on Body Warming

The effects of concentration can be seen in the ancient practice of *gTum-mo,* still performed today (Benson et al., 1982). *gTum-mo* gives the ability to generate body heat psychically. Tibetan Buddhists learn how to visualize so vividly that their bodies act like human batteries, generating physical heat. These skills are tested. Practitioners sit outside on an icy night. A wet sheet is placed directly on the meditator's bare back. With the power of concentration, the meditator generates enough body heat to dry the sheet. Accomplished practitioners can dry many sheets, one after the other.

These practitioners show us that body temperature can be controlled by focus and concentration. The procedures used in *gTum-mo* are complex, but can be experimented with by trying the first steps involved in the skill. This exercise teaches how to become free from the constraints of temperature.

HAND WARMING MEDITATION

Sit quietly for a moment. Begin by testing the temperature of the palm. Touch the palm to the upper arm. Notice how warm or cool the palm feels. Now, place the two palms together, pointing outward in the lap. Close the eyes. Visualize warmth arising between the hands. Visualize a fire in a fireplace, warmth from the sun, or even a heater. Draw upon an image that is vivid from personal experience. Imagine the warmth spreading up the arms. When ready to stop, test the palm temperature again and compare it to how warm it felt when you started. With practice, you will be able to feel a difference.

Once this skill is gained, perform the exercise with hands held apart, palms facing. Generate warmth using a complete visualization. A vividly imagined sensation may be enough. Keep the attention focused and follow the procedures above.

Conclusion

The ability to focus the attention brings many positive benefits. As skill in concentration improves, mental faculties sharpen. Physical coordination may also become more graceful and balanced. Paradoxically, with practice in the art of narrowing the focus of attention at will, mental capacities intensify and broaden.

8

The Eightfold Path: The Method to Travel

Rouse thyself by thyself, examine thyself by thyself.

(*Dharmapada* quoted in Yutang, 1942, p. 322)

Buddhism's Eightfold Path offers techniques for a meditative orientation. The exercises in this chapter draw from this ancient tradition, providing therapists with methods they can adapt. Sometimes the client is addressed directly to provide guidelines for use. Therapists and clients may find some of these methods overlap with what they do in therapy. The first steps help to orient as the process begins. Later steps can intensify and clarify therapeutic experiences.

The Eightfold Path Simply Stated

The Eightfold Path is the fourth of the Four Noble Truths, described in Chapter 2. Briefly restated, the first truth is: life is suffering. Truth two is that the root of suffering is self-centered desires and clinging to permanence. The third truth is that understanding impermanence and all that it implies will stop suffering. The Eightfold Path, the fourth truth, gives a distinct method for disentangling from the causes of suffering and bringing about healthy growth. The path involves eight distinctive yet interrelated steps: Right Views, Right Intention, Right Speech, Right Action, Right Livelihood, Right Effort, Right Mindfulness, and Right Meditation. We use the word *Right* from the traditional translations. "Right" here means whole, complete, and perfect. A moralistic connotation is not intended; rather a holistic conception referring to comprehensive unity is closer to what is meant. The wheel of Dharma is often used as a symbol for the Eightfold Path, with each spoke representing one of the steps interrelating together in a nonlinear way.

This chapter presents the first six steps. Chapter 9 covers Mindfulness. Many of the other chapters contain the meditation methods of Right Meditation.

Figure 8.1. Wheel of Dharma.

Right Views

Right views will be the torch to light his way.

(Sermon at Benares, quoted in Stryk, 1968, p. 51)

The first steps on a meditative path introduce people to the Right Views offered by the Noble Truths. They learn that the problem they think they have is not the real problem. Many problems are actually illusions, created by faulty thinking. They also gain a realistic hope for change. Life will be better when pointed in the Right Direction, by following the Eightfold Path. To begin an inner transformation, people must first orient themselves with Right Views. They do so by introducing themselves to what lies ahead.

A 25-year psychotherapy research project at Johns Hopkins University Hospital found a measurable advantage to orienting clients to therapy (Frank et al., 1978). The research showed that giving a correct view of the process of psychotherapy through a Role Induction Interview helped clients benefit more from treatment. This pretreatment interview clarified what the real problem was, what the treatment would involve, and described the likely course of events. The role induction interview initiated a therapeutic relationship, raised client's expectancy for successful treatment, and oriented clients to the therapeutic direction. Right Views give an expectancy that is important for therapeutic transformation.

Buddhists prepare themselves for a meditative transformation by reflecting on their views. People form views about themselves from parents, education, and the culture as well as from personal experiences. As the years pass, these views become fixed into attitudes. Studies have shown that attitudes tend to remain stable (Frank & Frank, 1991) and influence future actions (Krosnick & Petty, 1995). As anyone involved in therapeutic processes surely knows, changing attitudes can have a profound effect at many levels. Buddha taught that altering attitude involves being free from prejudice, superstition, and delusion. By letting go of false views, we clear the way for a truer, deeper insight into our nature.

To Begin with Awareness, Examine Attitudes

The Eightfold Path begins by examining commonly held views or attitudes. This can take many forms, depending on the problem being addressed. For most forms of therapy, one might begin by questioning attitudes about change itself.

EXERCISE: EVALUATING ATTITUDES

Buddhism distinguishes between wholesome and unwholesome views. Wholesome attitudes foster the ability to live well, in accord with life as a whole. Other attitudes lead to pain and suffering. These views are called unwholesome since they lead away from a unified aware life. The guiding ideal should be the ideal in general, not just a specific ideal. The ideal is found in perfection itself, as a universal, not a particular view or attitude to follow.

DEVELOPING RIGHT ATTITUDES

In order for a plant to grow, it must be given the correct conditions, such as the right amount of light, water, and nourishment. Then the plant can reach perfection. Similarly, the Right Attitudes will foster endeavors and wrong Attitudes will hurt them. So, for example, a view that people never really change would be in conflict with the inner transformation the Eightfold Path is encouraging.

Exploring Right Attitudes

The following are some questions to explore right attitudes for therapy: Can people change themselves? If not, why can't they change? What are your personal attitudes toward change? If you think you cannot change, investigate whether there is some circumstance that prevents change. If you believe outside forces prevent you from changing, is this belief reasonable? Often people who feel helpless to change have projected their abilities out into the environment, outer circumstances, or onto other people. Sometimes the belief that change is obstructed has a reasonable basis, and should be addressed. Challenge false views that cause barriers to growth and development with attitudes that are more open and conducive to an aware, awake life.

Right Intent

Right aims will be his guide.

(Stryk, 1968, p. 51)

To seriously contemplate overcoming suffering, people must feel from the heart that this is what they want to do. Harold Greenwald (1910–1999), a renowned therapist who created Direct Decision Therapy, believed that decisions are the key to understanding personality and problems (Greenwald, 1975). The individual is free to change decisions throughout life. At some time in their lives, people make a decision that begins the problem, and if they return to the point at which they made the decision, they can make a new decision that corrects the problem. In order to begin the process, people need to make a decision at a deep level to do so. The decision is the primary force that activates the process of change. Right Intent involves making primary decisions, with whole-hearted commitment.

Right Intent engages the emotions as well as the intellect. By caring deeply about something, people find it easier to follow through even when faced with obstacles. Wholehearted commitment directed from Right Attitudes propels us in the Right Direction.

Examining Intent

Examining intent uncovers deeper motives. This examination will help in pursuing benevolent motives and preventing ego-centered ones. For example, many people donate to charity to help others, but, surprisingly, the benevolence may be lost if the intention is ego-centered. When people expect personal reward for their charity, the action lacks true benevolence. D. T. Suzuki (1960) recommended doing anonymous, secret acts of kindness to keep intention pure. Do not take any personal credit, nor seek recognition. Perform a kind act not for personal gain or ego, but just because it is the right thing to do.

Summoning Right Intent through Visualization

The client can summon the right intent by using these guidelines: Ask the client to sit quietly with closed eyes, and to consider her or his decision to do therapy. Is there a wholehearted intention to make whatever changes are needed? Or is there a secret wish to just do the minimum to "get by"? Does the decision to undergo therapy come from within or is there another motive, perhaps to please someone else or to satisfy some legal or academic requirement? If the intent is found to be incomplete, insincere, or irresponsible, examine the intention honestly and thoroughly. The client needs to consider making a change toward a more positive, heart-felt intention. Perhaps a stronger inner resolve is needed. Or maybe problems and difficulties have led to a permanent pessimism. If the client questions these attitudes then the possibility for other options opens up.

Enhancing the Intent

Motivation to do something is strengthened by knowing it is possible. In a recent study, seventh grade students performed better in their schoolwork after hearing a brief discussion about the malleability of intelligence and the brain. When they knew it was possible to improve, they did (Dweck, 2006). This research is in line with a large body of expectancy and placebo studies (Frank & Frank, 1991; Rosenthal & Jacobson, 1968). When something seems possible, even if it is challenging, people are more likely to put in the effort and achieve it. Motivation builds as people recognize their potential to be free and happy. The gate is open and nothing blocks the way (paraphrased from the *Mumonkan* in Sekida, 1977).

Visualizing Right Intent

Sit quietly with eyes closed. Visualize being free of problems: feeling capable and motivated, peaceful and happy. Allow this fantasy to take form in the mind. Perhaps there is goodwill for others or resourcefulness not usually available in everyday actions. What is this experience like? New personal understanding can be discovered in the imagined experience, even though only imagined at this point. Since this experience arises within your mind, there is something to be found. Trust the process.

Right Speech

Right Words will be his dwelling place along the road.

(Stryk, 1968, p. 52)

The next step on the path is to notice speech. People often talk without really listening. Access to inner experience is gained by listening while speaking.

Becoming Aware of Speech

Right Speech begins with awareness of the act of speaking as it occurs. Listen to yourself speaking, and to speech as it occurs, to begin to know yourself and others. Start this training at home between sessions or in the office during the therapy session. Pay close attention to your voice and words while speaking. Listen for the tone of voice, and to the words. Think about the intended meanings. Are the words sincere, truly reflecting the inner intent of the communication?

Now try to extend listening to others. Begin with the person you are conversing with. Pay attention to his or her actual words and voice tones. Try to give the other person space to communicate fully, before considering what you think are the intended meanings. Extend this awareness to other conversations in various situations. It may be more challenging to listen closely in less familiar circumstances, but in time attentive listening to others will become easier and habitual.

Overcoming Obstacles to Listening

For those who have trouble listening at the same time as speaking, try talking into a recording device, then listening to the playback. Sometimes a deliberate act of speaking and listening will help to get the process started. Some will find the process easier than others. Use what works, and vary the situation appropriately.

Notice anything that might be interfering with attention to speech. Do related or unrelated thoughts intrude? Or do judgments and comparisons interrupt the ability to sustain listening? Are any emotional reactions clouding awareness? Answer these questions without being too self-critical. For example, if there is trouble listening, don't get angry or judgmental. The path is one of compassion toward others, and that includes compassion toward oneself. Keep trying with sincerity, and in time, awareness develops.

Just listening is not enough. People should be aware of when they speak with negative intent, and try to understand why they did so. When people gossip about a friend, for example, they are being defensive, alienated from pure being. By questioning a negative comment about a friend, deeper motivations may be uncovered. Continued awareness and self-examination can help in communicating more positively, more harmoniously with true nature. Right Speech is an essential step along the path to change.

Changing Speech

While paying attention to speech, do you detect hostility or deceitfulness? When you do, try to alter such expressions toward greater compassion and honesty. When speaking in anger, and you realize that you are, stop. Instead of getting lost in the irritation, stay attuned and inwardly ask yourself where the anger comes from. Does the anger stem from attachment? Think about the roots of suffering in the natural wish to hold onto pleasure or avoid pain. Search for a different interpretation that might alter the angry feelings now. Then speak from this perspective, with compassion.

Keep in mind that the changes are intended to bring wisdom. Defensive lying, for example, dissociates us from what is really happening, lessening real understanding. Staying in touch with the reality dispels ignorance, which makes us vulnerable to suffering. Insecurity, fear, and arrogance dissolve in the process. As defenses lessen, harmony with the world develops and angry responses will lessen.

Start from where you are. At first it may be difficult to avoid; for example, gossiping, criticizing, insincerity, or lying. But keep making an effort toward correct speech. Over time, the words and meanings will reflect the true intent, in harmony with what is really present in the situation.

Right Action

His gait will be straight for it is right behavior.

(Stryk, 1968, p. 52)

Right Action means understanding behavior and its underlying motivations. Buddha recognized the importance of improving the quality of behavior. Outer actions reflect inner being, and so Right Action is a powerful inroad to profound inner change.

Much can be inferred from observation of action and conduct. This step on the Eightfold Path resembles cognitive-behavioral therapy methods for observing actions. The skills developed for Right Speech will be useful for observing actions. Change in behavior is begun and sustained by means of awareness.

When people begin to pay attention to what they do, they are often surprised to learn many of the things they do take place habitually without conscious intervention. Sometimes habits are helpful, like driving a car or tying shoelaces. But at other times, unconscious action can lead to trouble. Recognizing the difference begins with observation. When people do the right thing, and try to live in accord with Right Conduct, their suffering diminishes.

Next, reflect on these observations by asking what motivated this action. Try to stop being motivated by ego. Instead, consider the welfare of others.

Studying Behavior

Study various types of typical behaviors while in the midst of doing them. In attending to behavior in the midst of doing them, new aspects appear. Observe the behavior in various circumstances; for example, while walking around a store, when getting together with friends, or when alone.

Next, study the quality of the actions. Are actions rushed without thought about what is being done? Are the thoughts ahead of the actions or behind? Or perhaps the actions are performed in a sloppy manner? Some may discover that actions are hesitant. What else is noticed?

Take note of behavior with others. Are actions self-centered or are they considerate of other people? Personally relevant observations will come to mind. Use these suggestions as springboards for further discoveries.

Correct Action: The Five Precepts

Buddhism has certain fundamentals of behavior called the Five Precepts. These precepts are important guidelines for behavior. Most people will find them a common denominator with other traditions. The precepts are: avoid destroying life, don't steal, never lie, don't engage in sexual misconduct, and don't abuse intoxicants.

If a client is having trouble abiding by any of these precepts, encourage him or her to set change in motion by overcoming ignorance, by learning about the problem. So, for example, if someone is struggling with intoxicants, he or she needs to learn all about their negative effects on the body and mind. Encourage the client to try to learn about personal motivations. Help him or her to apply the insights of the Noble Truths. For example, is the client clinging to intoxicant use, falsely believing that they are the source of pleasure? He or she needs to reconsider attachment to pleasure and aversion to discomfort (see Chapter 17). During therapy, look for the middle way between the two. Combining therapeutic methods with the precepts as a guide can be a helpful pathway to a mind free of conflict and disturbance.

Making Changes

Altering negative behaviors is only one side of Right Action; altering behavior to become more benevolent is the other side. Kindnesses should be performed whenever possible. This can be done through randomly selected small actions, such as giving bread crumbs to a wild bird or helping someone carry a heavy package. The range of kind actions can gradually be expanded. Acquaintances can be treated with courtesy and consideration, friends and family can be helped whenever possible. Make sure the client understands that as integration between thought, feeling, and action develops, it becomes easier to express benevolence.

Right Livelihood

His refreshments [benefits] will be the right way of earning his livelihood.

(Stryk, 1968, p. 53)

Right Livelihood is the fifth step on the path. The Bodhisattva is a helper of humanity, and so work should reflect this commitment to some degree. Buddha believed that people wouldn't become enlightened if they spent most of their day working at a profession that is contrary to wisdom. Any field that is in direct conflict with the five precepts should not be pursued. Buddha named certain prohibited jobs, such as poison peddler and slave trader. Translating his criteria into modern terms is straightforward: Any occupation that does not harm oneself or others is compatible with the Eightfold Path. This criterion leaves room for most modern forms of work. Fields that help other people are especially compatible. For example, people who are involved in manufacturing, building trades, and arts are creating something for the use, convenience, or enjoyment of others. Service professions such as medicine, psychology, and public relations are helpful to the world. Business can be positive for the culture as well.

Most occupations have the potential to be helpful when done sincerely and well. But people can turn a potentially positive job in the wrong direction. For example, a merchant who cheats customers always has the choice to stop doing so. Just as much opportunity exists for doing Right Actions as for doing wrong ones. Some wealthy CEOs help their employees and support numerous charities, while others run their businesses dishonestly. Every individual makes a personal choice about how to act in his or her occupation. But if the job situation does not permit right action, consider changing it or leaving.

Assessing the Occupation

Ask the client to think about the work situation in terms of the Eightfold Path criteria. Is there the opportunity to be honest and do good work? The job itself need not be perfect, but it should not interfere with becoming aware and compassionate.

Making the Most of the Work Day

Wisdom does not just happen on one's time off: personal growth is part of everyday life while living it. Thus, walk the Eightfold Path even at work. By enhancing awareness through the day, thinking becomes clearer, allowing work to be accomplished more efficiently. And there is less inward conflict.

Performing a Work Task with Awareness

Pick a small work task. Before beginning, sit down and close the eyes. Feel the sensations of sitting in the chair. Be fully present in the moment. Then, when calm and steady, open the eyes and begin to perform the task. Notice everything about the work while doing it, such as movements and thoughts. Work efficiently without rushing or lingering. When finished, sit down again and close the eyes. Sit quietly for a moment until ready to return to the regular work. Try to keep awareness attuned throughout the day.

Being More Compassionate at Work

Encourage the client to extend compassion into the workplace. Try to be considerate and helpful with fellow workers. Whenever there is a choice between self-centered action and other-centered action, try to plant the seeds of benevolence. Action takes place in a community with others, and kindness may inspire others. Enjoy the fruits of such actions with a more comfortable and harmonious work environment.

Right Effort

Right Effort will be his steps.

(Stryk, 1968, p. 53)

Mumon (author of the famous koan collection the *Mumonkan*) said, "If you are brave you will dive right in without being worried about the risk. . . . However, if you hesitate, you will be like someone watching a horse gallop by the window. In a twinkling of an eye it has already gone" (quoted in Low, 1995, p. 21).

Right Effort is the sixth step. Buddha believed that when people make efforts in the right direction, positive changes begin to take place. But if they try for the wrong goals, they follow a path inevitably leading to unhappiness and suffering. Buddha encouraged his followers to put themselves into what he called wholesome efforts that include helping others and avoiding unwholesome efforts that involve greed and crime. Always make the correct efforts and eventually you will succeed. "Earnest among the thoughtless, awake among the sleepers, the wise man advances like a racer, leaving the hack behind" (*Dhammapada*, quoted in Yutang, 1942, p. 329).

Right Effort involves wholehearted engagement in the correct direction. Enlisting Right Effort involves resolve and attention. Once a decision is made to do something with Right Intent, attention must be drawn to the thing to be done along with a continuing commitment to keep doing it.

Focusing Attention

Actions performed with attention are more readily carried out. Follow-through becomes easier when carefully attending to what is wished for, and holding that idea firmly in mind. As William James, said:

> The essential achievement of the will, in short, when it is most voluntary, is to attend to a difficult object and hold it fast before the mind. The so-doing is the fiat; and it is a mere physiological incident that when the object is thus attended to, immediate motor consequences should ensue. . . . Effort of attention is thus the essential phenomenon of will.
>
> (James, 1896, pp. 561, 562)

ATTENTION WARM-UP EXERCISE

Learn to direct and hold the attention with this exercise. Look around the office or living room. Let attention move from thing to thing without stopping. Then pick one object and keep attention focused on it for several minutes. Don't think of anything else; just keep focused on this one thing. Maintain active interest and awareness of the chosen object. Practice this exercise at different times during the day.

UTILIZING ATTENTION

Attention can be directed to any object of choice. Choose to direct attention to steps on the Eightfold Path. For example, when practicing Right Speech, deliberately direct attention to speech. Don't divide the attention by talking while doing something else. Experiment with placing undivided attention on the chosen task, whatever that is.

Unifying Right Effort

Right Effort unifies all capacities. Combine actions with thoughts, emotions, speech, and lifestyle to facilitate change. All of the steps on the Eightfold Path work in conjunction with each other. For example, when engaged in Right Action, the mind is directed to behavior, emotions are engaged, and speech is congruent as well. But how can everything be coordinated in this way? Mindfulness and meditation, the last two steps on the Eightfold Path, integrate mind, body, and spirit. If resistance emerges, recognize that the resistance has emerged, and note what the resistance is. Try to do whatever is needed. The Eightfold Path and psychotherapy go hand-in-hand. Anything is possible to a willing mind.

Pacing

Right Effort involves correct pacing. Marathon runners know to not start out too fast. They must pace themselves correctly in the beginning, or they might find themselves out of energy midway through the race. Similarly, becoming deeply aware of every word and act can be taxing, even disturbing at times. Buddha encouraged his followers not to overexert themselves before they were ready. Be diligent, but always in accord with personal readiness. The therapist provides guidance to help find the best pace for each client, without eliciting uncomfortable self-consciousness.

9

Mindfulness: Of Body, Emotions, and Thoughts

> Mindful he breathes in, mindful he breathes out. Whether he is breathing in
> a long or a short breath, he comprehends that he is breathing in a long or a
> short breath.
>
> (Mindfulness in *Majjhima-nikdya I*, quoted in Conze, 1995, p. 59)

A Zen student had been studying Zen for a number of years. He was considered an accomplished master who was to be recognized for his achievement and promoted to teacher. One rainy day before his promotion was to take place, he made a visit to his first Zen teacher, whom he hadn't seen in a long time. Before he entered he respectfully left his shoes and umbrella outside the door and entered barefooted. He bowed to his instructor and said a warm hello. His instructor was visibly glad to see him. Then he asked, "Tell me, on which side of the door did you leave your shoes and umbrella?" The student thought for a moment and then bowed his head in shame. He had been so excited to see his old teacher that his anticipation had interfered with his mindful awareness of where he was placing his shoes and umbrella when he entered. He decided to postpone his promotion and went back to his meditation until he could sustain his awareness no matter what the circumstances. Eventually he did become a true master, mindfully aware in whatever he did.

Mindfulness is an approach to life, a way of orienting with alert awareness and complete presence. Life without mindfulness is foggy and vague, driven by conditioned responses to outer circumstances. But mindful awareness opens a vast vista of potential for wisdom, freedom, and compassion. Mindfulness can deepen every experience of life.

The word *mindfulness* implies mind *full* ness, a method for filling the mind completely with each moment. So, mindfulness is not just a matter of what one does, but rather how mental attention and concentration are applied while doing it.

Modern mindfulness has a neutral, neuroscience-based interpretation. Siegel (2007) described mindfulness as a way to shift from the typical top-down cognitive categorizations and abstractions to a simpler, bottom-up perception. This allows for more direct experiencing that is immediate, concrete, and new.

There are a number of theories about the prefrontal cortex (PFC), where top-down brain processing is thought to take place (Squire et al., 2003, pp. 1373–1375). The somatic marker hypothesis (Damasio, 1994) is one theory of PFC processing that may help to explain the modern view of mindfulness. The orbitofrontal PFC is responsible for labeling people, objects, or situations with an emotional significance by associating feeling-laden memories of the past with current experience. The somatic markers can be helpful for making decisions, but sometimes interpreting the present in terms of the past interferes with direct perception. Mindfulness unlinks the connections so that the present moment can be experienced on its own. Mindfulness begins with experience, here and now.

Work with the exercises to develop the skills. Use the body, feelings, thoughts, and objects of thought. In time, awareness will spread into every moment, like a light that illuminates the darkness. Regular practice of mindfulness will lead naturally into deeper meditation.

Maintaining a Nonjudgmental Attitude

I open the windows of my senses,
Then light can enter.

(C. Alexander Simpkins)

Mindfulness is an opportunity to get to know about all of life's actions, thoughts, and feelings as well as gain understanding of other people. But after learning to observe more deeply, some may not like what they see. And as a result, they may be tempted to pass judgment concerning themselves or others before they fully understand what they are judging. But passing judgment will not help on the path to mindfulness. In fact, it may interfere.

Mindful awareness should be nonjudgmental. Like a researcher who is gathering data, set aside judgment. Do not jump to conclusions or use the new information gained to form biased opinions. Suspend judgment until more data is gathered. Trust the process of awareness and cultivate an open mind.

If you notice a trait that you don't like, take note of it. This may be a quality to change, but do so without self-criticism. There is an important difference between simply observing something that may need changing versus evaluating whether it is good or bad. Nonjudgmental observation often brings a lessening of defenses and a more open attitude. So while performing the mindfulness exercises, try to observe without making evaluative judgments: just become aware in the situation, without taking a position.

Body Mindfulness

MINDFULNESS WARM-UP I: NOTICING BODY POSITIONS

Warm up to mindfulness with a generalized sense of body awareness. When going about daily activities, take a moment to notice body sensations. Start by noticing the body positions and movements at times while sitting, standing, lying down, and walking. People often pay little attention to such fundamentals. But body sensations are part of every activity, an important and valuable inroad to attuning. So, when first awakening in the morning, begin by taking a moment to experience lying in bed. Then pay attention to the process of sitting up, stepping onto the floor, and slowly standing up. Take note of various body positions whenever possible through out the day.

MINDFULNESS WARM-UP II: EXPLORING A BODY POSITION

Delve a little deeper and pay attention to the body sensations of being in a certain position. For example, when sitting on a chair somewhere at home or at work, stop to pay attention to posture. Notice the quality of sitting: Is it straight, leaning, or slumping into the chair? Do you take support from the chair or push down on the seat? Where are the feet? Pay close attention to all the details.

FOSTERING MINDFULNESS BY ACCEPTANCE

To become aware of what is there, keep observations clear and descriptive. Learn to accept each experience, without making comparisons or criticisms. Then, the finer qualities of experience can be fully appreciated, just as they are.

To apply this nonjudgmental attitude to mindfulness, survey yourself from head to toe and recognize all the different parts. Traditionally, Buddhists counted 32 body parts. Describe each part. Notice, for example, the hair, its color, texture, style; the eyes, the eyebrows, and so on. But stay factual. For example, observe that the hair is, long, dark brown, and curly. Try not to use evaluative terms, such as unattractive or attractive, too long or too short, or perhaps, not straight enough. What happens?

This exercise might be easy for those who are young, attractive, or physically fit with few faults. But therapists may have to guide clients toward a more neutral attitude when they want to reject their appearance or believe they have serious flaws. The Zen Buddhist teacher, Lin Chi, often told his disciples that nothing is missing (Watson, 1993). Problems occur when people step away from what is actually there. Everyone is fully equipped to be mindful. And if they are willing to truly just notice without adding anything extra, they will find that their negative appraisals will dissipate.

Mindful Breathing Exercise Series

One of the most widely practiced meditation traditions is mindful breathing. Many people find that paying attention to breathing is one of the easiest ways to begin the process of mindfulness. Relaxed and controlled breathing was described in Chapter 6. Mindful breathing adds another dimension that can help to access more varieties of experiencing.

Sit down and close the eyes. Observe a breath, beginning with bringing the air in through the nose. Feel the air in the nasal passages and then follow the sensation as the air travels down into the lungs. Concentrate on the movement in the chest and diaphragm as the air enters. Follow the air as it moves out. Note how the diaphragm pushes down as the air travels up and out through the nasal passages. Feel the sensation of air pushing out as it leaves the nose.

Treat each breath as a unique experience to be noticed fully and enjoyed for the first time. Approach the next breath as a completely new experience. Follow the air as it moves in and out, with fresh interest. Each moment is distinct, different from the past moment, and unique, open to new potentials. And so every breath is completely new and worthy of full attention.

After following each breath in this way for several minutes, people often experience calm and ease. This sense of inner peace can become a resource.

Opening Intuition Through Mindful Breathing

Mindful attention to breathing at key moments in the day can become a helpful therapeutic tool. Attention to breathing puts people directly in touch with what is happening within. By turning attention to breathing at various times during the day, people will become aware of different qualities in their breathing, and in so doing, be able to recognize deeper feelings that may be occurring, expressed subtly. For example, when hurrying to accomplish tasks, the breathing rate quickens, with shorter breaths. By stopping to notice, other feelings such as impatience might emerge.

When feeling tense or anxious, a moment of mindful breathing might reveal tightness in the chest or breathing passages. After a few minutes of close attention, a previously unnoticed feeling of disturbance might begin to surface. Emotional responses are usually accompanied by certain patterns of breathing, deep or shallow. Breathing late at night is probably different from breathing early in the morning. As breathing patterns are experienced and accepted by quietly noticing, some or all of the discomfort may ease.

Always start from where you are, without trying to alter anything. With patient, mindful breathing, changes will happen. Remember that each moment is new, so even an uncomfortable breathing pattern or feeling will eventually transform. Turn the attention to breathing for a few minutes here and there through the day to gain new intuitive understandings.

Mindfulness of Feelings

Emotions are an important component of living, and so mindfulness must include attention to feelings. This gives a strategy for dealing with emotions in a way that will overcome suffering from uncomfortable feelings and maximize fulfillment from positive ones. Mindfulness is key with a clear method for applying it.

Feelings can be evaluated as pleasant, unpleasant, or neutral. People tend to cling to pleasant feelings and reject unpleasant ones. And this clinging and rejecting sets in motion a secondary reaction that interferes with awareness and causes suffering. Instead, pay attention to the feelings themselves. Don't add evaluations. Then the secondary reaction that follows can be dropped. The process leads to more comfortable reactions.

The Impermanence of Feelings

Think about how feelings are impermanent. From the perspective of impermanence, feelings, like every other aspect of human experience, are actually a series of fleeting moments. Clinging to a pleasant feeling will inevitably lead to frustration because the feeling always ends. Conversely, trying to avoid an unpleasant feeling will also bring suffering, since there is no escape from moment-to-moment experience. So face the feeling, moment to moment, and do not try to change its character.

Identify Feelings (Affect Labeling)

Mindfulness of feelings begins with first identifying the feeling being experienced. Studies show that altering the labeling and appraisal of emotions lowers the activation of the amygdala, the area responsible for emotional experiencing (see Chapter 14 for the details). This meditation develops the skill of affect labeling by identifying the feelings using this technique.

To start the process, sit down for a moment and close the eyes. Turn attention inward. Try to put a name to the emotion or mood. Then match the description with what is felt. If it is not quite right, modify the label until satisfied that the description fits the feeling.

While doing so, try to be like a benevolent kindergarten teacher who watches over her students as they play on the playground. When two children begin fighting, she does not become angry with them. Instead, she tries to calmly attend to their needs. Benevolently observe all feelings, even the ones that could be labeled unpleasant.

Mindful Attention to Feelings

When out of touch, emotions seem to take on a power of their own, pushing and pulling in many directions. Awareness puts people in the center of their experience, giving greater ability to understand and manage feelings in a mature fashion.

Begin by noticing pleasant feelings. While in the midst of a pleasant experience, stop and take a moment to observe. Feel the accompanying sensations. You may want to sit down and close the eyes. With practice, it gets easier to sense a feeling without needing to stop.

Next, try noticing neutral feelings. Work gradually toward becoming aware of the unpleasant ones. For example, practice being aware of mild annoyance before trying to become aware of strong anger. Build awareness skills gradually, and they will be ready when needed. Mindfulness responds to practice.

Pay close attention to the feeling. Notice that the feeling is not just one quality, but rather is a collection of different sensations. For example, when annoyed there may also be accompanying sensations such as butterflies in the stomach, quickening of the breathing, and heat in the face. Get to know the feeling and all its accompanying aspects. In time, you will be able to discern that even the strongest feeling is a combination of sensations. Notice as many aspects as possible, without judgment. With careful, objective attention that deconstructs the feeling into sensations, the strength of the emotion as seen in all its parts, tends to ease.

Stay with the feeling, moment-by-moment. Often the feeling begins to change under close observation. Notice how each moment is different. The annoyance felt at first may be altered now. Observe the differences. Embrace the feelings and accept them as just what they are, this feeling now, and that feeling later, an ongoing transformation.

Mindfulness of Mind

Mindfulness of mind involves observing mental activity itself. Cognitive psychology is a modern discipline devoted to understanding the nature of mental processes. These methods of mindfulness of mind are compatible with the findings of cognitive psychology about how the mind works.

Mental processes take on many different forms, filling our minds with one thought after another. At times, we think with clarity while other times our thoughts are confused. Sometimes the mind is filled with emotion and other times it is completely unemotional. But if you step back and look at the broader picture, you notice that all of these different states of mind are actually mental processes. For example, if you look at a flower, the flower you see is really a product of your cognitive activity, constructed by your mind. In fact, everything you perceive is partly mentally constructed. Through mindful awareness you can step outside the usual mental constructs that seem to fill each moment.

Become Aware of Thoughts

Mindfulness begins by first recognizing thoughts while thinking them. Sit quietly and close the eyes. Notice each thought as it occurs. Follow the flow of each thought. Be like someone sitting on the bank of a river watching leaves and twigs flow past. Don't jump into the river but stay back on shore observing. Keep observing and letting each thought drift past. If you find yourself drifting downstream with a thought, climb back on shore and resume the observing as soon as possible.

Recognize Mental Construction

Next, try to understand the cognitive process itself. People do not usually experience the world directly. Rather they recognize it through a combination of sensory experiencing and brain processing. The term *recognition* comes from the Greek, *gnosis*. Knowing involves a two-part sense of re-cognizing. We now know that primary cognitive processing is complex and multifaceted. The brain disorder of visual agnosia can serve as an example of how perception involves the combination of the visual system and cortical action. Visual agnosia causes blindness, even when there is no injury to the eyes. The brain plays a vital role in vision. Seeing takes place *through* the eyes, not just *with* the eyes. Similarly, other areas of the brain are part of hearing, smelling, tasting, or touching.

Thus, when viewing a flower, the flower is perceived through the brain's participation with the information received from the senses. Perception involves meanings of flowers, both personal and shared with the culture, with sensory experience of the flower.

Experience is constructed, and mindful awareness of perceptual processing can clarify how this occurs. The sense of permanence comes from these mental formations—the concepts, the meanings, the abstractions that endure in the mind.

Wholesome and Unwholesome Constructions

Some mental constructions are wholesome, tending to wholeness, fullness, completion, thus happiness and fulfillment. Others are unwholesome, and partial, leading to unhappiness and suffering. Buddhism categorizes some mental processes as tending to the whole, unity: love, forgiveness, faith, humility, self-respect, diligence. And others are partial and tend to the unwholesome: greed, hatred, ignorance, pride, doubt, as a few examples. They divide and separate, disrupting the unity. You can probably consider many others wholesome or unwholesome, as well.

Some processes can go either way. For example, diligence is wholesome when it helps to stay with work that needs to be done, but it can be unwholesome if it endangers health from overworking.

Right Mindfulness involves first becoming aware of the thoughts and then considering whether they are wholesome or unwholesome. Look more deeply into each thought and trace it back to its roots. If an unwholesome thought is discovered ask where it came from. Perhaps it is a learned idea, or maybe a culturally shared one, or perhaps it comes from personal insecurities. Trace the thought back to its origins for a more complete understanding.

Cultivate wholesome thoughts and encourage them while also discouraging the unwholesome ones. Be like the farmer who nourishes his plants with the proper fertilizer and keeps away the weeds.

Mindful Thinking

Mindfully observe the thoughts again. Think about this statement from a Buddhist sutra, "A thought is like lightning, it breaks up in a moment and does not stay on" (Conze, 1995, p. 163). Observe the fleeting nature of thoughts as they come and go. Notice how every thought lacks staying power. Even if the content of a present thought resembles earlier thoughts, each actual momentary thought is new, brief, and then gone.

Meditating on Thought

Apply mindfulness by turning attention to thinking. Sit quietly and observe beyond the content of thinking. Turn to thought itself.

MINDFULNESS OF THE OBJECTS OF MIND

Typically, thinking is always intentional; thinking about something. When feeling an emotion, it is directed toward something or someone. Similarly, sensory experiences are of an object or a person. Consciousness is filled with an object of mind. The Chinese word for perception is made up of two ideograms: *sign* and *mind*.

When we try to experience the world outside of consciousness, we discover that we cannot easily do so. How can we step outside consciousness and know the world? The objects we think are outside of ourselves in the world are actually in relationship to us, connected as the objects of mind. Through the mind, experience of the world comes to be. Mindfulness gets one in touch with this constructive process, and meditation helps develop the vision to see beyond what appears.

Mindful in the Moment

Now bring all the ways of being mindful together in the present moment. Scan the body to raise body awareness. To become mindful of emotions, observe the feelings. Notice mental activity: thoughts and perceptions. Pay close attention to the objects of the perceptions. It doesn't need to take too long to perform these four qualities of mindfulness. Once centered in the moment's experiencing, let all this go and just be present.

Notice how experience transforms, moment by moment. Whenever possible, turn the attention to experiencing. Get in touch mindfully as often as possible. In time, mindfulness will become habitual and natural. In balance with oneself and the surroundings, accept the flow of life as it comes and act in harmony with what is needed. Stay anew with each moment of experience.

10

Working with Qi: Activating and Centering

All things have darkness at their back [yin]
and strive towards the light [yang],
and the flowing power [Qi] gives them harmony.

(*Dao De Jing*, quoted in Wilhelm, 1990, p. 46)

The ancient Chinese believed that Qi flows from the dynamic interaction between yin and yang. The word *Qi* corresponds to the Greek word *pneuma* and the Sanskrit word *prana*, meaning breath, respiration, wind, vital spirit, or soul (*Webster's Unabridged Dictionary*, 1998). Qi is manifested in every area of living, from inner health and vitality to the environment and outward. Everything in the universe both active and still is part of the vast sea of Qi.

The texts of ancient Chinese medicine hold that when Qi flows freely, everything works smoothly as it should. Health is maintained by living in accord with yin and yang as they occur in nature. Disease happens when Qi is blocked. Surpluses build up in some areas and deficits in others. The meditative methods of Qi Gong foster the free flow of this internal energy to keep people healthy, thereby preventing diseases from happening. In fact, the most effective form of treatment is prevention. The Yellow Emperor's advice is just as true today as it was thousands of years ago:

Thus, the sages do not treat a formed disease, but treat an unformed disease; they do not treat a formed disorder, but treat an unformed disorder. That is just so. If medicines are only used once a disease has formed, or treatments are only taken when a disorder has formed, this condition is just like digging a well when one is thirsty, or like casting knives when one is about to fight. It is late, isn't it?

(Yellow Emperor; Ming, 2001 p. 295)

Qi Gong is an ancient Chinese art of meditation and gentle movement combined with breathing techniques that help people to maintain and restore the correct flow of Qi. The uninterrupted flow of Qi is natural and healthy and can be maintained through correct habits, including the practice of Qi Gong. Since problems develop when the flow is blocked, diminished, or overly stimulated, Qi Gong may be prescribed to treat both psychological and physical problems. It is also recommended as part of a healthy regime.

Modern research has shown the effectiveness of methods that work with Qi (Mayer, 1999; Sancier, & Holman, 2004) and so therapists and clients can be confident that these methods may prove useful at many phases of treatment and beyond.

Chinese tradition holds that the Yellow Emperor Huang Ti (2700 BC) was the first to record the ancient practices of healing that formed the foundation for Chinese medicine. He practiced exercises for health that involved using gentle movements combined with breathing and meditation (Liu, 1986). These ancient exercises developed into martial arts such as Taiji Quan (Tai Chi Chuan) and the health practices known today as Qi Gong. To lend support to the idea that these practices are indeed ancient, several artifacts were discovered in the late 1990s: a carved cylinder from 380 BC and a silk scroll dating back to 168 BC, both of which show figures performing Qi Gong exercises (Gascoigne, 1997).

"Gong" means cultivating, working with, or developing, and thus Qi Gong is a practice of cultivating Qi. According to Qi Gong theory, learning how to develop and direct the Qi is the foundation for much greater health and well-being (Gascoigne, 1997, p. 67). Qi Gong methods offer new options for enhancing vitality.

Cultivating Qi involves sensitizing to a different aspect of functioning. We are accustomed to attending to what we are doing, where we are going, and what we are thinking. But sensing energy is usually done in a vague, nonspecific manner: We feel energetic or tired, but the subtleties are missed. Qi Gong opens up perception to this important dimension of functioning by raising awareness of Qi energy as it flows through the body. Awareness is the first step to working with energy flow.

The Qi Gong exercises that follow will help to attune to energy flow and then to use it for what is needed. When stressed and vitality is low, there are methods to become more energetic. When overly stimulated, Qi should not be raised more.

Two Types of Qi Gong: *Wei Dan* and *Nei Dan*

Qi Gong has two broad categories of practice: Wei Dan and Nei Dan. Both methods can help raise Qi and then enhance and circulate it through the body, but they do so by using different methods.

Wei Dan is the external form of Qi Gong. Wei Dan increases Qi by stimulating areas of the body. The Qi builds up in that area and then spills over through the meridians. This energy can be thought of as a healing medicine that nourishes and vitalizes the whole body.

Nei Dan is the internal form of Qi Gong. These methods begin by generating Qi in an energy center of the body located in the lower abdomen. Then by focusing attention, Qi is guided around the body through the two major vessels called the Conception Vessel and the Governor Vessel.

Wei Dan

PRELIMINARY WEI DAN EXERCISE: RECOGNIZING THE FEELING OF QI
Clapping can draw the Qi into the hands, raising the energy level in the palms. Clap the hands together for 15 seconds. Then stop, and close the eyes. Concentrate attention on the sensations in the palms. Take a few moments to feel the sensations.

DEVELOPING AWARENESS OF QI
The previous exercise emphasized the physical sensation of Qi, but the true art of working with Qi is subtler, using the mind. Mind and body are unified and interrelated, so when attention is focused on an area of the body, energy will tend to flow there.

Conception Vessel

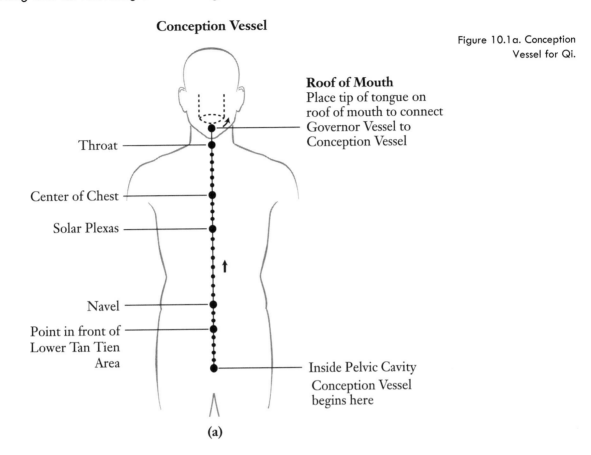

Figure 10.1a. Conception Vessel for Qi.

Roof of Mouth
Place tip of tongue on roof of mouth to connect Governor Vessel to Conception Vessel

Throat

Center of Chest

Solar Plexas

Navel

Point in front of Lower Tan Tien Area

Inside Pelvic Cavity Conception Vessel begins here

(a)

Sit in a quiet place with hands resting on the knees. Focus attention on the palms of the hands. Feel how warm they are, and whether they seem heavy or light. Keep attention focused on the hands. After a few minutes, do you begin to notice some tingling in the fingertips? Or do you feel a slight warming? These sensations can be indicators of the Qi flowing into the hands, directed by focusing attention there.

Experiment with other areas of focus. For example, focus attention on the feet. Does an experience of warmth or tingling develop there? With practice, a response develops in an area of the body as soon as the attention is focused there. With more practice, directing Qi becomes easier.

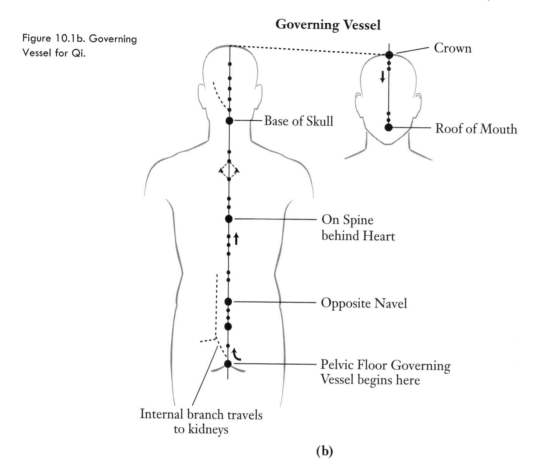

Governing Vessel

Figure 10.1b. Governing
Vessel for Qi.

Crown

Base of Skull

Roof of Mouth

On Spine
behind Heart

Opposite Navel

Pelvic Floor Governing
Vessel begins here

Internal branch travels
to kidneys

(b)

MOVING WEI DAN: EIGHT PIECES OF BROCADE

Traditionally, Wei Dan is performed by doing sets of movements that involve tensing and relaxing of muscles. Wei Dan is most effective when one is calm and relaxed. Therefore, before beginning, do one of the exercises given in the book to clear the mind of distraction and relax the body.

After a brief relaxation meditation, try this series of traditional Wei Dan exercises known as the Eight Pieces of Brocade. These exercises date back to the Sung Dynasty

(960–1279) in China. Brocade is a cloth with finely woven patterns of great beauty and value. These gentle exercises are beautiful patterns that have been used for centuries to improve health and well-being. When performing these exercises, don't push or strain. Do only what is comfortable. Progress happens over time.

Stand quietly for a few minutes. Let the breathing become calm and natural. Keep the back relatively straight. Perform the movements slowly, keeping the body relaxed. Repeat each piece three to five times and then proceed to the next one. Continue until the series of eight is complete.

These eight exercises, performed in sequence, activate the entire body. Be sure to concentrate on the movement because the mind is an important component for raising Qi. A slight change in energy can be experienced as warmth or tingling sensations.

Piece One, figs. (a) and (b): Stand with feet shoulder width apart, hands dropped straight down at the sides and inhale. Exhaling, rotate the head to the left without straining. Keep the rest of the body still. While inhaling, bring the head back to face front, then exhale again while turning the head to the right. Finally, inhale while turning to face front.

Piece Two, figs. (c), (d) and (e): Intertwine the fingers together with palms facing out, inhale, and then carefully swing the arms up overhead while exhaling. Then inhale, bringing the hands back down in front of the body.

Piece Three, figs. (f) and (g): Place the hands palm up in front of the body, elbows bent, and fingertips touching and inhale. Exhale, moving the left hand up overhead with the palm facing up while simultaneously moving the right hand down in front, palm down. Then inhale and return the hands to their original position. Exhale and reverse, raising the right hand overhead palm up and the left hand down palm down.

Piece Four, figs. (h), (i) and (j): Begin with the fists held at the waist, palms facing up. Inhale and step to the left into a slightly wider stance, known in martial arts as horse stance. Let the knees bend slightly. Exhale and turn the body slightly to the left, crossing the arms out to the left side. Then open the left hand, palm facing away from the body while drawing the right hand back to the chest, as if shooting an arrow. Now inhale again and return to face front with both fists at the waist and left foot drawn back in to shoulder width apart. Pivot to the right and repeat the pattern while exhaling, stepping out to the right, extending both hands to the right, and pulling back the bow. To finish, turn back to face the front while inhaling.

Figure 10.2a–s. Eight
Pieces of Brocade.

(a)   (b)

Piece Five, figs. (k) and (l): Step to the left into horse stance. Let the hands rest on the thighs. Exhale and lean to the left without raising the feet. Inhale and return to center. Exhale while leaning to the right. Inhale and return to center.

Piece Six, figs. (m) and (n): Bring the legs back to shoulder width apart. Raise the hands, palms up, fingers touching as in Piece Three and inhale. Then gently stretch forward while exhaling and place palms so they face the floor. As flexibility increases some people will be able to touch the floor with the palms, but don't try to go further than is comfortable. Inhale and return to standing.

Piece Seven, figs. (o) and (p): Inhale from a horse stance position with fists at the sides, then exhale while slowly punching to the left with the left fist. Turn the head to watch as the fist moves outward. Inhale while returning to the original position, then punch to the right and exhale. Finally, inhale and return to center.

(c)   (d)

Figure 10.2 Continued.

(e)

Figure 10.2 Continued.

(f)   (g)

Piece Eight, figs. (q), (r) and (s): For the final piece, inhale, stand with the feet together, hands at the sides and keeping the legs straight, raise up on the toes while exhaling. Then inhale and lower the heels slowly to return to standing.

STATIONARY WEI DAN: MIND LEADS THE QI

Wei Dan can be performed by sitting quietly, imagining the motions without actually performing them. In this way, Qi moves to different areas more subtly. Once familiar with doing the Eight Pieces of Brocade, try sitting quietly and imagine doing the exercises. Do not move the body. Instead, simply visualize doing each exercise. Imagine doing the exercises even better than when actually performing them. Imagine correcting mistakes as well. This will not only begin circulating Qi but will also help to improve performance of the exercises when doing them actively. As a side

(h)   (i)

Figure 10.2 Continued.

(j)

Figure 10.2 *Continued.*

(k)

(l)

(m)

(n)

(o)   (p)

Figure 10.2 Continued.

benefit, this visualization can be performed in conjunction with any physical activity, such as martial arts forms, dance patterns, tennis serves or strokes, or weight lifting. This may also activate ideomotor mechanisms to help improve psychomotor coordination.

Nei Dan

Nei Dan has its roots in alchemical Daoism. The outer alchemical process of heating a cauldron to melt elements that would be drunk as elixirs for health and longevity was reinterpreted with these exercises as a symbolic, internal transformation of spiritual elements to bring about health-giving effects (Simpkins & Simpkins, 1999a).

Figure 10.2 Continued.

(q)   (r)

(s)

WARMING THE DANDIEN

There are three main energy centers in the body: upper in the head, middle in the chest, and lower in the abdomen. This lower area known as the dandien is located an inch and a half below the navel and one third of the way in. This lower area is an important center used in martial arts, Eastern medicine, and Qi Gong as a source for power and energy. Qi energy is thought to be stored in the dandien. A number of exercises are devoted to concentrating on this vital area.

One of the best ways to begin getting in touch with internal energy is by warming the lower dandien. The lower dandien is like a central furnace that heats the body. Meditation helps to fuel this internal furnace and bring about warming. With attention concentrated in this area, energy will gather and can then be circulated around the body.

MEDITATION ON WARMING THE LOWER DANDIEN

Locate the dandien by laying the hands across the abdomen so that the fingers touch, forming an empty triangle between them. The fingers will be placed over the lower dandien.

Now place the palms over the dandien and focus all the attention on this area. Imagine warmth and energy building in this area. A visual image may be helpful, such as remembering a warm fire or recalling a hot day in the middle of summer. Imagine that a source of comfortable heat is located

Figure 10.3. Dandien.

in the abdomen. Imagine warmth beginning in a small area and then spreading outwards. Suggest that the warmth is building. With practice, the dandien area will become literally warmer as Qi accumulates.

EXTENDING QI

Extend the Qi, using an energy ball (Figure 10.4). Traditionally, this was imagined as a Golden Ball, but we often encourage people to imagine something more familiar, such as a beach ball. Begin with the hands over the dandien until the feeling of warmth begins. Then extend the hands outward, palms facing each other as if holding a ball of energy in the lap. Warmth and tingling will develop in the palms of the hands as the attention is focused on the energy ball. Let the energy ball begin to move by shifting the hands around so that one hand holds from above and the other hand holds from below. Advanced practitioners let the energy ball float, causing the hands to move upward.

Figure 10.4. Energy ball.

SMALL CIRCULATION MEDITATION

Most forms of Qi Gong consider this exercise to be an important skill. Once some warming or tingling of the dandien is experienced, a next step is to circulate the energy around the body. Visualize the energy moving up from the dandien along a pathway up the middle of the body (see Figures 10.1a and 10.1b). Visualize each acupoint and focus the energy about an inch deep. Pay attention to the area and wait for a feeling of tingling or warmth to develop. Some people may find it easier to imagine a small ball of energy, about the size of a golf ball, rolling around at the point.

Move to each point in sequence, concentrating on the point for a minute or two. At first, just do one or two points. Don't rush the process. Proceed only as it feels comfortable. If there is difficulty or discomfort after several sincere attempts, stop the meditation and seek guidance from a Qi Gong teacher.

Integrating Wholeness Contemplation

Qi Gong not only allows for the integration of the body, but also brings unity for the whole being, one with the universe. The world, as the Daoist would say, is one with Dao. When performing the Qi Gong exercises, contemplate the connection. With each inhalation, note how the air and energy that enters the nose and circulates down into the lungs comes from the world. Each breath out sends the energy back again to the world. Contemplate the flowing relationship, where the boundaries merge.

FREE FLOWING QI EXERCISE

Qi Gong can be a creative process. Artists can utilize the flow of Qi when they create. For example, painters can flow their brush strokes in harmony with Qi for inspiration, thereby expressing patterns of Qi in landscapes as well as poetic calligraphy. Qi can also be expressed in body movements that are harmonious and natural.

People have performed many different traditional patterns of Qi Gong for centuries. But ultimately, these patterns are merely the form—an empty container to be filled with Qi. Just as with Dao, the shape of the container is not what is important. Like Dao Qi goes everywhere. Skillful practitioners spontaneously create Qi Gong patterns to let the Qi flow freely.

Find a place with some open space. Stand in a relaxed position and meditate on the dandien for several minutes until warming begins. Then allow the Qi to begin to circulate, as in previous exercises. As it does, let the body move with it, as it wants to. Don't try to move, simply wait for movement to happen. If movement does happen, enjoy the flow. If not, enjoy the stillness. After learning to let Qi inspire motion spontaneously, it can be used for many purposes, such as calligraphy, painting, sculpture, and other arts.

11

Engaging the Symbolic Through Mandalas and Mantras

It is only possible to live the fullest life when we are in harmony with the symbols; wisdom is a return to them. It is a question neither of belief nor of knowledge, but of the agreement of our thinking with the primordial images of the unconscious.

(Jung, 1981, pp. 402–403).

Symbols surround us. They guide us to the unknown, and through the known. Since its early beginnings, psychotherapy has used the power of the symbolic as a looking glass in which to see deeper meanings, reflected by methods such as dream analysis, which was foundational in psychoanalysis. Symbols are also used metaphorically to stimulate associations and new potentials in such therapies as Ericksonian hypnosis. Meditation also utilizes symbols as a doorway to deeper levels of consciousness. The great meditation traditions of Yoga, Daoism, and Tibetan Buddhism have produced highly evolved symbolic practices to guide meditators along a journey of discovery. Many may be familiar with the traditional symbols through Eastern art: Symbolic diagrams known as mandalas appear in paintings and tapestries, and mantras, which serve a similar purpose, are heard in traditional chants. The classic *I Jing* can be expressed as a circular diagram, a mandala known as the *Pagua* (Cleary, 2000b) (figure 11.1).

Recent discoveries in modern physics and psychology have led to the scientific position that perception doesn't reflect reality as it truly is. As researchers

Figure 11.1. Pagua.

continue to investigate the interrelationships among phenomena that our senses cannot detect, we recognize that there is still much to discover and learn. Thus, it is not outside the realm of possibility that some interconnections, invisible to our senses, might exist. Symbols expressed as mandalas and mantras offer a different kind of tool for accessing what is often inaccessible to the typical linear, rational approach. These methods of meditation offer a nonlinear, immediate presentation of interrelated ideas that are held in mind all at once. In this way, a different kind of access is given which the ancients considered more direct and revealing of some of the hidden elements of reality and mind.

How Symbols Represent Reality

Order is intrinsic to the universe. Images and sounds are an expression of these underlying patterns. Life is a meaningful expression of this universal harmony, beyond any one individual conscious conception. Symbols such as mandalas and mantras represent the intrinsic order of the universe. They can act as a direct gateway to deeper patterns without conceptualization. The symbol serves as a guide, directing the meditator through a process that engages directly with nature.

This Eastern insight has a counterpart in the West in the work of the pre-Socratic philosopher Pythagoras (570–490 BC). Pythagoras saw mathematical relationships in everything around him and developed a theory, parts of which have stayed with us, woven into the fabric of Western thought. Pythagoras believed that numbers are not just points on a line, a quantity or measure to be used. He thought that numbers actually *are* the nature of the universe, the basis of all things. Pythagoras observed an intimate relationship between things and numbers everywhere in everything. For example, he recognized that the relationship of notes on the musical scale was always in exact ratios. He tested this out on a simple string that he secured at two ends. The string vibrated as a unit when plucked. Then divided in half, it produced a half tone. Dividing the string into thirds, fourths, and so on, Pythagoras produced all the overtone series of the musical scale. The sound of the note was related to the length of the string.

Pythagoras' theories showed that the deeper nature of the universe could be revealed in numerical relationships. Similarly, mandalas act as a bridge that links consciousness to higher realities through archetypal relationships presented in circular geometric diagrammatic patterns. The images of the mandala activate the wisdom of universal knowledge through symbols, leading to a better link with the world through consciousness.

The source of these patterns does not have to come only from the traditional symbols of ancient art. Meaningful symbols can be found in everyday life. They may be external or internal. We can learn to be sensitive to the symbolic. Then, everything that takes place, whether outside or inside, can become an opportunity to learn. By harmonizing with the symbols in our own lives, we return to having contact with the source, a wellspring for transformation. All the experiences of life can be viewed as symbols to be utilized to deepen meditation and enhance the therapeutic process.

Engaging in symbolic practices involves identifying with archetypal roles, reaching beyond the narrow confines of typical patterns to merge with larger, universal potentials. We play many roles in life; some limit our options, others open up new ones. When you are a father, or a mother, for example, be the best parent you can imagine, the higher form. Or if you are in the role of a son, be that role at its best. By identifying with the better, the larger, the higher roles, we extend beyond our limitations. We gain a sense of new possibilities for ourselves, beyond the role.

Mandalas

The choice of the circular shape for a pattern intended to depict the universe is not accidental. The circle, the only figure that does not single out any particular direction, is used spontaneously everywhere to depict objects whose shape is uncertain or irrelevant, or to depict something that either has no shape at all, any shape, or all shapes.

(Arnheim, 1966, p. 234)

Carl Gustav Jung (1875–1961) incorporated the symbolic realm extensively in his work. He believed that archetypal patterns are fundamental to the inherited collective unconscious, symbolizing the central pole of the self, the axis of the inner universe. He encouraged his patients undergoing deep analysis to express themselves and their transformation through the pictorial imagery evoked in mandalas. Many of his patients created their own personal mandalas to express the transformative therapeutic process. He found that the practice facilitated analysis and higher synthesis of the personality.

Mandala as Symbol

Mandalas are ancient. There are representations of them in the earliest recorded history. They contain symbolic patterns, figures, abstract designs, and letters. Every culture has some form of mandala. The root word of mandala, *manas*, means mind. The mind is central to meditation and mandalas diagram the unconscious, giving a clear depiction of the inner mind. The word *mandala* in Sanskrit also signifies circle, sphere, territory, group, and collection. The circle has come to symbolize the journey into the mind, beginning from the outer fringes and penetrating deeply to the central core. The mandala collects many symbols together into one collected whole, often representing a compendium of teachings.

Mandalas are created from uniform divisions of a circle. The divisions are symbols that reveal the inner workings of nature and the inherent order of the universe.

The Avatamsaka or Flower Ornament teachings expressed conceptual imagery to evoke this larger perception of relationships known as interpenetration. The analogy of Indra's net illustrates the perception well. Imagine a net of interconnected jewels, connected with each other, as in a geodesic dome. Each jewel is reflected in every other. Similarly, every event is seen as a composite of all the smaller events. Even events that seem to be different may be similar in principle. In this way, each individual perception is not an isolated event but is also understood as part of a more comprehensive perspective. Through the therapeutic process this global understanding of difficulties, a conceptual mandala, may develop for use.

Types of Mandalas

The Daoist *I Jing* is well known as a book that reveals principles for understanding the ever changing nature of reality and how human beings can understand their own minds and adapt to the change. *I Jing* mandalas were developed as a practical tool for mental development. Each mandala contained an integrated array of images and insights from the combinations of yin and yang in one completed pattern (Cleary, 2000b).

Yantras, widely used in Hinduism, are a particular type of mandala that use strictly geometric patterning. They are a visual representation of the harmonic tones used in mantras. Directing thoughts to these archetypal patterns is used to attune consciousness to the harmony of the universal. Shri Yantra is the most revered of all the Hindu yantras. It is sometimes known as the Yantra of Creation. The Shri Yantra is believed to be the image of the Om mantra (figure 11.2).

A Tibetan Buddhist mandala is a highly developed art form that often pictures a meditating buddha in the center surrounded by geometric patterns representing a way to the understanding. Through perception of an organized set of images, the viewer can move from the particular image to universal understanding. Understanding arises, not from magnifying any one individual object in the image but rather by making a symbolic shift from the specific to the broader meanings.

The Wheel of Existence mandala is one of the best-known mandalas that depicts a model of the universe based on the doctrine of Tibetan Buddhism. This type of mandala reflects a microcosm of existence that reveals the entire continuum of life in one picture. A personified image of death usually sits above the circle, watching over it.

Figure 11.2. Shri Yantra.

The designs are complex, filled with the many facets of both conscious and unconscious life. The shapes and symbols visually communicate a code of meaning that allows a special relationship between the concepts and the viewer. These symbolic images can be read as visual shorthand, directly experienced beyond concepts by using pictures and experience.

The Rasa Mandala (Figure 11.3) pictures a mythic dance, known as the rasa dance, that was performed in a circle with Krishna dancing along with the people. It has come to symbolize joyful togetherness with others sharing in the divine. It

Figure 11.3. *The Rasamandala* (from a Bhagavata Purana). (Opaque watercolor on paper, ca. 1690. 9–1/8" x 13–31/32." Central Indian school, India, Madhya Pradesh, Malwa. Edwin Binney III Collection, 1990: 964. San Diego Museum of Art.)

often pictures couples, as in the rasa mandala pictured here, which may be useful for couples therapy.

Mandalas are incorporated into practice by drawing the viewer into the meditative process, in a process we call *invisioning*. The well-constructed mandala induces the observer to imagine motion to center, the source of the circle. Tibetan Buddhists speak of entering the mandala, which implies that the mandala is not just a map: It is an opening to another dimension of being. The mandala also shows the Way. Entering the circle of the mandala initiates a process of inner transformation. It invites letting go of limitations and expanding potential.

Mandala Meditations

INVISIONING INDRA'S NET

Through working with individual problems, we recognize the complex, nonlinear, and multifaceted nature of problems in general. This meditation offers a method for pulling together many levels of understandings into one intuitive interrelation-ship. The development of this skill leads to awareness that is capable of taking in multiple dimensions all at once. Through such awareness, the client may be able to shift beyond a narrow, redundant pattern to form a new understanding at another level.

The first step is to turn attention away from linear, rational thinking. Perform one of the methods to change the focus of attention such as attention to breathing, one-pointed awareness, or clearing the mind as described in other chapters. Next, meditate on Indra's net, an image of a jeweled interconnected net with all the jewels reflecting all the others. Visualize this, allowing the awareness to expand outwards to include more and more jewels.

SHRI YANTRA MEDITATION

Place the picture of the Shri Yantra in clear view (figure 11.2). Sit in a comfortable posture on the floor or seated on a chair while maintaining a straight spine. Breathe in through the nose and out through the mouth, but do not force it at all, just let the breath flow normally. Look into the center of the Yantra, trying to blink as rarely as possible. Don't look at the particular details, just keep the gaze directed to the center and observe the whole Yantra at once. Do so for up to 15 or 20 minutes. Let the Yantra meditation absorb the complete attention. *Invision* the Yantra. With practice you may have an experience of nonduality, when the Yantra is experienced as within and without at the same time.

RASA MANDALA MEDITATION 1

In this meditation, entrance begins from the peripheries and gradually penetrates to the center. At first the meditator takes on a role through identification with the symbols. Through the unification, the mandala becomes the self in transformation as it guides the process.

Begin by gazing at the mandala (Figure 11.3). Use the skills of one-pointed awareness from the previous chapter to keep attention focused on the mandala. Start at the outer edges and study the patterns carefully. Gradually move the gaze inwards until the entire mandala has been observed.

RASA MANDALA MEDITATION 2

Gaze at the mandala with eyes half open. Take in the whole picture without focusing on any one item. Allow the entire image to enter into consciousness. Encourage the process, with an open, welcoming attitude. Sit quietly and let the unconscious flow. If this seems difficult, review Chapter 5 on unconscious flow and then return to this exercise.

The process is more important than its content. Meaning is not necessarily dependent on form. Content is not form. But form includes content. Form can give information about all kinds of things, through meanings given to the symbols and by relationships between the objects and symbols. Thus, use symbolic sources that are personally meaningful. Thinking can be stimulated by meditation on these symbols in this nonspecific, open-ended manner.

Mantras

> Mantras do not act on account of their own "magic" nature, but only through the mind that experiences them. They do not possess any power of their own; they are only the means for concentrating already existing forces—just as a magnifying glass, though it does not contain any heat of its own, is able to concentrate the rays of the sun and to transform their mild warmth into incandescent heat.
>
> (Govinda, 1960, p. 28)

The nature of the universe is also symbolized in sound. Hindu theory has long held that the universe is in harmony. Modern physics agrees in principle. Each particle, each molecule, and each object has its own vibration, its own frequency. A great singer can shatter a glass by singing a long note in harmony with the correct frequency for the glass. A platoon of soldiers marching over a bridge assigns one soldier to be out of step so that the vibration they generate as a unity will not shake the bridge apart. Research shows that sound affects the chemistry of the body to bring about alterations in thought patterns and emotional responses. Properly used, sound has great potential for healing.

A mantra metaphorically opens a window and shows a primordial image. The primordial image becomes a mirror that reflects the inner essence, the heart of the universe. In mantric theory, sounds are not apart from this essence of reality: they are intimately unified with reality. By chanting certain sounds in patterned combinations, the corresponding experience of meaning is evoked. Mantras provide an experience to listen to, so the practitioner can hear the universe itself with direct awareness. The word *mantra* comes from the Sanskrit roots, *Manas*, mind and *tra*, tool. Mantras are tools of the mind to unify everyday consciousness with higher consciousness.

Sounds get our attention directed towards reality. Since each particle has a frequency, and the heart of the universe is a complex musical harmony, then chanting is a way to focus attention and direct oneself into union with enlightened consciousness. The mantra is a powerful way to focus consciousness and resonate with the music.

Mantras utilize natural dynamics. We may spontaneously yell with happiness or anger, shout to release emotion or stress, or sing when happy. We hear our names and respond. Some people hum instinctively while going about their work. Mantras utilize this spontaneous capacity, to deliberately focus attention and consciousness at will. Certain sounds are fundamental to the human condition. Sounds tell us about what is happening. According to a well-regarded theory held by linguist Noam Chomsky (Cook & Newson, 2007) certain sounds are innate and universal to all human beings, worldwide. These sounds, uttered soon after birth, are the basis for the patterns of systems of language and communication.

Om

Om is the original mantra from Hinduism and expanded in Tibetan Buddhism. *Om* stands at the beginning of many mantras in Buddhism, symbolizing the wholeness of things, the infinite and perfect.

Om Mani Padme Hum

Om Mani Padme Hum, which translates literally as "Hail to the Jewel of the Lotus," is a root mantra for Tibetan Buddhism. The universe begins with Om and ends with Hum. The world's fundamental vibrations are expressed in this mantra.

CHANTING OM MANI PADME HUM

Begin by breathing comfortably for several minutes. For the chanting, do not breathe deeper; just breathe naturally. Inhale, and then exhale while chanting Om (ohm).

Then, inhale and exhale while chanting Mani (mah nee). And smoothly inhale and exhale while chanting Padme (pahd may). Without pausing, inhale and then exhale while chanting Hum (hum). Feel the vibration in the lips and vocal chords. Keep each word timed together with each breath, in and out. Let the lips remain relaxed and the breath natural. Allow breathing and chanting to become rhythmically in tune. In time, the flow of sound and air becomes natural and comfortable. Keep attention engaged, enjoy the process. Repeat continuously several times.

Whispering Mantra

Once at ease with chanting, try whispering the mantra following the same procedures as chanting. Begin whispering Om with an exhalation and continue through the mantra, repeating for a comfortable period of time.

Silent Mantra

Next, perform the mantra in silence. Keep the attention focused with a silent Om while exhaling, Mani while exhaling, Padme while exhaling, Hum while exhaling. If the mind wanders, bring it back gently. In time, a rhythmic harmony develops between silent sound and soft breath. In the silence, discover an inner quiet and clarity.

Chanting with Reflection

Each mantric syllable has meaning, both literal and symbolic. The Dalai Lama encourages people to meditate on the meaning of *Om Mani Padme Hum* while reciting

Figure 11.4. *Om Mani Padme Hum.*

it. *Om* symbolizes the impure body, mind, and speech of everyday unenlightened life along with the pure body, speech, and mind of an enlightened Buddha. *Mani*, which translates as jewel, signifies the method of directing oneself toward becoming enlightened, compassionate, and loving. *Padme* translates as lotus and means wisdom. The final symbol, *Hum* means indivisibility and signifies that purity is achieved by uniting the method with wisdom.

While reciting each syllable of the mantra, keep the meaning in mind. Consider the ramifications of the meaning for personal development. Keep the mind focused on the meaning while reciting the mantra.

Chanting Combined with Visualization

The mantra is more than just sound; it also has a visual image in the language script itself. Each mantra syllable can invoke a corresponding color while it activates a related chakra or center of spiritual energy in the body. The mantric syllables are pictured within the complex visualization of energy centers in order to direct consciousness to experience circulation of energy. These practices are also used to promote healing. The meaning is identical with the sound and the image and the essence of mind. All components resonate together like a gong, which is reality itself. Modern science holds a corresponding view of reality. What we see and hear are actually waves of energy, resonating in harmonic patterns that our senses interpret as different colors and sounds.

Visualizing Sound

With each inhalation while chanting, visualize fresh, clean energy flowing into the body and down through the spine. Then with the exhalation while chanting, picture used, old energy flowing up through the spine and out. Color relates to the energy. Brighter colors enter with inhalation and darker colors exit with the exhalation.

Conclusion

Mandalas and mantras serve the meditator in many ways. The sound and its image are not two separate things. The mantric vision is a vision of harmony. The mandala guides us into the center of harmony. And the harmony can be found within as well.

12

Empty the Mind

Make your will one! Don't listen with your ears, listen with your mind. No, don't listen with your mind, but listen with your spirit. Listening stops with the ears, the mind stops with recognition, but spirit is empty and waits on all things. The Way gathers in emptiness alone. Emptiness is the fasting of the mind.

(Zhuangzi quoted in Watson 1968, p. 58)

One of the great traditions in meditation is to clear the mind. But clearing the mind is not just a matter of pushing out thoughts or stopping thinking. This famous story illustrates the point:

A Zen student was trying very hard to make his mind clear like a mirror. He sat quietly and tried to think of nothing. But thoughts inevitably kept distracting him. Feeling in despair, he complained to his master, "No matter how hard I try, I cannot clear my mind! What should I do?"

The master picked up a tile that was on the ground and began polishing it with his robe. Confused, the student asked, "Master, what are you doing?"

"I am polishing this tile to make it into a mirror."

"That's impossible! You cannot make a tile into a mirror," said the student.

The master smiled. "Nor can you make your mind into a mirror!"

Correctly clearing the mind activates a capacity that is already potentially there. Think of the mind as similar to a lake that seems murky when sediment is stirred up. The nature of water does not change when it has sediment stirred up in it. The potential for clarity is there, but when the sediment is stirred, the clarity is obscured. All that is needed is to allow everything to settle. When the water is analyzed into its parts, its molecule is a stable substance, in its relationship of two hydrogen atoms to one oxygen atom.

Emptiness

Meditation finds meaning in emptiness. For Buddhists, all things are empty, without form in their true nature. The Daoists saw the significance of emptiness when they said that the usefulness in a cup is in its emptiness. Once the cup is filled, it can no longer be used. Thus, attune to the empty to get to something useful, with infinite possibilities.

Figure 12.1. The Empty Cup: Empty your cup so that it may be filled. (Artists: C. Alexander & Annellen Simpkins, San Diego, CA, 2007; walnut burl and maple burl, wood on wood)

But emptying is only half the truth. The Heart Sutra points out that form is emptiness and emptiness is form (Conze, 1995). Paradoxically, emptying the mind leaves the mind open.

This conception has many indirect, positive effects. Normally, the mind jumps from one set of associations to another. The Buddhists had a name for this common condition: monkey mind. Clear thinking is lost in a sea of associated thoughts rushing around. With the mind-chatter from the minor concerns of daily life silenced, thinking clears. Less scattered, more single-minded and self-directed, solutions to problems are easier to recognize without distracting thoughts. A more realistic and direct response to the situation becomes possible. Meditation fills the mind with new understandings as it empties the mind of unnecessary problems that derive from illusions.

The untrained person experiences thoughts as occurring automatically, beyond control. Psychology and meditation teach that the contents of the mind can be influenced, just as readily as a sculptor can shape a piece of raw wood into an object of beauty. The interaction of the artist's inner vision with the qualities and capacities of the wood makes this possible.

Step on the path with confidence. As Zen master Lin Chi, founder of the Rinzai Zen sect, told his students, "When students today fail to make progress, where's the fault? The fault lies in the fact that they don't have faith in themselves" (Watson, 1993, p. 23).

Experiment with the exercises that follow to develop this skill. Be patient, these exercises do respond to practice. And keep in mind that stable, consistent practice is healthy. Focus on the experience of the exercise itself, not just as a means to an end. Without a goal in mind, simply enjoy each experience for itself and let abilities develop naturally.

Focus On A Color

This meditation is one of the first that we present to people who are just beginning to meditate. We have also taught this to children, who have enthusiastically practiced it.

Sit comfortably in a quiet place and find a comfortable position. Close the eyes. Focus attention on one color: either a favorite color, or any one that you select at this time. For those who have difficulty visualizing a color, think of an object that is that color, such as a blue sky or green grass at first. Then perhaps the color itself may become available to focus on as an object. If unrelated thoughts or feelings intrude, notice it as soon as you can, then try to return attention to the chosen color. At first, concentrate on the color for a brief time only. When ready, open the eyes.

Begin with a very short span of time, such as 30 seconds. Once the attention can remain focused on the color for 30 seconds, increase to 1 minute, then 2 minutes, then gradually to as long as 30 minutes or more. Practice this several times a day at several different sittings. Some people like to do this twice a day, for 15 minutes morning and evening. Find your own rhythms.

Visualizing Beyond Thought

In this exercise, use a peaceful visualization to slow down the mental chatter. Several scenes are offered, but feel free to use something that is personally meaningful if this is preferred.

Sit or lie down comfortably. Close the eyes. Think of the mind as a vast river and thoughts as small leaves or branches floating along. Watch from the banks of the river and allow the leaves and branches of thoughts to simply float past, with little notice except to observe that they do move past. Keep applying the same procedure: notice the thought, think about it briefly, but disengage from it and return to concentration as soon as possible. The task is to stay focused. Eventually the stream of consciousness clears, and no new leaves or branches appear as thoughts clear. Remain in meditation, watching the quiet stream. If a thought intrudes into consciousness, notice it, think about it for a moment, and then let it go. Return to focused attention: poised, observing the stream until ready to stop.

Another image that many people find helpful is a vista of grassy hills, rolling as far as the eye can see. The clear blue sky meets the green hillside. All is quiet, still. In fact, it is so quiet that you can almost hear your own heart beat. The muscles relax a bit, without effort. The colors are soothing; the breeze is soft. Just looking at this peaceful scene, thoughts tend to slow—leaving an experience of calm and stillness. Do not do anything; simply enjoy the scene.

A pond is another apt metaphor. Sit quietly with eyes closed. Imagine sitting on the shore of a pond. The pond is alive with activity. Frogs croak; crickets sing; birds fly overhead; a fish jumps out of the water, feeding on insects, splashes back, and jumps again after a bit, in another spot. Wind whips over the water, stirring up the muddy bottom. All is movement. Then gradually as the day passes, the conditions begin to shift. The wind dies down. The frogs settle in for a nap, the crickets are silent, the birds perch in the trees, the fish stops jumping and waits. The pond is quiet. The murky rippled surface calms as the mud sinks to the bottom, and the water is again crystal clear, reflecting the natural surroundings. All is stillness. Imagine this scene vividly. Stay with the quiet, crystal clear water.

Classic Zazen

Zen Buddhists have practiced a form of clearing the mind called *zazen.* This form of meditation continues to be a well-traveled path for calm and insight. Here are the classical instructions that have been given for centuries.

Zazen is best performed in a quiet room that is not too hot or too cold, nor too light or too dark. You should not have eaten or drunk too much immediately before beginning. Clothing should be loose but neat.

Set a thick pillow on the floor, and then add a second smaller one on top. Sit down on the pillows and cross your legs. Place the hands on the lap with the left hand on top of the right, middle joints of the middle fingers together and thumbs together, lightly touching. The hands will be shaped like an oval. One reason for crossing the legs and hands is to make the body a unity, with no distinction between left and right, no beginning and no end. The mouth should be gently closed, the eyes half open. Do not focus the gaze on anything in particular. Remain relaxed, but alert.

Keep the body straight, without leaning to one side or the other. Allow the spine to be straight, Relax the shoulders and keep the head straight aligned in the center without tilting. Don't strain. Breathing passages should be free and unrestricted as the breathing becomes calm and steady.

Begin by simply sitting and not thinking about anything in particular. If a thought or wish arises, bring it to consciousness, notice the wish or thought as it is. Do not evaluate it. Simply observe that it is. Then allow it to leave. In doing this you will begin to become aware of both thinking and not thinking. Gradually, consciousness settles into a no-mindedness that is neither thinking nor not thinking. Eventually the thoughts will clear, leaving a calm consciousness.

Dogen, who we described in Chapter 2, wrote: "If you practice in this way for a long time, you will forget all attachments and concentration will come naturally. That is the art of zazen" (quoted in Dumoulin, 1990, p. 76).

Classic Koan to Clear the Mind

Koans are another method used in Zen to discover a clear mind. This classic koan is drawn from the famous koan collection, *The Mumonkan,* composed during the Sung period (960–1279) in China. This koan is usually presented at the beginning of Zen study, to enter what is often called the gateless gate or *Mu.*

"A monk asked Joshu, 'Has a dog the Buddha Nature?' Joshu answered, 'Mu'" (Sekida, 1977, p. 27).

Mu is translated roughly as *no* or *nothingness.* While thinking about it, summon every effort to concentrate on mu. This effort involves setting aside the usual ways of thinking. But don't think of mu in a negative sense—nor is it a vacuum. The way to contemplate mu is by meditation, not rational thought. The instructions for meditating on mu are to sit comfortably as in the zazen instructions above. "Breathe in normally and exhale in a long, slow, quiet breath. Follow this simple practice until your own method develops from within yourself. Do not be impatient" (Sekida, 1977, p. 29)

The Koan Way to Clear the Mind

Some people might relate well to a modern koan. On first hearing it, people often smile. Approach this mind-twister with a sense of humor!

Think of nothing, but don't think anything about it. Contemplate this deeply.

Indirect Mind Clearing

The purpose is to see things as they are, to observe things as they are, and to let everything go as it goes. This is to put everything under control in its widest sense.

(S. Suzuki, 1979, p. 33)

Some people may find the exercises in this chapter difficult to do. If you have been unable to clear the mind, don't become discouraged. An indirect approach might be more accessible. The following meditation is indirect. It will help to discover the quiet mind that may already be there when the time is right.

Rhythms of vital energy, of circulation, and of breathing are appropriate in various circumstances; cycles that are part of us in ways we hardly know. Everyone has rhythms of the body and of mental functioning. At certain times of day, or perhaps during the week, or even over the months and seasons, people are spontaneously more physically or mentally active. Some people do their best creating late at night. Others get up early to do creative work. Many want to get out and do things in the summer, while others prefer the winter. These natural tendencies can be utilized. The meditation that follows uses a Daoist strategy of letting be and allowing.

To Overcome Resistance with an Indirect Approach

Notice a time with no immediate responsibilities or obligations coupled with less spontaneous mental activity. Look for such a moment, perhaps at night, just before sleep, during a lunch break, a time alone with nothing that has to be done. Another possibility is to find a time when attention wants to drift or the mind feels blank. At moments like these, people might try to force themselves to do a chore or task. But instead, such a moment can be used as an opportunity to develop a quiet mind.

Spend a few minutes permitting the mind to be blank for a moment and explore how expansive that blankness can be. Do not try to discern what it is exactly, but allow this spontaneous tendency to do nothing to be. This state of mind may happen sitting, standing, or even when waiting in line for a long time. The important thing is to notice the blank moment and permit the experience to take place when the circumstances occur.

Let the thoughts drift. Don't do anything and don't think about anything in particular. Simply sit quietly, allowing this experience to develop. Let the breathing be comfortable and the let body relax of itself. After allowing the naturally occurring blankness, even if only for a brief time, you may find that you can deliberately access this mental quiet at other times as well. If successful, go back and try some of the other meditations in this chapter again.

Conclusion

A clear mind, once experienced, can be practiced anytime, anywhere. Consider varied situations as opportunities to practice, to extend calmness deliberately throughout the day.

13

Meditation Through Ritual and Art

But when we consider how small after all the cup of human enjoyment is, how soon overflowed with tears, how easily drained to the dregs in our quenchless thirst for infinity, we shall not blame ourselves for making so much of the tea-cup.

(Okakura, 1989, p. 31)

Traditionally, when Westerners were taught meditation in the 1940s and 50s, they were encouraged to learn a meditative art. Westerners are accustomed to doing something, and a Zen art involves participation in an activity that is associated with meditation. By participating in a meditative art, a skill is learned directly, and a new way of eliciting the meditative state develops, indirectly.

Many meditative arts are practiced today. Some of the best known are *Cha-no-yu* (the art of tea), *haiku* (poetry), calligraphy, and martial arts. There are also meditative arts such as gardening, *Koto* (incense), *Sumi-e* (ink painting), *Kyudo* (archery), *Shakuhachi* (bamboo flute music), *Noh* drama, and *Ikebana* (flower arranging). Some involve sports or physical action; others involve creative expression in art. They seem very different. But all Zen arts share in training the mind and evoking meditative states.

Participation in a Zen art is an excellent doorway for pragmatic clients to enter into the meditative experience. Two traditional methods that lend themselves well to the psychotherapeutic process are the tea ceremony and haiku. Both can be integrated at some point into psychotherapy. A story may convey the spirit better than just factual description, for meditation's unifying processes may evade such constraint.

Meditative Tea

This whole idea of Teaism is a result of this Zen conception of greatness in the smallest incidents of life.

(Okakura, 1989, p. 71)

Imagine that you are walking though a beautiful garden. You notice plants carefully arranged. You feel like each step takes you further and further away from the clamor of the outside world. Fragrant aromas tantalize your senses as you walk along a stone path. You come to a water basin, set low. You kneel down to carefully wash your hands and face in the crystal-clear water. Feeling cleansed and somehow humbled, you arise and continue along the path. Just ahead, you observe an unpretentious thatched wooden structure standing by itself. You duck down to enter through a low doorway. The diffuse light softly illuminates a calligraphic scroll hanging alone on a wall. A flower rests in a stoneware vase on the floor. As you enter the room and notice a teakettle sitting on a fire pit, you hear water bubbling. The master enters, carrying several simple utensils. He bows quietly, sits, and you bow, and then sit down on the mat with him. He begins to prepare the tea, moving effortlessly yet precisely, wiping the bowl dry with a clean linen napkin, ladling in water, spooning the tea, stirring it carefully. A meditative silence pervades the room. Subdued sounds of clinking and tapping gently massage your senses. You find your attention turning inwards, yet you are also becoming intensely, fully aware of the sights, sounds, and smells around you. All is in harmony with the surroundings. The master offers you a cup of tea. You are surprised and delighted by the delicate, subtle tastes. When the ceremony is over, you feel renewed, completely at peace with yourself and the world. This is the tea ceremony, Cha-no-yu, an ancient tradition that has carried the spirit of meditation into the modern day.

Tea Instructions for an Adapted Tea Ceremony

The water that fills the kettle is drawn from the well of the mind whose bottom knows no depths, and the emptiness which is conceptually liable to be mistaken for sheer nothingness is in fact the reservoir of infinite possibilities.
(Teamaster Rikyu (1521–1591) quoted in Suzuki, 1973, p. 298)

The spirit of tea transcends any particular technique or method, even though traditional tea ceremonies had specific practices that could take many years to master. You can perform a modern ceremony to use with clients or even to teach the client to perform at home between sessions. This simple ritual is enjoyable and will bring about a calm, clear mind.

In the past, Japanese tea ceremonies were performed in a special separate teahouse: a small, wooden structure, often likened to Thoreau's Walden cottage in its rustic simplicity. However, the tea ceremony can be adapted and performed in any quiet location, even in the office. If there is no suitable space indoors, pick a quiet place outdoors. The outer environment can help to intensify the experience but the ceremony can be performed in various settings. The spirit of tea is the central organizing principle; individual details are meaningful in terms of the whole, if they enhance and communicate the spirit. The suggestions that follow can be modified to suit the available situation.

Find a quiet corner of the home or office and make a few modifications ahead of time. Clear a space of furniture. Place a plain mat on the floor and bring in a small plant, a simple flower arrangement, or one picture. A light, soothing incense can be used as well. Keep the decorations minimal and unadorned.

Gather the utensils ahead of time: a teapot, teacups, small bowl, ceramic spoon, hot water, and tea. You will also need a source to heat the water, such as a small hibachi, hot plate, or hot coals in a fireplace. When no heat source is available, preheat the water and bring it in a thermos. Prior to the ceremony, pour the hot water into a pitcher. The traditional teas were powdered and stirred with a whisk. Most tea today comes as tea leaves, prepared by steeping. Use whatever is available. We have often used peppermint tea for its pleasant aroma and soothing qualities. If a tea bag is used, remove the tea from the bag and empty the tea leaves into the bowl prior to the ceremony. A cookie can also be served to each person to accompany the tea.

Figure 13.1. Tea ceremony.

We have often served almond cookies, but any type of cookie can be used. Practice the tea ceremony until the motions can be performed smoothly, with calm and confidence.

The Ceremony

When ready, bring in the participants. In Japanese teahouses, the entry door is so low that people have to crouch down to enter. Traditionally, emperors and peasants alike entered with head bowed. Everyone is equal in the tearoom. Try to foster this atmosphere of mutual respect at your own tea ceremony. Do not engage in extra talking, except for simple greetings and instructions. Invite everyone to sit on the floor, facing each other. Encourage them to pay close attention while the tea is being prepared and to meditate on what they see, hear, smell, feel, and taste.

Place the pot, bowl with tea leaves, ceramic spoon, and hot water on a placemat on the floor as pictured. Place a teacup in front of each person including the tea server. Begin by lightly tapping the spoon three times on the side of the bowl and then three times on the side of the pot. There will be a pleasant ringing sound from each. Then take one scoop of tea from the bowl and place it into the pot. Repeat the tapping and scooping until most of the tea leaves are in the pot. Place the spoon back in place, lift the water pitcher, and slowly pour the hot water into the teapot. There will be a sound of pouring water and an aroma of tea. When the teapot is filled, carefully return the pitcher to its place on the mat and put the top on the teapot. Then turn the teapot three times in a clockwise direction and then turn it three times in a counterclockwise direction to stir the tea. Lift the teapot and pour tea into each cup, with the server last. When all cups are filled, with cups placed on the mat, each person turns his or her cup three times clockwise and three times counterclockwise. When all have finished turning their cups, drink together. If cookies have been served, they can be eaten at this time as well. Savor the tastes, smells, and sounds. Enjoy the tranquility and quiet sharing. Following the tea, with mind cleared and awareness sharpened, many will have renewed energy as well.

We encourage clients to perform a simple tea ceremony at home between sessions. Taking a few moments to clear the mind in this way can offer an oasis away from the usual pressures and concerns of daily life. Being centered and aware in the moment may generalize, to help in developing a better adjustment. Pay the same attention to detail if using another activity as a calming, meditative ritual. Tea is not the only possible one.

Gardening, cooking, or crafting are other activities that can be practiced in a Zen way without special training. For more traditional practice, study a Zen art such as martial arts, Sumi painting, archery, or flower arrangement with a master.

Meditative Poetry

A poem is a painting with a voice, and A poem is a voiceless painting.

(Zen poet and painter, Yosa Buson (1716–1784),

quoted in Fontein & Hickman 1970, p. 14)

Poetry is another path to the meditative moment. Poetry can be a way to express an ongoing experience, created spontaneously in a particular moment. Zen developed forms of poetry that allowed for the expression of a meditative moment. First, the classic forms: Haiku, traditionally a group of three lines of 17 syllables of verse, is the best known. Renga, which means linked verse, is another form of poetry that is created with a group of people. There are other interesting varieties of these poetic forms: Senryu, verse that includes subtle humor, and Haiga, a diagrammatic picture or sketch often with some phrases of haiku that illustrates a haiku directly or expresses implications. Finally, Haibun, or story telling, gives anecdotal material used for koans in Zen practice.

Early Development of Poetry

Renga became a popular form of poetry in early Japan. Renga was developed in the courts of Japan, which organized poetry parties. Early creations had a formal and elegant quality. The formal structure of traditional renga includes three lines of five, seven, and five syllables followed by two lines of seven and seven. The pattern repeats for up to one hundred lines. The links between verses are not always direct; the chains of association can be the ending line, implicit meaning, color or tone, leading to the first line of a new group of lines. Each new additional verse, as a result, dissociates from the original meaning intention of the first group of lines, creating a new unity. Today's renga may not follow the formal pattern, but retains the sensitivity and depth. Many variations of length of lines and form are acceptable. Renga can be shared continuously as a poetic dialogue over time, as well.

Haiku, originally called hokku, was a simplification of renga and even a simplification of the shorter verses of human relation known as tanka, which were 31 syllables long. Hokku consisted of only three lines of about 17 syllables on one subject. Much later on, Shiki Masaoka (1867–1902) popularized this poetic form and gave it the name haiku that we use today. Many other contributions have been made. Poetry also found its way into the world of the samurai and monks, who wrote haiku, death poems (poems written near the time of one's death), and enlightenment poems, expressing pivotal moments.

There were many great masters of haiku, one of the greatest of whom was Basho (1644–1694). His insightful poems impart a meditative moment to all who read them. For example, in these poems, Basho suggests impermanence and emptiness without thought:

Those who see the lightning
And think nothing:
How precious they are!

(Holmes & Horioka, 1973, p. 70)

The skylark
Sings in the field:
Free of all things.

(Holmes & Horioka, 1973, p. 111)

Other Haiku Poets

Haiku continued to be a popular form of artistic expression. Yosa Buson (1716–1784) was one of Japan's finest painters. He painted rocks and landscapes as living, breathing, weightless mystery. He also applied his skills with sensitive depth and beauty from painting to his poetry, giving it breathtaking visual detail. Buson is considered among the greatest haiku poets.

Two butterflies:
They dance in the air till,
Double-white, they meet.

(Holmes & Horioka, 1973, p. 45)

Issa (1763–1827) led a life with many personal tragedies, including loss of fortune and important persons he cared for, but he rose above the adversity through creative expression in poetry. His poems are timeless metaphors, personal and compassionate.

They continue to touch the souls of readers through the ages, extending the range of their feelings about personal and universal themes.

> All creatures!
> They squirm about among
> The flowers in bloom.
>
> (Holmes & Horioka, 1973, p. 31)

By the 19th century, haiku were disparaged as low class literature. Shiki's profound and prolific haiku inspired his readers and helped once again to elevate the form. Although Shiki's life was cut tragically short, he left an indelible mark on haiku. He devoted himself fully to haiku, composing more than 25,000 of them. Shiki's poems expressed sketches of people, culture, and nature.

> As innocently as the clouds
> He tills the field:
> Under the Southern Mountains.
>
> (Holmes & Horioka, 1973, p. 30)

These four masters of haiku are like Zen patriarchs, representing a broad range of possibility. Their steps on the path of poetry helped to made modern haiku what it is today.

Poetic Use of Language

In meditation's poetic expression, language can become painting or drawing, in story or song. Form and formlessness melt together, so that as we experience the poem, we may enter a timeless moment.

Shiki's view of haiku as a kind of sketch opened a new way to create and use haiku for meaning. Language can be used in many ways, not just for literal reference. So, poetry can use language to allude to experience, by cadence and rhythms of words, like musical tones.

Instructions for Haiku

Haiku is a record of a moment of emotion in which human nature is somehow linked to all nature.

(Henderson, 1977, p. 14)

Several different criteria exist for what makes a good haiku, but generally, the instructions are simple. Form in traditional haiku is five, seven, then again five syllables in three lines, while modern haiku varies more, sometimes as two lines, sometimes more.

Haiku expresses a moment of experience. This moment might be surprising, awe inspiring, beautiful, tragic, or humorous. The descriptions should not explain the moment; just evoke the experience or a reaction to it.

Haiku are spartan in the number of words, especially adjectives and images. In their simplicity, a world of experience is communicated. So keep the number of images as two or less. The lines should be simple and strong. If you use metaphors, make your metaphors vivid. You can imply meanings by the words, spacing, and even what is left out.

Traditional haiku always includes a reference to nature and a season, sometimes implicitly. Innovative, modern haiku is more liberal and expresses personal experience, which may include a reference to nature and a season, but may not.

Creating a Haiku

Gather a pen and paper and then sit down to meditate. Become centered in the moment, in touch with feelings right now. When ready, write the haiku.

Some may find it easier to write in the midst of a natural setting. Experience what is there meditatively; then express the experience on the paper.

Haiga: Poetry and Paintings Combined

If the client is artistic, creating a haiga might help to express inner feelings. Match a picture with a few lines of verse, or the haiku with a picture or diagram.

Figure 13.2. Lotus. (Daqian Zhang,
Chinese, 1899–1983. Ink and color on
paper, 1958. 52–2/8" x 26–2/4."
Gift of Ambassador and Mrs. Everett F.
Drumright, 1986: 44. San Diego
Museum of Art.)

A story can be told with a very brief few lines for the poem part of the haiga. As noted above, the classic form of haiku is expressed in syllables grouped as five, seven, and five in three lines. Modern forms vary.

Classical haiga paintings have themes of nature rendered with landscape, animals, famous people, or often with plants such as bamboo. Haiga may be created using many forms of expression including caricatures, abstractions, and other variations. A Zen moment may be expressed quite well in this medium.

Creating A Haiga

For those who enjoy painting and writing, try creating a haiga. Either begin with the painting and then let the poem be inspired by the painting or start with a poem and then create a painting inspired by the poem. Haiga can also be created by using someone else's poem or painting as the inspiration. Experience fully what is evoked by the one piece of art to create the other. The two should complement each other on a deep level. Be creative and enjoy the process!

Renga

Renga can be created with a group to capture the experience of the moment. Modern renga do not have to follow a strict form. Simply begin with two or three lines that express a felt sense of the present, and then pass the paper to the next person. Each person responds to the line before and then writes his or her own experience. When everyone has written, read the renga aloud. This can be varied as a dialogue between two people, and in other ways as well.

PART III

Balance in the Void: Applying Meditation

Blowing on the ten thousand things in a different way, so that each can be itself—all take what they want for themselves, but who does the sounding?

(Zhuangzi quoted in Watson, 1968, p. 37)

Each chapter in Part III is organized around a specific problem area that can be treated using meditation. The problems we chose to include have been studied empirically to verify the efficacy of meditation as a major component in the treatment. The nature of the problem area is explored by discussing Eastern and Western theories. Eastern and Western conceptions of treatment may overlap. But sometimes the Eastern view differs, opening new options. Key neuroscience discoveries about the problem and relevant meditation research are given next, to show the scientific findings.

Meditational techniques are described with cases and brief explanations to guide in applying these methods. Sometimes the exercises are worded as if we were talking directly to a client, to give the therapist a sense of how these instructions would be presented. Then the therapist can use the patterns in ways that make sense to him or her. Methods can be varied and combined creatively to individualize. Another alternative is for the client to follow the exercise under the guidance of the therapist.

Choosing the Meditation Method

In meditational therapy, the whole includes the components together in a multidimensional field. The theoretical distinctions that people differ about tend to obscure a larger unified pattern that is there. As Zhuangzi advised, don't take sides! Petty details obscure our view of the Way. But there is a therapeutic path to follow through the client's troubled emotional life. This path is where the therapist can join with the client to help bring about change. It doesn't matter at what point you enter, only *that* you enter. Alternate variations of meditation techniques can be effective if the individual client's needs are met. So, therapist and client can work together on the physiological level, the brain level, or the cognitive level and bring about change. Varied methods drawn from the traditions can be applied in therapy to specific problem areas, but must always be individualized to the client. Therapists should realize that what seems easy or difficult to them as a technique may not be so for the client. Don't take talent or the lack of talent for granted.

Yoga meditation, with its emphasis on focus and concentration, cultivates stable mental states, which may be disengaged from the world if needed. For example, by focusing on breathing, consciousness can be withdrawn from overconcern with disturbing external circumstances to become more centered in inner experience. These methods may be most helpful when a client must cope with a troubling but real, external situation such as a death or illness. Or they may prove helpful for clients with wandering attention problems. But these techniques may not be suitable for those who lack a firm reality sense, such as psychotic or paranoid tendencies. However, modern methods now use open eyes to include grounding the mental state in a reality sense of the external world, thereby extending the usefulness of these methods to other populations.

Buddhism offers a different alternative by cultivating mindful moment-to-moment attention to all experience. Attending to every experience without condemnation or assessment can lead to a calm steadiness. Mindfulness helps clients to accept themselves, freeing the mind of disturbing thoughts and emotions. This form of meditation has been helpful for people overcoming addictions and impulse disorders, where craving for one thing has led to neglect of other things. By attending equally to all experiences, a more normal balance is restored and the problem lessens. The ability to be nonjudgmental can be helpful to clients suffering from anxiety and emotional disturbances as well.

Zen develops awake, aware perception, free of constructs, and capable of spontaneous action. Learning to let go of thoughts and be present in the moment may help those whose thinking becomes entangled in problems. With nothing in mind to interfere with perception, clients can develop a capacity to be aware of themselves and their circumstances. Behavior becomes more adaptive and can flow spontaneously when needed. Clients suffering from mood and anxiety problems will find Zen meditations tend to open awareness and facilitate letting go of resentments and negative interpretations that get carried from the past to cloud the future. Relationships may also benefit from Zen and mindfulness meditation.

Daoist philosophy encourages that practitioners flow with the moment, letting it be, attuning to the inevitable currents, in touch intuitively with the nature of things. Through the gentle, permissive methods, Daoist meditations restore balance, ease tensions, and lessen the grip of an overly controlling mindset. This approach may be helpful with clients who are inhibited or who make even small tasks into an ordeal. These meditations can also be helpful in grounding clients in the realities around them. Qi meditations can be used to balance energy when clients suffer from too much or not enough vitality, often experienced with mood problems. These methods are also helpful for stress reduction, which has been shown to be an imbalance in the stress pathway. Relationships are enhanced as well, with active techniques for sensing the other.

Symbols and rituals, applied meditatively, can also facilitate the therapeutic process. For example, mandalas, mantras, and ritual, as in tea ceremonies, can help access the calm experience as well. Art is another way, such as in writing haiku.

In summary, some meditation methods give strategies of concentration and detachment, others offer techniques of mindful engagement, while others show how to release and be free of problematic constraints. There methods overlap. Distinctions are made in order to help map the way through the territory. As therapists become more familiar with the different meditations, by doing them, they will be able to adapt them well to the individualized needs of the client.

The therapist decides with the client what aspect to work on. Here, clinical judgment is important. For example, some people are more body oriented, so working with body awareness will flow most naturally. Others may be cognitively oriented, engaging in thought readily, and so mindful meditation that works with thinking may be best. However, sometimes the client is excessively cognitive, creating a troubling reaction from thoughts, and correspondingly out of touch with the body and imagery. So the therapist can help establish a better functional balance, using techniques that stabilize and quiet thought, use visualization, and focus on relaxing.

The balance may shift as treatment proceeds. With many varied methods to choose from, therapist and client will find useful techniques that can be applied through the process. Part III will describe this more fully.

Regarding the Inclusion of Research

Scientific experiments on the effectiveness of meditation for therapeutic applications have shown that many types of meditation are effective for various types of problems. These studies indicate that by using meditation in therapeutic treatment, clients can become emotionally and physically healthier.

Regarding the Inclusion of Neuroscience

Revolutions come and go, and while the dust from the cognitive revolution has long since settled, another revolution appears now to be underway. In the last decade, emerging technologies have allowed us to begin to peer deep into the living brain, thus providing us with a unique opportunity to tie phenomenology and cognitive process to its neural substrates.

(Lieberman, Gilbert, Gaunt, & Trope, 2008)

Today's therapist is well aware of the new brain science. The modern technology such as fMRI, although still approximate in its imaging capabilities, when combined and enhanced with mathematical estimation methods, is getting better all the time. As therapists, we can use the new discoveries to help attune better to the world of the brain that is revealed. Just as the perceptual, emotional, and cognitive responses have been the tools of the therapeutic trade, so now we can also open ourselves to brain responses as sources for more information.

In Part III, the neuroscience mechanisms given in each chapter describe how the brain is understood to affect psychological processes. Many clinicians and clients are familiar with brain anatomy, but to accommodate those who are not well versed in anatomy, we have presented some basic information along with diagrams, to make the subject matter more comprehensible.

Research reveals how meditation affects the brain. Some of the areas that are involved during meditation also play a primary role in overcoming various psychological problems, helping to inhibit overactive pathways, and excite underactive ones, directly intervening at the neurological level to help with overall improvement.

Bringing Together Specific and Nonspecific Factors

As the specific techniques are mastered, they can be utilized to help correct deficits, add abilities, and build skills. But successful therapy transcends the specific technique, to bring about a more general transformation. Clients usually find unexpected changes. For example, one client who wanted to stop smoking discovered that he had a talent for dancing. Another client who was trying to control her impulsive overeating found that she had an unsatisfied love of learning. General, nonspecific effects can reach far beyond, to be felt over a lifetime. Experiences of well-being are common in meditational therapy. With both the specific and nonspecific factors in mind, we invite the therapist and client to apply this method to problems as shown in Part III. Use these approaches as stepping-stones, to be integrated into treatment methods. We encourage creative individualizing.

14

Transforming Through Emotions and Moods

Activities that are graceful, heroic, terrifying
Compassionate, furious, and peaceful—
And passion, anger, greed, pride, and envy—
All these things without exception
Are the perfected forms
Of pure well-illuminating wisdom.

(Shaw, 1994, p. 28)

Carl Jung defined emotion as "an activity of the psyche as a whole, a total pattern of the soul" (Spiegelberg, 1972, p. 10). Thus, as a fruitful gateway to inner experience, feelings are of vital importance to therapy. Probably one of the main reasons that people seek psychotherapy is that they do not feel emotionally comfortable. Through meditation in the context of therapy, people can learn to feel and express their emotional nature, helping them to overcome problems with their emotions.

Theories of Emotion

Theories of emotion have a long established history from both East and West. Several prominent Western theories of emotions continue to be important today. The variations in theories of emotion attempt to explain how emotions take form. These theories include certain components, as the reader will notice: a physiological response, some kind of brain reaction, and certain cognitive interpretations. The theories may differ about priority, sequencing, and other details about how these interact, but they agree that these components are involved. Perhaps individuals differ in their pattern of interaction.

Some of the most relevant representative theories of emotion are included here. Each theory suggests different strategies for altering emotions, addressed by the varied meditation methods included in the book. Individualizing of technique then becomes possible. We encourage the reader to incorporate other theories, if they make sense, with an open mind.

The James–Lange Theory

The James–Lange theory of emotion, established by William James and Carl Lange, is probably the best known, with its principle that emotion is not simply a feeling in response to a situation, as common sense might suggest. Rather, we have physiological sensations such as muscle tension, increased heart rate, perspiration, and so on, in response to a situation. Emotion is experienced because of the sympathetic nervous system responding, rather than being the cause of these sensations. Emotion is the perception of feeling this response to bodily changes.

For example, the physiological response to a charging tiger brings a rapid heart rate and a strong impulse to take action, such as to run away. Fear is the perceived total nervous system experience, not just the wish to run away, nor just a felt experience without any impulse to action. The emotion of anger is a feeling in response to certain sensations experienced when participating in a perceived annoying situation. Anger may bring the impulse to vent, perhaps just by strongly criticizing the situation with a raised voice. But the less anger is vented, the less anger will be expressed in future similar situations. In James's view, if anger and angry behavior is regularly engaged in and thus practiced, an angry response may become habitual. But if happiness and positive behavior is regularly engaged in, then that can be expected to become a habit. This is a general pattern for role-playing and behavioral learning theories of change.

The Cannon–Bard Theory

Walter Cannon and Philip Bard proposed a simultaneous sequence in an effort to refute the James-Lange theory. The Cannon–Bard theory, based in the organism's need for constancy and stability, states that when the body receives a stimulus through the autonomic nervous system, a physiological change takes place. Equilibrium is disturbed. The muscles respond in a pattern of corresponding activation while the thalamus sends a signal to the amygdala. This gives the emotional feeling, and information for restoring stability, and thereby, emotional homeostasis (Bard, 1929; Cannon, 1927, 1932). Homeostasis in the biological context is analogous to homeostasis in the social context. In both contexts, homeostasis is a natural ongoing process. Cannon believed that the health of society, like a living organism, should be addressed, just like the health of the individuals who make it. Then the inner wisdom of society, expressed in social homeostasis can guide social policy, leading to a vibrant society that fosters fulfillment of the highest human potential. Gestalt therapy draws from this for the basis of an innate mechanism within the human organism that should guide as well as help to maintain emotional and social life. The seeds for the rationale for family systems therapy can also be found in this theory.

Two-Factor Theory

The two-factor theory of Stanley Schachter and Jerome Singer combined the Cannon–Bard and James–Lange theories. Emotion involves two components: physical arousal and cognitive labeling of the arousal. Cognitions are the way people give meaning to the physiological reactions to the outside world. Thus, the first step is to experience physiological arousal. Then, we often try to explain the feeling by observing what we are experiencing.

Schachter and Singer performed a pivotal experiment (1962) that helped them formulate their emotion theory. An experimental group was told they were being given vitamins to test their vision. One group was given an adrenaline injection, which caused increased heart rate and rapid breathing. Another group was given a saline injection with no side effects. The adrenaline group was divided into three, with some subjects apprised of the realistic effects of adrenaline, some misled to think they would feel a headache and numbness, while others received no information. Following the injections, the subjects sat in a waiting room with confederates of the experimenter, who acted either playful or angry. Subjects who were either misled or naïve about the effects behaved similarly to the confederate. Those who had accurate information about the effects of the adrenaline did not behave like the confederates (Schachter & Singer, 1962). Emotion came after the inchoate, ambiguous sensation of physiological arousal was interpreted. Schachter and Singer believed that their experiment showed that physiological arousal leads to different emotions, depending on how the arousal is interpreted. The psychotherapeutic implication is that interpretation can lead to very different emotions.

Cognitive Appraisal Theory

The cognitive appraisal theory, also known as the Lazarus theory after its founder, Richard S. Lazarus (1989), challenged the simultaneous principle of the Cannon–Bard theory, while correlating with Schachter and Singer. Lazarus's theory holds that cognitive appraisal or interpretation of a situation is the primary source of emotion. Lazarus did extensive experimentation and research to verify his theory concerning healthy adaptation to stress by means of better coping. His view of stress and coping was actually an extension of his more general approach to emotion (Lazarus, 1991; Lazarus & Folkman, 1984).

Lazarus believed that a person's interpretation or appraisal of an experience, object, or situation comes first. Then, the appropriate emotion or feeling follows. For example, a remark by someone is experienced and interpreted or appraised as annoying followed by the emotion of anger in response. So, an emotion can be positively coped with by reinterpreting the situation or object through strategic cognitive appraisal. The emotional response transforms. Then the reaction to the situation that the person finds himself or herself in can change. Strategic therapy and other active approaches to psychotherapy draw from this as a rationale for the therapeutic value of reinterpretation (Lazarus, 1989).

Each of these theories approaches the situation of emotional response from different patterns of combination of person, situation, and reaction, but they are linked.

Eastern Theories of Emotions

The Buddhist view of emotions is an ancient one, dating back beyond the earliest Theravada sutras. These theories show an advanced comprehension of human experiencing that adds a thoughtful supplement to contemporary views.

As has been shown, Western theorists tend to view emotions as states that are caused by some combination of physiological, neurological, and cognitive processes. In contrast, the Buddhist view, not starting out from the same basis, begins instead from emptiness, and therefore does not view emotions as fixed states. Emotions are created anew in each instant as a moment-to-moment combination of factors, arising from a coming together of body sensations and mental events within the larger context of the greater world of interaction. No fixed state remains *after* each moment. Meditators should focus attention mindfully on each feeling reaction as it happens.

There are six senses: seeing, hearing, smelling, tasting, touching, and a sixth sense, the mind. These senses bring input with every passing moment in new and different combinations. Even though the inputs are separate and unique, they tend to be brought together as an experience. We form concepts of emotion as if they are real, but in truth, there is no constant individual that reacts, nor a fixed unchanging situation to react to. The concept does not even refer to anything that is graspable, exactly. So emotions are only moment-to-moment states in a process of change, just like all things. And in this sense, there is really no problem.

Yoga philosophy views the individual as like a drop of water in the ocean of the universe. Individual feelings and thoughts are reflections of the greater whole. Transcending a narrow perspective to comprehend within a wider universal context will transform emotions. For example, think of a young child who feels angry because mother takes away a cookie that the child wanted to eat just before dinner. If the child could gain a more mature knowledge of the importance of proper nutrition, the feeling of anger would probably dissolve. Similarly for all the emotions: From the larger, enlightened perspective, petty emotions are transcended and wisdom can be found.

For Daoists, all manifestations of the unchanging Dao are changing, flowing between yin and yang. Thus, emotions are always changing as well, understood as a dynamic balance between what they are and what they are not. So, happiness is only possible to know because we can know sadness. And similarly, we need to be able to understand sadness to understand happiness. Thus, there is a rationale for feeling the full spectrum of emotions. When we select one feeling over another, we move away from contact with the whole. Seek the balance between the individual and the world, to bring about a healthy, happy flow, at one with Dao. These theories share common ground: flowing change with emotional reactions.

Theories of Mood

Mood and *emotion* are two terms that are often thought of as synonyms, but they should be distinguished from each other. The quality that distinguishes a mood from an emotion is its constancy over time, somewhat independent of changes in circumstance, not just a subjective quality. The quality of stable endurance of the state is essential. If a feeling is or becomes state-bound, it is not just a passing feeling or emotion. The feeling then has the stable quality of enduring that is a property of moods. When using meditation for psychotherapeutic purposes, as in other forms of psychotherapy, the distinctions are important for deciding how to address the client's needs. But the apparent endurance of a mood may be a misunderstanding of the person having it. Sometimes moods are useful as a positive way to cope. The exercises later in the chapter will address these issues.

Biological Theories of Moods

One of the prominent views of mood today is the neurochemical theory. Depression has been linked to disruption in norepinephrine and serotonin, two neurotransmitters that are important for arousal, attention (norepinephrine), and mood, pain, aggression, and sleep (serotonin). The norepinephrine system is one of the most global, traveling throughout the entire brain. Serotonin is made from an amino acid in the diet, tryptophan, so it is one of the few neurotransmitters that we have control over: the right diet leads to the right amount of tryptophan in the brain. Drug therapy uses SSRIs to block the reuptake of serotonin in the limbic system. Bipolar disorder has been treated successfully with lithium carbonate and other compounds. Twin studies have shown that depression and bipolar disorders have strong genetic components. Katz and McGuffin (1993) found that 52% of depression variance and 80% of bipolar variance was due to genetics.

Cognitive Theories

Most people agree that there is a neurological component to moods. However, more recent studies have shown that drug treatment is no more effective than psychotherapy. In a large NIMH study, 250 patients were randomly assigned to one of four 16-week treatment conditions: interpersonal psychotherapy, cognitive behavior therapy, imipramine hydrochloride plus clinical management (as a standard reference treatment), and placebo plus clinical management. Patients in all treatments showed significant reduction in depressive symptoms and improvement in functioning over the controls (Elkin et al., 1989).

A meta-study reviewed a wide range of comparative studies and also found that there was no difference between pharmacological treatments and psychotherapy, even when it was severe depression. Cognitive-behavioral therapy had a slightly better result from other psychotherapies. They also found that psychotherapy was more effective than medication in developing social skills and in relapse prevention over time (Antonuccio, Danton, & DeNelsky, 1995).

In light of the research findings, the cognitive-behavioral approach has been used widely in treatment of depression. Beck proposed a triad theory of depression consisting of self, situation, and future. People make cognitive errors such as distortions in thought processes, overgeneralization, and overpersonalization.

Seligman (1992) put forward a theory of learned helplessness based on research he did in 1965 with dogs. The dogs were conditioned to salivate to a tone as Pavlov had conditioned dogs to do, and then given a shock when the tone sounded. The researchers expected the dogs would feel fear when they heard the tone and would run away. Instead, the dogs just lay passively, having learned to be helpless. This theory was extended to people suffering from depression. Similar to the dogs, depressed people have learned that their efforts are futile, they have no control, and they are bound to fail. People can overcome depression by undergoing cognitive therapy that challenges the false beliefs that have led to feeling helpless, and instead develop beliefs that lead to "learned optimism" (Seligman, 1990, 2002).

The cognitive theories seem to correlate with the neurochemical views. In one experiment, (Weiss & Simson, 1985) found that rats exhibiting learned helplessness behavior also had decreases in norepinephrine.

Neuroscience of Emotions and Moods

The hypothalamus, the brain stem, and the limbic area are the three main brain structures involved in emotion. The hypothalamus, located under the thalamus, is a deep brain structure made up of a number of nuclei. One of the functions of the hypothalamus is to integrate emotional responses with the forebrain, brain stem, and spinal chord. Emotions involve areas of the brain from the brain stem all the way up to the cortex.

The hypothalamus takes relatively unprocessed input from the cortex and then outputs to the reticular formation located in the brain stem. The brain stem is a web of more than 100 cell groups that control arousal as well as the sleep–wake rhythm and attention. The reticular formation receives hypothalamic and cortical signals and then outputs to the somatic and autonomic systems, such as those that regulate the heart and other functions that don't require conscious thought. The limbic area is the deep structure consisting of the amygdala, hippocampus, and mamillary bodies located around the corpus callosum (the connector between the hemispheres) and encircling the upper brain stem. The limbic system links between higher cortical activity and lower systems. It also integrates information from the cortical association areas.

The amygdala, located in front of the hippocampus, connects to a number of areas: the olfactory bulb and cortex, the brain stem and hypothalamus, the cortical sensory association areas, and the emotion association area. Mirror neurons (see Chapter 18) in the somatic motor and autonomic system are also connected indirectly. The amygdala is involved in fear, emotional judgments, and the recognition of situations of potential threat. It is also involved in instrumental learning.

Research on Meditation and Emotions and Moods

Meditation has effects on the areas that are involved in emotions. Many studies have been performed measuring the effects of meditation on emotion and moods. Here are a few studies that represent some interesting findings about how meditation alters emotions themselves. Studies on the therapeutic use of meditation reveal that

Figure 14.1. Brain
structures involved
in emotion.

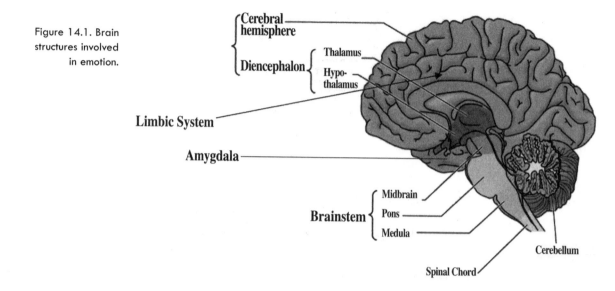

meditation enhances positive feelings. In a mindfulness experiment, meditators developed a measurable quality of consciousness that is related to a number of well-being constructs that was different from that of nonmeditators. They found that meditators had better regulation of their behavior and positive emotional states (Brown & Ryan, 2003).

The specific effect of meditation on emotions has been studied as well. One study examined how long-term meditation practice was manifested in EEG activity under several conditions. The nonemotional arousal condition included eyes closed and viewing a neutral movie clip. The emotional condition induced negative emotions by viewing an aversive movie clip. They found that changes in electrical brain activity associated with regular meditation practice showed that meditators had better capabilities to moderate the intensity of emotional arousal (Aftanas & Golosheykin, 2005). Meditators were also shown to have greater emotional clarity, meaning that they were better able to accurately discriminate among their own feeling states and label them correctly. Furthermore, the length of meditation practice correlated positively with clarity. The researchers also speculated that meditation may offer clues as to how

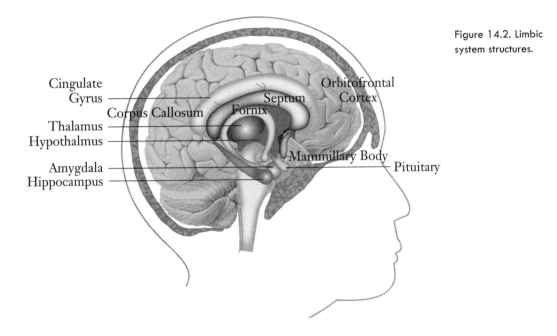

Figure 14.2. Limbic system structures.

emotionally ambiguous information is processed, regulated, and represented in awareness (Nielsen & Kaszniak, 2006).

Love has been shown to promote health and well-being (Esch & Stefano, 2005). Thus, meditation, which helps people to become more loving and compassionate, may also prove to be good for health in general.

Working with Emotions Meditatively

Both Eastern and Western theorists conceive methods as strategies for altering emotions, but coming from a different starting point as they do, the methods are sometimes different. When working on emotions using the tool of meditation, the wisdom from the Western and Eastern models can be interwoven together. Utilize any one or all of the Western components in combination. In so doing, the path

Figure 14.3. Brain
structures that mediate
emotions.

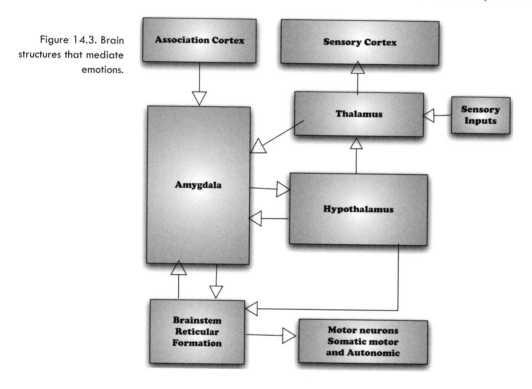

is transformed. For example, an acupressurist might treat a backache through massaging points on the sole of the foot, around the anklebone, and on the shinbone. This intervention might seem unrelated to healing a backache, but in the larger Eastern model of healing by correcting the flow of Qi, the components are related. So work with the different components as points of entry into the larger model of correction of mind to lead to therapeutic change.

The exercises address all three of the emotional components (behavioral, brain, and cognitive) in varying ways. These strategies are possibilities. We encourage you to draw from other meditations included in this book as well. There is much room for creative adaptation as the therapist and client discover together what is most appropriate for the person, the situation, and the reaction.

Accepting Feelings

For every yin, there is some yang. We can appreciate the complete fullness of Dao, by knowing both yin and yang. Similarly, with human emotions, each polar opposite reveals an aspect of the greater whole, and in this sense, it is a source of information, a way of attuning to the world. The great Japanese swordsman Tesshu gave a Zen perspective on human emotional nature:

> When there is happiness, be happy. When there is anger, be angry. When there is sorrow, be sad. When there is pleasure, rejoice in it. This is acting accordingly free of hindrance.
>
> (quoted in Stevens, 1989, p. 144)

Problems with emotions arise when people are dissociated from them. They lose a valuable tool that attunes them to their environment and other people. But people often take sides: They are willing to feel the pleasant feelings, but unwilling to feel anything uncomfortable. Anger, sadness, and frustration are feelings that people often do not want to experience; understandably so. But in the attempt to avoid discomfort, people often miss something important. The prickly cactus produces some of the world's most beautiful flowers. Emotions become meaningful signposts when accepted and felt through. Learning to tolerate and embrace the range of emotions can bring greater control. Clarity is also gained and can help to guide action. When the emotional dimension is included, it becomes easier to decide whether to accept a situation or try to change it.

BEGIN WITH AN INWARD GLANCE

An important beginning is to notice the feeling. Turn attention inwards at various times throughout the day. Take an inward glance at what is being felt, using a meditative focus. Try to comprehend the experience within, with its meaning, but not just in words. Concentrate attention on the feeling in a sensible, attuned way.

When feeling slightly frustrated, annoyed, or unhappy, but before reaching the point of taking action to resolve the inner reaction, pause for a few moments of meditative focus. As meditative skills improve, this process becomes easier to apply even when having a stronger intensity of emotion.

Sit down and sense the emotion in the moment. Remember not to evaluate it, but simply sense what is there. If describing it is helpful, do so. Breathe comfortably while sitting.

ONENESS WITH EMOTIONS MEDITATION

When successful with the exercise above, try the next exercise for help with deeper attunement. Next time you are in the midst of a feeling, notice any accompanying sensations in the body, such as tension in the stomach, neck, or back. Become aware of what thoughts are going through the mind and observe them as they occur. Allow the feeling and simply notice whatever is there without thinking beyond it; stay concentrated on the feeling and its accompanying sensations and thoughts just as they are.

Gradually the feeling will begin to alter, usually opening a window to deeper emotional being in that moment. Stay with the feeling and perception, allowing it to change with each new moment.

Don't stubbornly try to hold onto the original situation or feeling. And try not to make something rigid or fixed out of experience. For example, perhaps a sad feeling began when a partner, friend, or parent left. Pay attention and the emotion may change or reveal deeper meaning. Continue to concentrate and wait, allowing a meditative focus to develop. A feeling, when concentrated on with free-floating focus, may bring clarity and attunement. Start from the first sense of the feeling and meditate. Any moment is a good time to begin.

Both the therapist and the client can meditate whenever having feelings that may be important to therapy. Keep working on the emotions meditatively. Accept each feeling as an integral expression of the whole.

Taming a Temper

People often come to therapy in order to do something about a troubling emotion. The typical cognitive approach considers the thoughts, assumptions, and beliefs about the individual's situation and the self. A meditational approach drawn from Zen offers a different option, working on philosophical grounds, as this classic exchange between the great Zen master Bankei (1622–1693) and a monk illustrates.

A monk consulted master Bankei for help with his short temper. The monk said, "I know I should do something about it, but I was born this way and there's nothing I can do!"

Bankei asked him, "Show me your temper now."

The monk replied, "I'm not angry now. My temper just pops out at unexpected times, when someone provokes me."

Bankei said, "Well, if you aren't angry now and your temper comes and goes, you couldn't have been born with it. The only thing you inherited from your parents was your pure, original nature. Everything else you have created yourself!"

The monk was very surprised and felt hopeful that maybe he could change his temper. Bankei went on to explain that the source of the monk's feeling was that he took himself too seriously. People create their opinions, their tastes, and their insistence that things must be done a certain way. Then, if someone disagrees, they feel angry, sad, or frustrated. Let go of ego. Personal tastes should not be taken as universal truth but as personal preferences for actions that could be done in many possible ways.

LETTING GO OF PREFERENCES EXERCISE

Think about a personal taste or preference. Why is it important? What is this importance based on? Such questions usually lead back to ideas about the self: I'm this kind of person or I'm that kind of person, because I like this or dislike that. An honest appraisal will show that these qualities are not innate. They have been taken on over time for various reasons. What would life be like without this particular preference? Does the genuine person remain, without this preference? Usually it is found that nothing essential to the true nature is lost. Consider letting go of this preference. Does the mind become clear, or does the mind get less clear? This type of change can be explored in therapy over time. Let go of concern for trivial preferences. Most of them are unnecessary.

Nonattachment

Another way to moderate inappropriate emotional reactions is by becoming less attached to the reaction. Emotional reactions can be held under control by learning this skill. Sometimes people become accustomed to having a certain reaction, and even if it troubles them to react that way, they nonetheless form a certain attachment to it. With meditation training, it is possible to let go of the attachment while at the same time, permitting the feeling itself to occur. Then emotions can be felt as they are without anything extra being added. The emotions then become tools of insight. The Dalai Lama has said that these methods can be adapted to modern therapy and the quest for inner change (Komito, 1983, p. 4).

A middle-aged woman sought hypnotherapy to lose weight. She was an active volunteer in her community and had a full-time job as well. She always put the needs of others ahead of her own and felt she was a happy person, except for the weight problem. She learned hypnosis and practiced at home as well. But during trance she found that she had disturbing images of herself feeling anger toward the world and all the people she loved. The images shocked her. She felt upset to even think such things and wanted to push them away. When she tried to feel the emotions, she found them too disturbing.

Here was an opportunity to use meditation along with another form of therapy, in this case, hypnotherapy. We taught her nonattachment meditation. As a person who was already skilled in trance, she found meditation was not difficult to learn. With the calm and clarity of meditation, she could feel the feelings while remaining just detached enough to observe them and learn from them. Through the process, she unraveled some of the ways she had been kind while quietly feeling resentful. Applying mindful awareness during the day, she noticed the process as it happened. Over time, she was able to respond more fully when needed, and in so doing, truly felt comfortable. Her ability to lose weight was the confirmation!

NONATTACHMENT EXERCISE

Sit quietly in meditation and use meditations from Chapter 7 to focus the attention inwardly. When ready, turn attention to feelings. Notice an emotion that is being felt. If sad, for example, feel the sadness, but do not become overcome by it. Stay a little at a distance without losing touch with the feeling. Keep breathing calmly and deliberately relaxing as much as possible, while at the same time, staying aware of the feeling of the emotion. This skill takes practice; so don't be discouraged if the emotion takes over at first or if the emotion dissipates. Follow the threads of consciousness but do not pull too loose or too tight. The therapist can help the client to keep the tension just enough to feel the emotion but not too much to handle. By following and accepting the feeling while also staying centered, the feeling naturally begins to transform, to evolve. Repeat this meditation at other times to enlarge the perspective and include different aspects of the feeling.

Empty the Mind for Calming

Sometimes the feeling itself needs to be altered. Perhaps being angry is inappropriate to the situation. Often, after a client spends time in therapy a change is in progress and the usual reaction doesn't quite fit anymore. But reacting overemotionally seems to happen anyway. Meditation can help to make the change.

When feeling a troubling emotion, sit down to meditate. First, notice the feeling. Then, relax the body and clear the mind of thoughts. Whenever a disturbing thought or sensation appears, just let it go and return to no-thought. Use the meditations from Chapter 12 to empty the mind. Keep working at it until the emotional response slows down. Calming comes gradually.

Breathing with the Emotion

If calming down is difficult, the client can be encouraged to go to a calming situation, such as a quiet meditation room (or corner) with subdued lighting, incense burning, and soft meditation music playing, either in the therapist's office or perhaps, a place created for this at home. Then, these guidelines can be followed:

Sit in meditation and breathe comfortably. Pay close attention to the breathing. Feel each breath, in and out. If in the midst of a strong emotion, breathing will be different from when feeling calm. Notice the quality of each breath, the sensation of the air as it enters through the nose and down into the lungs. Pay attention to the sensations in the chest. Are there any sensations of constriction or tightness? A tense ribcage often accompanies strong emotion. If possible, let go of any muscle tension, but if not, simply notice the quality of the sensation.

As time passes, the breathing alters slightly. Notice any changes. With each breath, try to permit the breathing to become more relaxed and comfortable, to find its natural rhythm. Body relaxation may follow gradually. Be patient. Working with emotion by attending to breathing becomes more effective with practice.

Making Moods Work

As was stated above, emotions that are sustained over time may become moods. Normal mood can be an attunement, a feeling tone that may have an outer stimulus or not, at the time. Mood is a feeling tone. Mood as defined by Heidegger (1962) means an attunement to the world, at its best, to be immersed in caring interaction. To Heidegger, being human meant always being in relationship to the world; we cannot exist or conceptualize without it, he believed. Being is not apart from the world; first, being is in the world. And this relationship is one with feeling: One person is perpetually up beat, cheerful about life, and positive. Another is gloomy, with a dark cloud hanging overhead, so to speak. As a result, life may seem bleak, dark, and hopeless.

But there may be no outer source for the reaction. So, the mood is not a direct response to the person's experience of the actual outer physical or behavioral world. The mood may just be a personal feeling state that a person seems to already have. And sometimes, no obvious inner cause can be found either. The person just feels happy: in a good mood. Perhaps, on another occasion, the individual may feel unhappy or irritable, again with no obvious reason or outer stimulus-event to bring this about: In a bad mood. And no obvious inner cause is evident, either.

Meditation as an Option

Even though the term *mood* refers to a feeling state that may be more independent of outer circumstances to induce or maintain it, there still is a link. A wonderful, surprising visit from a good friend, for example, may bring about a happy mood that continues throughout the day and perhaps for some time afterward. Of course, this might not really need to be changed if the mood is pleasant or not very troubling. But usually people come to therapy because they want to change their mood.

Medication is increasingly being used to change mood. But meditation offers an additional option with methods for positive attunement, so that mood becomes a resource.

Working with Moods

In keeping with a flexible, flowing utilization mind-set, wise psychotherapists encourage their patients to use tendencies to be moody in a positive way. Sometimes, a calm, kind, and compassionate mood can be a very helpful resource in difficult circumstances, so that the person is able to endure inescapable discomfort for a time as needed.

A young man working at a large company had been diagnosed with bipolar disorder and was taking medication from a psychiatrist that he saw once a month. He decided to try meditation therapy as an adjunct. His psychiatrist was supportive. He began learning how to meditate and liked the feeling of calm that he could bring about. He felt encouraged that he could have some control over his moods or at least, his reactions to his moods. This was contrary to his usual experience that his moods just came on, swept over him, and impelled him into action to resolve his tension. Now he had new resources.

As he worked with meditation, he learned to recognize his moods. He became able to sense when he was starting to have an upward or downward swing, something he had never been able to experience before. In time, he could recognize the patterns of feelings and thoughts associated with his mood shifts. He felt the pleasurable energy surges, but instead of indulging in it as he used to, he deliberately meditated to steady himself, ate well, and got some rest. And when he felt the irritable, sluggish tiredness and negative energy pattern of his downswing, he noticed that too, and could moderate the effects. He included his wife in the process, listening to her, and so she was able to help him with accurate feedback to help him accomplish this. He also became aware of the irritability he radiated when his mood shifted downward, and he was able to work with meditation to help him control angry outbursts. As he gained more inner control, his confidence grew. Eventually, he was able to anticipate and prevent himself from indulging in some of the patterns that led to the swings. He found the up moods most difficult to relinquish, since he enjoyed the surge of energy. But as he learned to pace himself better, he found that he was less reliant on the ups to make up for lost time with things he used to let slide when he was down. He also improved the quality of his relationships with his parents and siblings, which helped ease tensions in his life. From a calm, meditative center, he developed a stable adjustment and was able to taper off medication. But he always had medication available if he needed it. Partnership with the psychiatrist worked well.

When a client is troubled by mood swings or with chronic sadness, anger, irritability, or other moods, regular meditation as part of treatment may help. Do not interfere with the use of medication or other treatments that are in use. If it is acceptable, and the client is willing, appropriate meditation can be an adjunct. Begin with several minutes a day, working up to 30 minutes. Regular meditation practice becomes a resource for greater calm, stability, and self-control. But it must be individualized and monitored for efficacy. Meditational methods for emotion can be adapted for moods.

Start Small

> Plan what is difficult where it is easy; do what is great where it is minute. The hardest things in the world begin with what is easiest; the greatest things in the world begin with what is minute.
>
> (*Dao De Jing*; Duyvendak, 1992, p. 135)

Small things can build up and lead to chronic moodiness. Daoism teaches us to take action when it is small. People who suffer from negative moods will find it easier to alter a mood by doing something just before and then while the mood is coming on. This requires that the client learns to recognize the signs and commits to change. Therapist and client can work together to uncover the typical signs of a mood about to start. A certain amount of trial and error is necessary.

Getting in Touch Mindfully

Once aware of what the signs are, the client can turn attention to the experience as it begins to happen and retrace the events that led up to a recent moody episode. Often, just thinking in therapy about a recent episode may trigger the experience. If so, utilize this as an opportunity to follow the mood together.

Notice the body sensations, the emotions, the thoughts, and any outer circumstances as they are happening. Stay in touch moment-by-moment and point out how the experience continues to alter. Don't add anything that is not there, but do try to notice the nuances of feeling and thought that take place through the process.

From Pratyahara to Concentration

As the mood begins to develop, it may become uncomfortable for the client to stay focused. This is a key point where people often turn away and stop noticing until the mood is entrenched. If the feelings become uncomfortable, use the pratyahara meditations from Chapter 7 to withdraw attention from other concerns and focus the concentration where it needs to be: on the inner experiencing as it occurs. But do not force awareness or insist on control, prematurely. Reassurance and support from the therapist can make the process easier to stay with and endure.

Reinterpreting the Mood

The mood is intimately involved with thoughts about the circumstance, other people, and life in general. As the cognitive appraisal and two-factor theories of emotion would predict, what is thought about the mood will influence its emotional tone.

Analyze thinking using the Four Noble Truths and the Eightfold Path. Here is a typical sequence of associated thoughts to an angry, irritable mood:

Do you believe that life should always satisfy the personal ego, to be just how you want it to be? And if things don't live up to your expectations, do you feel let down, angry, irritable, deprived, or depressed? Are you making negative judgments about the personal self? Or are you engaging in thoughts based in greed, hatred, or excessive pride? Perhaps you are clinging to unreasonable wishes for personal pleasures or trying to satisfy a need due to a rigid self-concept. Notice the views, intent, speech, and actions regarding these issues.

With regular meditation practice, people find it easier to apply the Eightfold Path under challenging circumstances. If the client is unable to stay with the discomfort or address the mood objectively while in the midst of duress, the therapist can suggest stopping and performing a calming meditation, such as a visualization of a peaceful place, or looking at a beautiful painting or photograph that may be hanging in the office. Then ask the client to try again, be patient, and keep trying. With guidance from the therapist, the process becomes easier over time. The therapist must be sensitive to the client's needs, and know when to move forward as well as when to withdraw. Like the back and forth flow of Qi-sao (Chapter 18), the therapist will be able to sense the situation best by staying closely attuned to the client.

BALANCING ENERGY

Often a mood involves an imbalance in energy. Clients in a depressed mood may experience a loss of energy. Others have too much nervous energy. Qi Gong exercises can gently and naturally help to restore the balance. Perform the Eight Pieces of Brocade. Breathe with the exercises, following the instructions given in Chapter 10. Repeat these exercises regularly to bring about balance.

RAISING ENERGY AT THE DANDIEN

Clients who are bothered by low energy from a mood may benefit from focusing on the dandien. Since Eastern medicine considers this area to be an energy center, concentration on it may help to energize. Then energy can be moved outward and circulated to help bring about a gentle increase of vitality. Follow the instructions for the Nei Dan series of exercises in Chapter 10 for warming the dandien, moving the energy, and circulating it.

A Mood for a Mood

Sometimes, without realizing it, a client forms a negative mood and perpetuates it more out of habit than from a real need. The Dalai Lama encourages people to cultivate a calm, happy mood, and believes that this mood will positively affect others as well. "All of the virtuous states of mind—compassion, tolerance, forgiveness, caring, and so on . . . cannot co-exist with ill feelings or negative states of mind" (Dalai Lama & Cutler, 1998, pp. 308–309). This theory resembles the James–Lange theory. Meditating on positive mental states may develop benevolent feelings and make it easier to recognize the positive nature in others.

An artist suffered from depression. His negative mood interfered with how he handled his life. He felt that he wasn't achieving as much as he would like, which added to his disturbance. As he worked with meditation, he discovered a deep feeling of inner calm. Gradually he began to recognize that he had a confident center. This became a resource for him. He found that he could bring about a positive mood when needed. With an improved mood, he was able to make changes. He formed his own company and developed his creative talents. Through the process, he addressed his insecurities, becoming confident and successful in his field.

Research shows that judgments can be biased by moods. Isen et al., (1978) performed an interesting experiment that illustrates this effect. One experimenter randomly offered people in the street small gifts. Another experimenter then asked them to participate in a "consumer survey" about how satisfied they were with their televisions, cars, and other possessions. People who had received the gift were more positive than those who had not.

When people are feeling optimistic and happy, judgments tend to be more positive, whereas when they are feeling irritable and disgruntled, judgments are often more negative. This can set up a downward spiral that perpetuates the negative mood with no way out. Thus, shifting the mood in a more positive direction can reverse the cycle: cognitions begin to support a more optimistic appraisal, leading to more constructive problem-solving and better choices, which in turn lead to more positive emotions with accompanying appraisal. Then, the therapeutic process can unfold under better circumstances.

Meditations to Transform the Mood

The therapist will be able to judge whether this is an appropriate technique. There are many times, as this chapter has shown, that emotions should be accepted, felt, and worked through as they are. In situations where a negative mood emerges, cultivating a positive mood to counter it may be the answer.

Performing a meditation ceremony such as tea, described in Chapter 13, can dissipate a negative mood. Then, begin the process of cultivating positive feelings. Utilize the methods from the Eightfold Path to replace unwholesome thoughts with wholesome ones. Moving Qi, from Chapter 10, or practicing the complete breath from Chapter 6 may also prove helpful in dislodging a stale, lethargic, or passive mood. Meditating on an inspirational symbol or chanting a mantra (Chapter 11) can bring a peaceful feeling of harmony that will permeate the mood to shift it into a positive direction. Another meditation that many people find inspirational and positive is found in Chapter 18, meditating on Oneness.

Look for a meditation method that has had the deepest effect and apply it regularly. People vary on what meditation method is most helpful. Be open and experiment until the most natural method is found. After becoming skilled with one approach, it is easier to expand into others. But the starting point is the first step. An old saying states it well: The journey of 1,000 miles begins with one step.

Using Humor to Transform

Sometimes clients become too serious in their pursuit. Humor may help them break out of patterned ways of thinking and feeling. Humor, like koans, can make people look at things differently without having to engage the intellect. Zen monks typically used a stick to hit students when they felt sleepy during meditation. One day, a monk proudly told Chao-chao, "I have never hit anyone with my stick!"

Chao-chao's answer was, "I guess the stick you carry is just too short!"

Jokes are often funny because they upend what is usually expected and force thinking on another level. When the punchline of a good joke is understood, a sudden shift happens. For a split second, usual thinking is transcended. A good laugh takes us outside of the self for that moment. We aren't thinking, we aren't feeling: We are just laughing. In this way, laughter is not far off from what Buddhists call enlightenment. Life itself is the guide, sometimes funny, sometimes serious. Both are possible.

Meditation for Any Moment

We take ourselves so seriously. But if there is no ego to bruise, many of life's predicaments can be lived with a smile. Take any incident, any moment in life to consider this perspective. Turn the problem upside down; look at it from the other side. Search for a humorous perspective and you may be happily surprised to find it!

15

The Way to Stress Reduction

The correspondences of the yin and yang, exterior and interior, inside and outside, and the zang-organs and fu-organs of man respond to the yin and yang of nature.

(Ming, 2001, p. 25)

This stress is an internal or external cue that disrupts the homeostatic status of the animal.

(Squire et al., 2003, p. 1043)

Human beings are part of nature's being. In Eastern medicine, the doctor utilizes this unity with nature to help keep the patient healthy. In meditational theory, the person is always interacting with the environment. Meditational practice returns the individual to inner and outer balance. The idea of balance is also incorporated in modern Western theories of stress. Although conveyed differently in terminology, both East and West conceive of the human being as having an internal balance that is also in balance with the environment.

Approximately two-thirds of clients who come into the psychotherapist's office complain of feeling "stressed." They suffer from troublesome symptoms, both physical and mental. For some, stress is the primary problem, but more often, stress is a secondary difficulty that adds to the main problem. And so, therapists often deal with a stress component when working on other problems. Mounting evidence shows that most forms of stress are helped by meditation. Therefore, therapists can confidently incorporate meditation, when appropriate, into the treatment regime.

Early Concepts of Stress: Homeostasis

According to Chinese medicine, the body is in an internal balance that is also in balance externally with the forces of nature. Balance is inclusive and in a dynamic flow. The opposites of yin and yang interact (e.g., light and heavy, cool and warm, acid and base, and so on). Internal equilibrium is a balanced and continuously balancing equation between the internal and external forces of nature. The doctor's role is to sensitively make the conditions favorable for imbalances in the body to become rebalanced.

This Eastern concept of balance has its counterpart in Western medicine's concept of *natura sanat* (nature heals), and the core principle of homeostasis, primary for the understanding of stress. Hippocrates recognized the body's innate ability to heal itself, and this ability takes place automatically if allowed to function. When a demand is placed upon the body, it responds by trying to reestablish balance.

An organism's tendency to come back into balance was researched extensively by the great French physiologist Claude Bernard in the 1850s. Bernard took Hippocrates's understanding further. He believed that the phenomena of living beings must be considered as a harmonious whole. He recognized the interdependence of social and behavioral life. Bernard sounded much like the Eastern doctor when he said: "Physiologists and physicians must therefore always consider organisms as a whole and in detail at one and the same time, without ever losing sight of the peculiar conditions of all the special phenomena whose resultant is the individual" (Bernard, 1865, 1957, p. 91). He believed that stability of the interior milieu of the organism is essential for life.

Walter Cannon devoted his career as professor of physiology at Harvard Medical School between 1906 and 1942 to researching this phenomenon and its mechanisms. He gave the name *homeostasis* to this natural wisdom of the body: When the balance is disturbed, the body instinctively tends to return to stability and balance. The Cannon–Bard theory of emotion is an integral part of this stability, essential for the survival and maintenance of the organism. Emotion signals that an imbalance needs to be addressed for the benefit of the organism (Cannon, 1927, 1932). Eastern medicine incorporates the principle of balance, but considers that the center of balance is the life energy or vitality, Qi. Qi flows in a dynamic balance of yin and yang within the individual, as well as with the environment.

The Development of Stress Theory

The theory of stress developed from the background of homeostasis and the natural tendency of the body to heal. The word *stress* derives from the Middle English word *stresse,* hardship, and the Old French word *destresse,* which referred to constraint.

Gradually, the idea of stress was applied to human difficulties. Sir William Osler, the famous 19th-century Canadian physician, equated stress and strain with hard work and worry. He said that every physician he knew suffered from it because of "the incessant treadmill of the practice of medicine, and in every one of these men there was an added factor—worry" (quoted in Hinkle, 1973, p. 30).

THE STRESS SYNDROME

Canadian physiologist, Hans Selye (1907–1982), is credited with theorizing the concept of stress as a distinct, nonspecific syndrome of its own, separate from disease and illness. As a medical student in 1926, Selye noticed that all the people brought before the students with different diseases seemed to share certain common symptoms, like tiredness and loss of appetite. It was not until the 1950s that Selye's research led him back to the implications of his early observations of a characteristic nonspecific reaction pattern. Whenever there is a continuous environmental stressor, he observed, the organism responds with this pattern. He called this reaction the General Adaptation Syndrome.

The General Adaptation Syndrome has three stages. First is the alarm reaction, when internal resources are mobilized in an attempt to return the body to its normal balanced functioning, homeostasis. Second is the resistance, when the individual uses whatever resources available to fight off the effects of stress. The third stage occurs if the stressor persists. Then the resources become depleted and the organism is exhausted. Selye believed that these three stages occur in any stress situation. This syndrome is a nonspecific reaction of the body as it adjusts to demands that are placed upon it, returning to balance. This view is still widely accepted today (Selye, 1974, 1976).

Wolff (1950), a contemporary of Selye, invented the concept of "life stress." He believed stress was the result of people's interaction with harmful agents or circumstances. For Wolff, Selye, and other researchers of this period, stress was an actual "state" that took place in the body. This theory has been accepted and expanded by more recent neuroscience findings.

Stress Can Be Good for You

These early theories of stress did not continue to bear out. For example, researchers did not consistently find a direct reciprocal correlation between hardship and the appearance of disease. Research conducted during the 1950s, in the post–World War II era, showed both the expected results of exposure to trauma and cases of the unexpected opposite. At times, soldiers and concentration camp survivors spontaneously recovered from existing illnesses such as ulcers, migraines, and colitis, diseases that were formerly thought to be caused by stress. This made it necessary to revise the stress concept.

Selye found that pleasant circumstances could also bring about stress. People feel just as much stress when experiencing pleasure, which he called *eustress*, as experiencing displeasure, or distress (Selye, 1974). Eventually, hard-playing as well as hard-driving people may suffer secondary difficulty from stress-related diseases such as ulcers, back pain, high blood pressure, and so on. Both positive excitement and negative tensions push us away from center. Restoring equilibrium is primary for healthy living. Stress is produced in either situation because the inner balance that is so necessary for life is disturbed. We need balance.

John C. Whitehorn (1894–1973), chief psychiatrist of the Johns Hopkins Phipps Clinic, believed that people actually need a certain amount of stress for optimum functioning. He pointed out that without challenge and "purposeful personal striving" (Whitehorn, 1956a, p. 647, 1956b), people become unhappy and often ill. Unmanageable stress tends to harm. But manageable stress can be beneficial, even stimulating.

Coping with Stress

How people interpret and handle the stressors in their lives seems to be a mediating variable. The interpretation and meanings people give to circumstances, physical predispositions, and life situation affect how well stress is handled. Dohrenwend and Dohrenwend (1981) noted in their extensive research that some people become ill when exposed to life stress but others do not. They hypothesized that expectations about the stressful event influence the effects. When a situation is appraised as a challenge rather than a threat, people cope better.

Janis (1971, p. 97) found that coping well is due to accurate perception. He followed the outcome of patients undergoing major surgery and observed that people coped well when they had realistic expectations, rather than unrealistically positive or pessimistically negative expectations. People who clearly perceived the truth about the stressor coped better, thereby lessening the harmful effects of severe stress.

Theorists have correlated stressful changes in the social environment with illness. Hinkle (1973) reported increases in respiratory illness at crucial stressful points in a person's life. Serious illness often follows separation of some kind (Frank & Frank, 1991). Supportive therapeutic interaction can help in coping with such life events, enhancing a positive, hopeful response. Support may come from family, intimate relationships, friends, or coworkers. All of us have been reassured and helped at times by others during trying circumstances, and a result we felt much more comfortable. This is one of the values of supportive counseling interactions. According to research, this kind of help stimulates feelings of hope and raises morale (Frank & Frank, 1991).

Lazarus pointed out that cognitive appraisals have an effect on coping with stress (Lazarus, 1991, p. 14). Adaptation to stress includes the interpretation (both conscious and unconscious) of the events or stimuli. He believed that how well people cope depends on how they appraise their circumstances and ability to manage them.

Lazarus distinguished between problem-focused coping and emotion-focused coping (Lazarus, 1991; Lazarus & Folkman, 1984). Stressors vary greatly, and require different coping strategies. For example, stress from the car not working when needed is best managed by problem-focused coping. The death of a significant relative requires an emotionally focused coping strategy. Successful coping strategies can modify whether the situation or stimulus becomes helpful or harmful to the individual.

Cognitive strategies are useful for coping, as well. Sometimes an attitude of detachment helps people manage a difficult situation (such as a serious loss of function from illness) until they can emotionally handle the knowledge about what they must inevitably live with. Lazarus pointed out that cognitive appraisals have an effect on the outcome. The actual physical body, in turn, may be positively affected by cognitive strategies. He believed that visualization of realistically positive changes in the body could even reverse negative physical or psychological processes (Lazarus 1991).

Useful Contemporary Stress Categories

The American Psychological Association (2000) has categorized stress as acute, episodic, or chronic (Smith & Miller, 1993). These categories can be helpful to the practitioner to help plan and design treatments for stress as part of the therapeutic regime.

Acute stress is temporary. It results from circumstances that typically occur in anyone's life, such as a fender bender, a heavy workload, or a child home with the flu. Acute stress can also result from positive experiences, such as skiing down a challenging slope, taking an exciting vacation, or planning a wedding. Acute stress is brief. People are well aware of the symptoms. They include emotional irritability, anger, anxiety, or depression and physical symptoms such as muscle tension, jaw pain, backaches, digestive system problems such as heartburn or irritable bowels, or elevations of blood pressure, dizziness, headaches, chest pains, shortness or breath, or cold hands and feet. These symptoms can be readily treated.

When acute stress recurs regularly it can become a habitual pattern, known as episodic stress. Worriers and "Type A" personalities are examples of those who experience episodic stress. Often such individuals become accustomed to feeling stressed and lose awareness of their reactions. Thus, such sufferers may be resistant to change. However, as treatment begins to bring some relief, these clients will often stay in treatment successfully.

Chronic stress is long-lasting stress that must be endured day after day over many years. People living in war-torn countries, extreme poverty, or with little hope of any relief for problems often suffer from chronic stress. But the stress may not be due to actual external circumstances. Sometimes people who have suffered trauma or neurotic adjustments in early life continue to carry the problems with them, similar to emotions transitioning to moods as they endure over time. These kinds of stress can lead to enduring mental disorders that require treatment with psychotherapy and involve a comprehensive change.

Neuroscience of Stress

Stress brings about a heightened physiological and emotional response in several main brain systems. The first line of defense, known as the flight or fight response, comes from the voluntary nervous system, which sends a message to the muscles. Faced with danger, the first impulse is to take some action.

The next system to respond is the autonomic nervous system, which becomes activated to prepare the body for action in two ways: The excitatory sympathetic response and the calming parasympathetic response. The sympathetic response excites the system by directing the adrenal glands to secrete epinephrine (adrenaline) and norepinephrine (noradrenaline). This causes the heart to beat more rapidly, muscles to tense, and blood pressure to rise. Breathing rate increases and pupils dilate. Blood flow is directed to the brain and muscles, away from internal organs and skin. The parasympathetic system helps maintain the homeostatic balance by calming the emergency reaction and keeping the normal maintenance systems going, such as digestion. These are normal responses that ready the body to either confront or flee from an experienced threat.

The neuroendocrine system involves a reaction pathway that mediates the stress response through the hypothalamus-pituitary-adrenal axis (HPA axis; Figure 15.1). The hypothalamus is a key center for regulating the stress response as well as a number of diverse physiological functions such as growth, metabolism, circadian rhythms, and osmoregulation (keeping the body's fluids from becoming too dilute or too concentrated). All of these functions are important in maintaining homeostasis between the organism and the environment. The hypothalamus maintains this balance by acting as an integrator. It receives converging inputs from the sensory and autonomic systems that are related to the internal and external environment. Then the hypothalamus responds quickly. Typically, neuronal cells in the brain release their transmitters

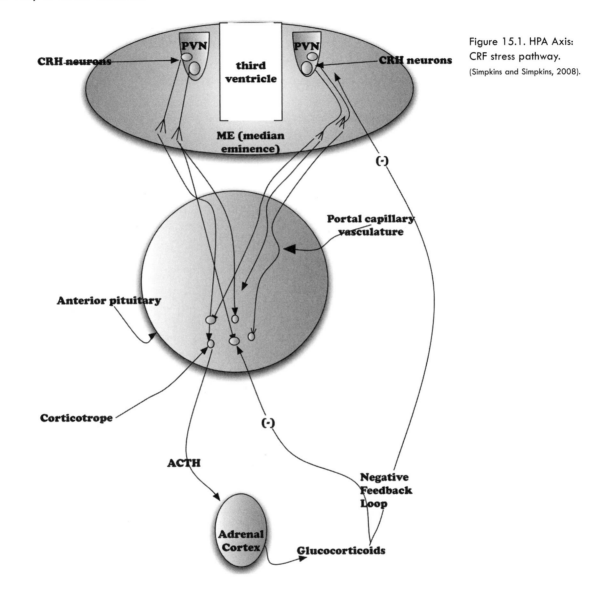

Figure 15.1. HPA Axis:
CRF stress pathway.
(Simpkins and Simpkins, 2008).

to other neurons through synaptic connections. But the cells of the hypothalamus do two things: they release neurotransmitters and neuropeptides to certain target areas in the central nervous system (CNS) and also into portal capillaries located in the anterior pituitary gland, which then go directly into the circulatory system for a fast response.

The hypothalamic hormone that controls the HPA stress axis is corticotrophin-releasing hormone (CRH; also known as CRF), which travels through the portal capillaries to the coritcotropes that have receptors for CRH along with another hypothalamic hormone, AVP. This causes the synthesis of ACTH, which is released from the pituitary gland into general circulation. Production and release of glucocorticoids are then produced and feed back into the brain and pituitary to negatively regulate

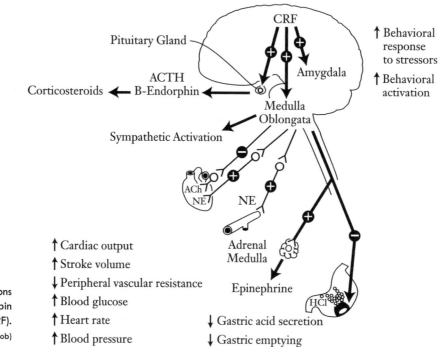

Figure 15.2. CNS Actions of Corticotropin Releasing Factor (CRF).
(Courtesy of George Koob)

(slow down) the synthesis of CRH and ACTH. This system is an example of a negative feedback loop.

The negative feedback loop of CRH, ACTH, and glucocorticoids is usually kept in balance. But when there is a stressor, the system responds rapidly with a large increase in activity along the stress axis. The increase is quickly down regulated by the negative feedback that brings it back to the baseline level as quickly as possible. Psychological factors can interrupt the system and prevent it from regaining the balance or help it regain balance more quickly.

Many other neurotransmitters, often associated with mood and anxiety disorders, are affected by stress such as dopamine, serotonin, norepinephrine, opiate, and benzodiazepine. The CRH system works as a mediator, and so in this way, treating the stress response often assists in the treatment of other psychological disorders as well.

Research on Meditation for Stress

Since stress seems to be a major contributor to other problems, dealing with stress by means of a scientifically proven and clinically evaluated method such as meditation can be useful as a part of treatment. Studies have evaluated the efficacy of meditation for stress. Included here is a selection of some interesting research.

Herbert Benson was one of the earliest researchers on the health benefits of meditation as a treatment method. Benson formulated a meditation method he called "the relaxation response" (Benson, 1975) that drew from the Yoga and Zen methods of following the breath and quieting thoughts. He believed these meditation practices could have relevance today for better health and did extensive testing for particular problems. Some of Benson's early studies showed that meditation could lower elevated blood pressure (Benson, Marzetta, & Klenchuck, 1974), one of the symptoms of stress. He also found that headaches responded to meditation (Benson, Malvea, & Graham, 1973), another stress related problem. Benson et al. (1982) studied body temperature changes resulting from meditation. His studies paved the way for mind–body medicine. Today he heads a center for mind–body healing that teaches these methods to treat a variety of health conditions.

Daniel Goleman also did some early studies testing the use of meditation to reduce stress. In one experiment, Goleman showed subjects a stressful movie and found that meditators had a reduction in stress reactions over nonmeditators (Goleman & Schwartz, 1976). Reduction of stress and anxiety has continued to be researched by different researcher groups using various types of meditation such as Benson (1978) and Dillbeck, Assimakis, Raimondi, Orme-Johnson, and Rowe (1986) with Transcendental Meditation (TM) and Miller, Fletcher, and Kabat-Zinn (1995) with mindfulness meditation.

Contemporary studies show the positive effects of meditation on reducing stress. In one study, 80 Chinese students were divided into two groups. The experimental group meditated for 20 minutes once a day for five days. They performed integrative body–mind training (IBMT), based in traditional Chinese medicine, similar to the Qi Gong exercises in Chapter 10 combined with mindfulness. Following meditation the experimental group had measurably less anxiety and lower levels of the stress hormone cortisol. Levels of anxiety, depression, anger, and fatigue also decreased (Tang et al., 2007).

Therapists are exposed to unusual stress, both occupationally related and at a personal level. Younger, more inexperienced therapists may be even more susceptible. Furthermore, stress can interfere with attention and concentration, two skills that are central for performing well as a therapist. Stress also contributes to professional burnout. Thus, therapists need methods for reducing stress just as much as clients do. A study found that mindfulness training three times per week over a 10-week period had a beneficial effect on reducing stress in therapists in training (Shapiro, Brown, & Biegel, 2007). Another study taught mindfulness-based meditation to medical and premedical students who were able to reduce stress to cope better with their academic demands (Shapiro, Schwartz, & Bonner, 1998).

With an ever-growing body of evidence that engaging in meditation reduces stress, therapists and clients will find it helpful in many contexts.

Improving the Handling of Stress with Meditation

Sometimes stress is unavoidable, as with temporary acute stress or chronic, ongoing stress that must be endured. The body's mechanisms of defense against stress usually help to regain homeostasis, but the life circumstances may not permit restoration of equilibrium or the stress pattern may be too deeply entrenched as a habit. Meditation can be an opportunity to help regain the homeostatic balance. Meditation draws on the ability to find calm amid the storm, and to activate the natural capacity for healing to take place as it should.

Inner Calm

A middle-aged woman sought meditation to reduce stress and lower her blood pressure. Her doctor warned that if her blood pressure did not drop, she would have to start taking blood pressure medication. She didn't want to have to take medication, but she felt so stressed by the demands of her life that she feared she might have to. She considered herself a victim in her family and spent time ruminating about it. She learned the calming meditations included below, to relax the body and mind. She described what she felt while meditating: "It takes me to a place where these problems don't exist." She learned to develop deep calm, giving her body an opportunity to find its natural balance.

She incorporated regular daily meditations into her routine, while doing chores such as folding laundry and washing dishes. In becoming aware of herself with mindfulness meditation, she realized how she had developed habits of inwardly fretting, worrying, and blaming others. As she became more aware, she also sensed her relationships with her husband and son. She realized that she had been overlooking the positive, loving times they spent together. In a matter of several months, she altered these negative thought patterns and took the time to enjoy what she had. Her blood pressure dropped back to normal and remained in the normal range.

BODY RELAXATION

These exercises develop skills in relaxation, first of the body, then of the mind. The first few exercises are designed to help relax the tensions that stress can bring. Any of the calming meditations in earlier chapters can be substituted or added, such as breathing meditations and Qi exercises. Take frequent short breaks to meditate. Meditate intermittently during the day and every day for a stronger effect.

Lie on the back, with knees drawn up, and feet flat on the floor. Some may want to add a small, thin cushion under the lower back to relieve tension. This position offers comfort to the back muscles, which often become tense when the body is stressed. A variation of this position is to lie on your side on the floor or on a soft rug, with the head on a pillow, legs bent, and knees pulled in. Again, a thin pillow under the hips or shoulders may help align the body comfortably. Close the eyes and allow breathing to be relaxed. Imagine, with every breath out, that tensions in the muscles ease. If any muscles in particular seem tighter, try to let go using the breathing. Rest comfortably for five minutes or so, breathing out tightness. When ready, sit up and stretch.

MIND RELAXATION

Sometimes a brief moment of relief from stress can help to ease the symptoms and allow the brain–body pathways to regain balance. Training makes such an interlude possible. Skilled meditators can create a peaceful moment no matter what mood they had before meditating (Kohr, 1977).

Evoke the moment of relief by filling or by emptying the mind. Fill the mind with a calming symbol, such as chanting a mantra or viewing a mandala. Alternatively, use one of the exercises for clearing the mind such as focus on a color for those new to meditation, or visualizing beyond thought (see Chapter 12).

RELAXATION BY DOING

Performing a quiet ritual may bring about relaxation seemingly without effort. Do the tea ceremony. Putting oneself into this situation of going through the movements and opening to the sensations can have a calming effect. We have prescribed a tea ceremony for clients to perform between sessions. Many have felt that it was especially helpful for an agitated stress reaction, when sitting still feels uncomfortable. Thinking about preparing and then performing the ceremony can offer relief, like visiting an oasis in the desert.

Meditative walking is another helpful option. It can be a 5- or 10-minute walk outdoors or even around the house. Walk slowly, aware of each step, focused on the sensation of the foot as it meets the floor, the arms as they swing by the sides, breathing in tune with each step.

Meditation can also be integrated into daily routines for stress relief. As our client discovered, the simple tasks of life offer a good opportunity to be awake and aware. Pay attention to each movement, such as in folding laundry. Feel the textures, temperature, and weight of the cloth. Look at the colors, smell the fragrances. Breathe comfortably and keep the muscles relaxed. The task becomes more pleasant to perform and much is learned in the process.

Mindful Appraisal: Finding Balance

Stress researchers such as Lazarus (1998; Lazarus & Folkman, 1984) and Janis (1971) showed that positive appraisal of the stressful situation improves coping. Thus, regular mindfulness meditation can be particularly helpful for altering long-standing chronic stress. Working with the therapist or with deep self-analysis will enhance the process.

Attend to breathing and body sensations until centered in the present moment. Then attend to feelings and appraise them. Are they pleasant, unpleasant, or neutral? Whatever the outcome of this appraisal, return to the more basic feeling with a nonjudgmental attitude. Sense it, as just an experience, without conceptualizing about it. Then, if concepts and judgments arise, perform mindfulness of mind. Question evaluations or other mental constructions that might be part of interpreting the sensations, such as, "I'm really stressed!" or "How awful this situation is!" or "My [mother, father, husband, wife, son, or daughter] is making me upset, and shouldn't." Then reflect on the judgmental response, and ask inwardly, "Does this bring about harmony, peaceful resolution, and better coping?" If disharmony seems inescapable ask, "Can I be more compassionate and understanding?" Try to empathize with the other's feelings and situation, not from a personal point of view, but instead, as the other person sees things, when at their best. Seek the harmony.

Next, let a clear meditative experience occur, without yes or no, good or bad. Just be aware, without assessment or judgment, clear, centered, and open to what is. In this open place, there is no stress or not stress, just being in the moment.

Mindful While Doing

The mindful meditation path can be helpful in dealing with stress throughout the day. People can lessen the stress response when performing daily routines, if they do so with such full attention that nothing distracts or disturbs them.

Become mindfully aware, utilizing the mindfulness meditations of body, feelings, and thoughts. Accept what is as it is and then try to learn more about it. Whenever possible, strive to refrain from interpretation when it is not necessary. Instead, approach each activity as calmly as possible. Most of the stressful aspects may dissolve away, leaving only the situation itself, which can be addressed in a more effective way when faced realistically. And with the attuned attention comes a better quality of action that is in step with and sensitive to the real needs of the situation.

Just Do It

Approach life wholeheartedly and just do it. There is to be no wavering, no conceptual evaluations, no "Should I" or "Shouldn't I?" Rather, mind, body, and spirit work together as one.

Mindful meditators are not troubled by many of the things that bother others, including stress. A difficult task is no different from an easy one—both are just tasks to be done wholeheartedly. Mindfulness can be performed with every activity throughout the day, including work, meals, and rest. This keeps the attention engaged in action leaving no extraneous thinking to distract.

Novices always wonder how to bring mindfulness meditation into daily life. An analogy may help. Think of a time when you were very thirsty but were unable to get a drink of water. Perhaps you were in the car on a long drive, and were running late. You tried to put your thirst out of your mind but could not. The more you attempted to put it out of your mind, the thirstier you felt. Eventually your mind was so entirely filled with thirst that you pulled off the road at the next restaurant to get some water.

With the same persistent intensity of that unsatisfied thirst, focus on here-and-now experience in life. Stay with it when walking, dressing in the morning, eating meals, spending time with family, or doing work. Gradually the mind clears and actions are just experienced as they are. Worries about activities drop away and you are left with just being in the moment. When completely immersed, thought and action are one.

Mazi (AD 709–788) taught Zen during its most creative period, the Tang Dynasty (618–907). He expressed this way of living when he said, "When hungry I eat, when tired I sleep" (quoted in Suzuki, 1969, p. 106). A student questioned a Zen master further about Mazi's statement, asking how this way of simply eating and sleeping was so different. The master answered as follows:

> When they eat, they do not just eat, they conjure up all kinds of imagination; when they sleep, they do not just sleep, they are given up to varieties of idle thoughts, that is why theirs is not my way.
>
> (quoted in Suzuki, 1969, p. 106)

Just Do It Exercise

Pick some small task that is performed often, to use for practice, such as washing the car or washing the dishes. Get everything ready ahead of time. Then, stop, sit, and clear the mind. When ready, begin the task and perform it without hesitation. Keep attention directed to each action while doing it. When the task is completed, put everything away. Then, sit again to clear the mind. The ability to ready oneself, take action, and then complete the action with awareness and without hesitation, can be extended into more challenging circumstances. A calm, confident way to do things will emerge naturally.

Letting Be

> Do by not doing, act by non-action, taste the taste-less, regard small as great, much as little. (*Dao De Jing*; Duyvendak, 1992, p. 135)

Sometimes clients fall into an unfortunate pattern. As therapy begins to reveal problems, some people react by thinking about the problems too much. They become overly self-conscious, which makes an already stressful lifestyle even more so. The harder they try, the more energy they expend, and the less they are able to accomplish. They become more disturbed and stress levels mount. A Daoist approach can interrupt this uncomfortable pattern with a radically different solution known as *wu-wei* or the way of nonaction. Sometimes the things that are done effortlessly turn out best. What seems difficult becomes easy. The next exercise guides in applying this principle.

Nonaction Meditation

This meditation begins a process of nonaction through letting be. Sit quietly. Is it possible to permit the eyes to rest, or are they watching? Notice this but do not change it. Pay attention to breathing, but do not alter it. Simply allow it to be as it is. Scan through the body. Notice any tension, but do not try to force relaxation. Allow the muscles to be as they are. How does the body meet the floor (or chair)? Do you let the floor (or chair) support the body, or is the body pushing against floor (or chair)? Notice these things.

Next, turn attention to thoughts. Note any thoughts that occur but do not attempt to direct them. Simply observe, allowing them to be as they are. Follow whatever awareness presents, but do not try to change. Be as you are. After sustaining this for up to 15 minutes, notice experiencing. Does breathing become easier? Are muscles relaxing of their own accord? Do you feel calmer? Without altering anything purposefully, change begins to take place. Allow what is natural to find its own balance, to regain homeostasis, as it inevitably will if allowed to.

Extending Wu-Wei to Daily Routines

Letting thoughts be in this way can be applied during a session. As a feeling or thought emerges, guide the client to stay with it, without altering anything. Follow the procedures described here to learn more about the problem.

By pausing to reflect on things as they are, without altering anything on purpose, something emerges. With time, the natural rhythms begin to reassert themselves. Laozi and Zhuangzi taught their students to overcome difficulties by letting things be. Allow nature to take its course, and it becomes a helpful guide. To become one with nature is to trust the nature within. As we begin to listen to the body, the rhythms of appetite, fatigue, and energy can become guides. A baby knows when it is tired or hungry, so we can regain the wisdom of the organism and help it to be expressed.

Often when stressed, the balance is lost. People force themselves into unnatural routines that put them out of touch with what is really needed. To regain attunement, become aware of rhythms, notice when hungry or tired, not just when the clock says it's time to eat or sleep. Readjust scheduling as much as possible to align more closely with what is natural. If tired when there is work to do, try resting briefly before starting the work. Don't ignore the inner signals, listen to them and try to accommodate when possible. This procedure applies to thoughts and feelings as well. Even small adjustments can help return to balance.

Finding the Individual Balance

But where is the balance point? Sometimes clients have unrealistic expectations about how they should be, based in stereotypes about the nature of a balanced, stress-free life. But in reality, the level of activity and demands, pace and timing will vary.

Therapists must also beware of imposing their own personal standards for balance and harmony onto the client. Attune with open awareness to what the client expresses. Look at the energy level where this individual seems to function best. Be open to individual differences.

An executive secretary sought therapy to help her alter her "crazy" lifestyle. She spoke quickly, laughed loudly, and was very direct. She sat sideways in the chair with her upper body leaning in one direction with legs crossed to counterbalance in the opposite direction. She told us that she lived "off tilt" and that her lifestyle was stressful. She felt annoyed with herself for being this way but was unable to prevent it. When she learned to use a letting-be meditation, she was able to get back in tune with her own personal way, her nature. She began to understand that she was imposing standards for normalcy that were interfering with her ability to truly sense what she needed—and then to let it be. This "off-tilt" woman found her balance point. The balance point began in dynamic activity, off-center. But from accepting herself as she needed to be, she became less stressed and more comfortable with her busy, often irregular lifestyle. Over time, she discovered she also enjoyed restful moments. She became comfortable without being off-tilt, and eventually found another person to meaningfully share her experiences with.

Meditative Retreat Exercise

Find a comfortable position, either seated or lying down. Close the eyes. Breathe normally, comfortably. Let go of any unnecessary tension. Recall a place or a time when you were relaxed and calm. Perhaps you were on vacation, with a good friend or loved one, or perhaps alone, but vividly imagine being there once again. Remember the feelings, what things looked like, any memorable smells or tastes: every possible detail. Filling the mind with this relaxing memory, the body spontaneously relaxes. Allow this to take place naturally. When ready, open the eyes and return to the present moment, relaxed and refreshed.

Discover harmony within so that life flows more smoothly. Each of us has an individually optimal balance point. Some people function at a very high energy level. Other people like to live a quieter, slower-paced life. There are times in life when even the quietest person is called upon to put forth an extra effort to meet a challenge. Learning to recognize personal rhythms, when to push and when to withdraw, makes it possible to accomplish more naturally and comfortably, without stress. Using meditation, the individual adjustment point that is optimal can be found, and followed as it changes.

Meeting Stress as a Bodhisattva

Some of the most useful learning can come when challenged. Hemingway defined courage as grace under pressure. It is easy to be happy and fearless when everything is going smoothly, but much more difficult when circumstances are demanding.

When dealing with stress, approach it as a Bodhisattva would, practicing warmth and kindness. Stay attuned and in touch with the situation as it unfolds. Begin with wisdom: Become informed about what is truly happening, listen to what others are saying, and consider the other points of view within a broader context of meaning that can encompass many perspectives, as one. Then pause, meditate for a few moments, and relax. Try to respond compassionately from a calm center. Address the situation without adding fuel to the fire. Sometimes other people's reactions are irrational. Instead of adding to the irrationality, pause to offer the other person the space and time to act more maturely. When the situation itself is stressful, consider ways to make improvements or help others to do so. With sympathetic input calmly offered, the dynamics of the situation are altered. Life's challenges can be met more effectively when you are aware, centered, and willing to find a more compassionate alternative.

16

Beyond Fear and Anxiety

There is no bodhi tree,
Nor stand of a mirror bright.
Since all is void,
Where can the dust alight?
(From the Platform Sutra of the *6th Patriarch of Zen*, Price & Mou-lam,
1990, p. 72)

To experience a fear-inducing situation and act bravely anyway shows true courage. After all, it does not take courage to experience and cope bravely with circumstances that one is not afraid of. This is a key emphasis: to face a fear or anxiety that is really there, meet the situation appropriately, and then act. This epitomizes the Western view. If people confront fear-inducing circumstances, they can overcome their reaction. There are times when this response is what is called for. But there are times when a different way of thinking from the East can also help when needed. Both have meaning, and neither negates the other.

Western Theories

The Western view has a long and venerable tradition. Ancient Greek tragedy, according to Aristotle, led to the valuable experience of catharsis. Feeling intense emotions such as terror, evoked by the drama, purified emotions so that people could be purged of troubling fears and anxieties. Both East and West emphasize the value and benefit of reaching deeper, albeit in different ways.

Dynamic Theories

Aristotle's theory found its way into expression in modern psychotherapy as well. A personal, meaningful variation of catharsis combined with insight is still considered a central part of the treatment of deep problems. In early dynamic models, fear and anxiety derive from an emotionally traumatic event. The link may be direct. For example, a victim of a near-drowning sometimes retains a fear of water. The link may also be indirect, as in a sexual conflict represented symbolically in a fear of snakes or a fear of intimacy, which can be unlearned by these means. During World War I and II, catharsis was a standard therapy for reactions brought on by war, then known as shell shock. People were guided to reexperience the inducing trauma and subsequently purge their feelings about it. Fear and anxiety dissolved when the roots of the trauma were faced and courageously worked through.

Existentialism

Existentialism, another root for psychotherapy, defined anxiety in two ways: existential or neurotic. Existential anxiety is the healthy recognition of human angst; the inescapable feeling that results from the conditions of life, with much that is unknown and beyond control. Here we see a parallel to Eastern ideas that we cannot know ourselves by using our usual modes of reasoning.

From the existential perspective, we all must face tragedy, vulnerability, and unpredicted contingencies. Neurotic anxiety comes from trying to avoid the realities of the existential condition, to falsely believe that there is security, that there are no uncontrollable contingencies. Trying to avoid the unavoidable tragedies in life inevitably leads to neurotic anxiety. Only by facing existential anxiety can life be authentic, in tune with what truly is.

Behaviorism

Behavior therapy shares a similar rationale, to face discomfort and overcome it with desensitization and exposure therapy methods. Anxieties and fears develop from some initial stimulus combined with an unconditioned response. When the two become paired, a conditioned response forms.

In behavioral approaches, fear and anxiety can be unlearned or extinguished by various techniques. Deep relaxation of the muscles is one way that is used to overcome fear. Progressive relaxation while in contact with or imaging the fear-arousing stimulus is a key method. Exposure has been more successfully used as a method of desensitization by guiding the sufferer through imagination in virtual reality, or in actual reality, to engage with the fearful experience. In general, stop avoiding the feared situation and the anxious conditioned response will extinguish over time. Meditative methods for immersion in the moment can also be used to enhance this process in many ways.

Cognitive Views

Cognitive therapy is one of the most prevalent methods. Cognitive factors, especially the way people interpret themselves and events, play a critical role in the etiology of anxiety (Barlow, Chorpita, & Turovsky, 1996). Therefore, how people perceive and interpret themselves in the situation can intensify or dampen the response. Mindfulness meditations that help to deconstruct the cognitive beliefs and patterns of emotional response coordinate well with cognitive behavioral therapies and therefore are being successively used (Kabat-Zinn, 2003).

Hypnotic Views

Anxieties can be approached indirectly and unconsciously using hypnosis. Many problems arise in the conscious mind, but the unconscious can be a reservoir of potential strength. By altering consciousness using hypnosis, clients bypass limitations to draw upon the natural potentials found in the unconscious (Erickson & Rossi, 2006; Simpkins & Simpkins, 2004, 2005). The altered state has some overlap with the phase of meditation where the deliberate effort becomes effortless, as in Daoism and Zen.

Neuroscience of Fear and Anxiety

Studies have shown that emotional processing in rodents (LeDoux, 1992) and in humans (Bechera et al., 1995) with brain lesions (Adolphs, Tranel, & Damasio, 1998) originates in the amygdala. The hippocampus is associated with emotion and memory and also plays a primary role in fear and anxiety by establishing intracortical linkages that integrate the systems together (McDonald & White, 1993).

The Fast Route and the Slow Route

There are two neural routes for an emotional stimulus to follow. In the fast route, sensory information enters the lateral amygdala directly from the thalamus. The information passes to the major output nucleus of the amygdala known as the central nucleus of the amygdala. The central nucleus projects, in turn, to multiple brain systems involved in the physiological and behavioral experience of fear. The reaction is rapid, connecting to different regions of the hypothalamus. This activates the sympathetic nervous system and induces the release of stress hormones activating the HPA stress pathway (see Chapter 15) that leads to the individual experiencing feelings of fear and anxiety.

When this occurs repeatedly, neurotransmitter patterns alter. People with anxiety disorders have changes in serotonin, norepinephrine, gamma-aminobutyric acid (GABA), corticotropin-releasing hormone (CRH), and cholecystokinin (Rush, Stewart, Garver, & Waller, 1998). Changes are compounded by the interaction: Alteration in one neurotransmitter system invariably elicits changes in another.

The slow route is a second possibility when a fearful stimulus is experienced. This route is mediated by the sensory cortex and hippocampus, allowing for further processing. Psychotherapy can help to slow down the fast route by teaching strategies that help activate the prefrontal cortex to regulate the arousal level such as with calming techniques or cognitive methods.

These neurological changes initiate body responses that activate types of defensive responses, as therapists well know. But these body responses can have helpful functions as well, such as suppressing pain in an emergency.

Neuroplasticity —the brain's ability to change over time—is now an accepted and acknowledged phenomenon. Understanding when and how neuroplasticity

Figure 16.1. Two pathways of fear. (Simpkins and Simpkins, 2008)

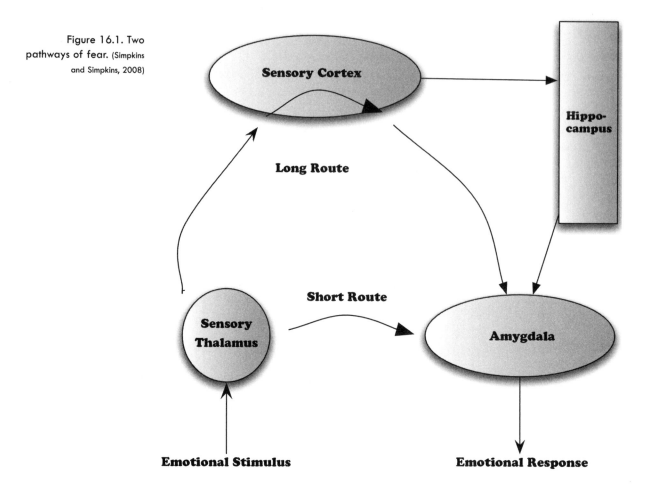

happens can help therapists make better interventions. Hippocampus size decreases in people with posttraumatic stress disorder (PTSD). When the hippocampus is reduced, the individual is less capable of drawing on memory to evaluate the nature of the stressor (McEwen, 1998; McEwen & Magarinos, 1997). However, recent research shows that the hippocampus can also increase in size. For example, one study found that cab drivers, who tend to be continually engaged in spatial orientation tasks—also a function of the hippocampus—had larger hippocampuses than people of the same age who were not cab drivers (McGuire et al., 2000). This research may indicate that if the correct learning experiences are given, the hippocampus can increase in size. Therapists who employ methods to stimulate hippocampal growth can help clients alter even difficult, entrenched anxiety patterns. Andrew Weil (2004) speculates that given the research that shows how meditation reduces anxiety and stress plus the capacity of the hippocampus to grow, especially when harmful inputs are removed and the correct ones presented instead, meditation may help the impaired hippocampus to regenerate (Piver, 2008).

Eastern View of Fears and Anxiety

The meditational conception of how to overcome fear and anxiety takes a different view that may be more helpful with some clients. "Wheresoever are material characteristics there is delusion; but whoso perceives that all characteristics are in fact no characteristics, perceives the Tathagata [the Buddha or truth]" (from the Diamond Sutra, quoted in Price & Mou-lam, 1990, p. 21). No anxiety or fear is really there. On first reading, this statement does not seem to make sense. Of course anxiety is there. The chronically anxious person knows this. But then, sitting quietly, after clearing thoughts, a glimpse, however brief, emerges when there is no anxiety or fear, and the impossible suddenly becomes possible. In this sense, a trained meditator has a way to experience what the Buddhist sutras claim about having no anxiety or fear. In the moment of true emptiness, there is no anxiety or fear either. How could there be, when there is no basis for it? After having experienced this, the thoughts or feelings that usually bring about anxiety and fear may decrease.

Meditation does not require the usual type of effort people make to accomplish things. Paradoxically, anxiety is reduced by quiet sitting instead of doing something about it. "The harder you strive after him, the further he is away from you" (Lin Chi; Sasaki, 1975). As has been noted in the *Dao De Jing*, the sage takes no action, yet nothing is left undone. This quality of meditation, the effortless effort, to try without trying and to do without doing, is paradoxical but not impossible. This does not mean just to just let things go badly. The sage remains engaged, immersed in the action, and at the same time, steps back to let nature take its course. Many of the anxieties people commonly experience will dissolve by using intuition instead of conceptual reasoning.

Research on Meditation to Treat Anxiety

Meditation has been tested with many different types of anxiety. Mindfulness practice appears to be a promising alternative technique for social anxiety, in which individuals are too shy to seek help or as an adjunct to psychotherapy (Arana, 2006). Yoga breathing has been applied as a public intervention to alleviate PTSD in survivors of mass disasters (Brown & Gerberg, 2005). Kundalini Yoga has been used for the treatment of obsessive-compulsive disorder (OCD) (Shannahoff-Khalsa, 2003). Research on worry, one of the components of anxiety, has indicated that detached mindfulness training helped to decrease proneness toward worry (Sugiura, 2004). Another study compared a meditation-based stress management program to an anxiety-disorder education program as an adjunct to pharmacotherapy. The meditation group showed significant improvement in scores on all anxiety scales over the education group. These researchers concluded that meditation could be effective in relieving anxiety symptoms in patients with anxiety disorder (Lee et al., 2007). A 20-week meditation-relaxation treatment program for elderly women suffering from anxiety and depression resulted in a measurable decrease in anxiety symptoms (DeBerry, 1982).

Many studies have measured the effect of meditation on anxiety. As noted, anxiety and fear engage a wide range of neural circuits involving the hippocampus, amygdala, and the stress pathway: the hypothalamic-pituitary-adrenocortical axis (HPA) described in Chapter 15. Researchers (Goleman & Goleman, 2001) suggest that meditation is effective because it helps to moderate the amygdala's emotional responses. The amygdala responds quickly with an emotion, whereas the prefrontal cortex takes slightly longer, but acts as a thoughtful mediator of emotions. Since many studies have linked meditation to increased activity in the prefrontal cortex (see Chapter 3), skilled meditators may be able to intervene by interrupting the amygdala's split second emotional response by providing a more constructive, realistic response. Another research group found similar results: The more mindful the subjects were, the greater the activation in the right ventrolateral prefrontal cortex and the less the activation in the amygdala (Creswell, Baldwin, Eisenberger, & Lieberman, 2007).

One interesting study analyzed the changes in EEG using Zen meditation in association with trait anxiety assessed by Spielberger's State-Trait Anxiety Inventory. Research on meditation has consistently showed the dual effect (described in Chapter 3) of increased attention with increased relaxation. All 22 subjects showed the dual effect of meditation. Their EEG results also indicated the following correlation: Subjects with lower trait anxiety more readily induced meditation with a predominance of internalized attention, while subjects who had higher trait anxiety more readily induced meditation with a predominance of relaxation (Murata et al., 2004).

Effects of Time

A study explored the effects of meditation over time. Beginners who meditated for one month or less, short-term meditators who practiced from one month to two years, and long-term meditators who practiced for more than two years were compared. The data from this study revealed increases in attentional absorption in conjunction with a decrease in trait anxiety across groups as the length of time meditating increased (Davidson, Goleman, & Schwartz 1976). Thus, the longer one engages in the practice, the larger the effect on anxiety.

Even brief meditation sometimes has an effect. One large study with 387 undergraduate students found that a single 20-minute session resulted in reduced state anxiety after exposure to a transitory stressor (Rausch, et al., 2006). Another study used a mindfulness-based stress reduction program over eight weeks. They found reduction in anxiety and related symptoms (Tory, 2004).

These numerous studies offer good evidence that meditation has undergone testing with anxiety and can be used either alone or in conjunction with other treatments.

Meditation Methods

When the goal is to ameliorate a problem with anxiety, regular meditation is needed. Therapists should encourage the client to meditate often during the day. For anxiety disorders, meditation when added to psychotherapy may facilitate the treatment considerably. Then the client has another resource to use for coping.

Therapists should advise clients to be patient about how long it takes to change anxious feelings. Many antianxiety medications take several weeks to begin affecting the symptoms. Similarly, meditation, which alters the neurological chemistry and psychological adjustment, may also take time. Sometimes the anxiety diminishes immediately during the meditation session, but since change of a habitual pattern is often more gradual, anxious feelings may not diminish right away. The client usually feels an easing of tensions later that day or only after several days or weeks of regular practice. Once activated, the natural healing abilities will take the time needed. Respect inner rhythms.

Minute Meditations to Start a Process

Begin the process with a very brief meditation performed at various times during the day. Regular brief practice sets in motion the possibility of a different experience, activating a changed sense of the fear or anxiety. Sometimes people feel that they have no extra time for meditation, but everyone can find one minute here or there!

Meditation can draw on the inner recesses of consciousness, a timeless experience that does not rely on the ticking of a clock. We have all felt this—for example, when a few minutes of a tedious meeting feels like an hour, or conversely, when a whole day of vacation seems to pass by in a flash. The nature of subjective time-consciousness allows regular, short meditative breaks to have a powerful effect. These exercises can be done almost anytime: at your office desk, in the evening just before sleep, during your child's nap, or as part of a coffee break. When working on a change in a long-standing problem such as anxiety, meditation needs to be performed often. Making these exercises, and many of the other exercises included in this book, part of daily routine can set the stage for a less anxious, calmer adjustment.

Meditation may offer relief: moments without the discomfort. One client who suffered from anxiety for many years said that meditation was like taking a minivacation. As she became more skilled in developing a calm, quiet consciousness, she felt that this ability become a resource that she could always rely on when needed.

She liked that she could meditate even for a minute here and there, and feel a moment of peace and calm. Gradually she brought the sense of no anxiety into her everyday life, and eventually she was able to stop taking antianxiety medication.

Minute Focus on One Thing

Pick one thing to think about: It could be an outer object or an inner sensation. Draw upon the focus meditations in Chapter 7. Keep the attention focused on this one thing. If the awareness shifts, stop meditating, rest for a moment, and then try again for a shorter period. Eventually, a time-span that is brief enough to sustain focus will be found. Build up the time gradually until enough minutes of focused attention are doable.

Minute Mind Clearing

Sit or stand and let the mind clear of all thoughts. Utilize the meditations from Chapter 12 to empty the mind, or the breathing meditations in Chapter 6. The beginner may want to imagine an empty space, a clear lake, or a single color. Others may prefer to allow the thoughts to settle and slow until clear. If a minute seems too long, begin with 30 seconds or even less.

Minute Mindfulness

Suggest that clients pick an activity of brief duration that is performed every day, such as brushing the teeth. Decide to attend to it mindfully, from beginning to end. Before beginning, stop for a few seconds and breathe with awareness of each breath in and out. Then begin the activity: notice the taste of the toothpaste, the temperature of the water, and the sensation of the toothbrush on the teeth. Feel the arm as it moves, and notice the body position at the sink. When finished, take a few seconds to pay attention to the sensation of the mouth and face. Another activity that lends itself well to a brief mindfulness is taking a shower or bath. Any activity that is performed regularly and doesn't take too much time to do can be a good place to start. Bring more mindfulness into each day by attending to other brief activities.

Minute Meditation of Choice

Many of the meditation methods in Part II can be performed briefly. If there is a particular method that seems most natural, begin there. Start small with what works best and build on the successes. Extend the time only after able to meditate briefly.

Minute meditations are also an excellent way to try something that seems more challenging. By taking off the pressure of having to sustain a meditation over time, learning can begin. Enjoy the process—not only are there satisfactions from experiencing something new, but also, very little time has been spent in the process! When ready, extend the time. Individualize and adapt the method in ways that make sense personally.

Meditation in Action

A little frog
Riding on a banana leaf
Trembling

(Kikaku [1660–1707], quoted in Suzuki, 1973, p. 231)

Some anxious clients find that trying to be calm makes them more anxious. Such individuals should work with meditation more actively, as in the following case.

A male college student was serious about his education. He was a motivated person, but he found that when he studied hard, he felt anxious. His thoughts raced, his stomach hurt, and his palms started to sweat. He had to get up every 20 minutes to use the bathroom. He wanted to do well in school, but the harder he tried the more anxious he became. He tried calming meditation, but he had the same anxious reaction. We taught him how to do active meditation, and he found that he could meditate well without feeling uncomfortable. As his meditative skills improved, he created ways to study more actively and was able to alter his anxious reaction.

Active Meditations

Pick an activity similar to one of the types of activities named here. The Eight Pieces of Brocade pictured and described in Chapter 10 is one set of patterns that can be performed to develop meditation skills. It gives a specific set of movements to follow while maintaining a calm active awareness. Another possibility is to use an activity that the client already practices, such as a martial art, sport, dance, a hobby, video game, or a simple work task.

Before beginning, stand quietly for a minute or so and do a whole body breathing meditation. With each breath in, imagine that the air spreads through the entire body. Then with the breath out, imagine the stale air exits, leaving the body refreshed and alert.

When ready, begin performing the activity, keeping the attention focused on it while doing so. Attempt to keep breathing steady. Make each motion smooth and deliberate, breathing lightly while moving. When performing an everyday activity such as typing or playing a video game, keep awareness focused on the stimuli and the sensations in the hands and body.

Go through a warm-up routine or training set that is a regular part of the activity. For a less physically active hobby such as painting or video game playing, make note of subtle sensations and experiences while performing the activity. As the anxiety patterns diminish, calming meditations can be added.

Deconstructing Anxiety

Anxiety sometimes involves linking uncomfortable body sensations in the chest to beliefs about what such physical symptoms usually signify, to worry about having a heart attack, expectations about that possibility, and so on. A real and existing pattern emerges from associating these components together, although not originally from an actual heart condition. Even if a medical checkup determines that there is no underlying physical cause, the sufferer still must believe and accept that there is actually nothing really there, to become free from the anxiety. The following case illustrates how to deconstruct this pattern of mental construction.

A medical practitioner came for treatment because of anxiety. Often when seeing his patients, he felt such intense anxiety that he had to leave the room. This problem was interfering with his work. His ribcage tended to constrict at his solar plexus, giving him sensations of difficulty when he breathed. As his body aged, his ribcage became less flexible, and when he experienced the sensations, he worried that he was dying, and could not dispel his anxiety. He sought medical treatment but was told that his problem was not due to a heart condition. He was referred for psychotherapy. Using meditation, he learned to become calm in the sessions, but still felt anxiety during the week. Gradually, as he improved his meditation skills, he began to recognize the sensation and experience it as simply that, a feeling of comfort or discomfort. The interpretation he was giving it—a possible heart attack or serious problem—was a further alarming evaluation that he made. When he combined his personal assessment of the sensation plus the negative meaning, he unwittingly was increasing his uncomfortable sensations. He learned to be more neutral as he observed carefully, without making any negative evaluations. In time, the discomfort lessened and eventually he lost his anxiety and fear.

Deconstruction Meditation for Anxiety

Meditation can be applied to relieve anxiety when medical examination has shown that there is nothing wrong. The first step is to contemplate the idea that sensation and cognition can be separated. A pure sensation and the thoughts about the sensation can be distinguished, and this helps manage the situation. Review the different forms of mindfulness: of body, of emotions, of mind and of objects of mind. Refer to the mindfulness instructions and practice these meditations when not feeling anxious. As skills build, it becomes possible to draw on them even while feeling tense, especially if already familiar with the meditation.

When practicing mindfulness, make special note of how each sensation is a new one. Start with breathing. Notice that each breath is a new and different breath. Even though the last breath resembles the next one, it is not the same breath. Everything is slightly different with each new moment. With the felt understanding of how each breath is unique, consider that each anxiety attack is unique too. Every time the anxiety occurs is a new time, a little different from the last one. Even though the experience seems to be exactly like the last time, it actually is unique and new. People often compress all the anxious experiences together into one dreaded experience. Follow each moment anew to discover how each moment the anxiety is happening offers a new opportunity to learn to let it go. Relax with each breath as much as possible.

Mentally break down the anxiety into its component parts. Anxiety can be thought of as a conglomerate of moments during which a frightening interpretation is added to describe an uncomfortable sensation. This process tends to increase the intensity of the sensation, leading to a further interpretation, such as, "It's getting worse." Each successive moment includes an interpretation followed by an even stronger sensation in reaction. First observe this spiraling process as it unfolds. Then as soon as possible, notice the separate parts: sensations, interpretations, and emotions. Try to recognize that the interpretations are separate from and are not the same as the sensations or the emotions.

Now extend the meditation. Notice how the components influence and are inseparably a part of each other: Worrying interpretations provoke more worry. And the worry brings on more discomfort, in a self-perpetuating cycle. Question the realistic certainty of this reaction with inwardly focused reassurance such as: "I know that my worry may not necessarily be what the sensation will bring; I have checked out my condition and I know that there is no physical problem."

Be patient with the process. Remember that time is a limiting factor. Recall a past anxiety attack when the discomfort passed after a certain amount of time. Remember that even when expecting the feeling to get worse, or that it might be a sign of terrible things, the anxiety sensations eventually passed.

Return repeatedly to staying in each moment as it comes, rather than anticipating what it might become. Allow breathing to find a natural rhythm appropriate to the moment. Try to carefully follow experiencing mindfully as it happens, including the periods of time that the feeling diminishes. Anxiety in general tends to become easier to handle and eventually lessens in intensity.

Indirect Treatments

Sometimes anxiety can be approached directly, by working on the symptoms such as in the minute meditations to begin the work and the deconstruction of how the anxiety is created, as in the exercises above. But often anxiety is best approached indirectly.

Show Me Your Anxiety

In the ancient times this was called the "freeing of the bound." There are those who cannot free themselves because they are bound by things. But nothing can ever win against Heaven—that's the way it's always been.

(Zhuangzi quoted in Watson, 1968, pp. 84–85)

A young woman who sought therapy for generalized anxiety usually felt uncomfortable. She had many successes in her life, but they were never enough. She felt compelled to achieve: She had to do what she did; she had no choice. She speculated about the reasons for her anxiety. Perhaps her parents' disapproval was the cause, or maybe it came from her ex-husband. This client eventually learned that she did not have to search for causes outside of herself: the answers were found within. She did not direct her efforts to not being anxious. Instead she just meditated regularly. In time, she came to feel relief when she sat quietly. She became more comfortable with who she was and what she was doing, which she discovered in those quiet moments.

Sometimes direct treatment of the problem is not the best way to get results. Thought may weave a pattern of misconception. Reduce misconception indirectly, by loosening the threads of thought, feeling, and body that weave the pattern together. Then make the necessary changes without hindrance.

Anxiety as Blocked Energy

Tightness in the chest or abdominal area often accompanies anxiety feelings. Generalized muscle tension may also be present. Look for unusual body tensions or complaints of low energy. Eastern medicine looks for blockages and helps to free them using the slow, meditative movements of Nei Dan and Wei Dan. Turn to these exercises if a blockage is suspected. Becoming aware of breathing can also help to release unnecessary tensions and relieve anxiety. These exercises should be practiced every day for a period of time for best results.

Learning to Relax

Greater relaxation is one of the expected effects of meditation. Regular relaxation tends to lessen tension and anxiety. Practice these relaxation meditations or any others from the book. Devote time to relaxation every day, several times a day. If the client has difficulty with relaxation, a more active form of meditation should be used. Short periods of relaxation may also initiate an ability to relax. Meditative breathing is one way that is often used, especially when allowing the breath to be natural and calm.

Breathing with the Whole Body

Let the body relax in a prone position. With each breath in, imagine that the air spreads through the whole body, all the way down to the toes. With each breath out, imagine that tensions flow out. Some may find it helpful to imagine that the air coming in is light colored and bright and the air going out is murky and dark. Allow muscles to relax and tensions to ease.

Dreaming

The mind is the pathway to deeper understanding. With mindfulness of experiencing, people often get in touch with what is needed. Next time anxiety arises, pay close attention to thoughts. Notice any tendency to internal conversations, perhaps in the imagination redundantly speaking to some person. Or again, perhaps you hear repeated reviewing of an avoided task. Become aware of any inner dialogue and listen! With mindful attention and an open, tolerant attitude, consider what actions are really needed. The anxiety may be indirectly trying to communicate something important.

Sometimes these understandings can be known directly, but more often the understanding comes indirectly, through the imagination, intuition, or a dream. Daoism uses dreams to help bring about a transformation. Being awake and being asleep are two sides of life, each of which serves an important purpose. In the West we have also thought that dreams hold the key to inner change. Psychoanalysis analyzes the symbols in dreams as reflections of the unconscious mind, resulting in deeper personal understanding. By experiencing a significant dream people are changed.

Sages used dreams to free themselves and those they advised to let go of limits in life by looking at things from a new perspective. Many teaching stories show the therapeutic use of dreams to help people transcend their everyday perspective and discover new possibilities.

A wealthy man treated his elderly servant very badly. He worked him so hard that the poor servant fell asleep each night, utterly exhausted. Yet, he was a happy man. A friend asked him how he could possibly be happy with such a hard life. The servant replied, "Every night I dream I am a king, ruling a large kingdom and living luxuriously in a beautiful palace. Since life is equally divided between waking and sleeping, why should I complain since half my life is perfect?"

Meanwhile, the wealthy man fell into a troubled sleep each night, worrying about his responsibilities. Every night he dreamed that he was a servant, suffering under the unmerciful demands of a cruel master. He slept so poorly that he eventually became ill. A friend advised him, "You have achieved much in your life, but your dreams seem to reflect the proper balance of your destiny." The man recognized the wisdom in these words. He lightened his servant's load and treated him with kindness. In time the wealthy man began to worry less, his dreams improved, and he became a much happier person.

One client who was working with anxiety had a dream about when she was a young child building sand castles on the beach. She also dreamed about building snowmen. During therapy she realized that she had lost her childhood ability to play and be happy. After she learned to allow herself to be more playful she found that her anxiety diminished.

MEDITATIVE USE OF DREAMS

Clients can be advised that just before it is time to go to sleep, they might like to place a paper and pencil by the bed or set up a recorder. Then they can invite a significant dream to take place during the night. While lying in bed, just before going to sleep, they should meditate using a method that they have found to be successful. The therapist can point out that the relaxation and calm of meditation is likely to naturally lead to falling asleep. When first awakening in the morning is the best time to record any dreams that are recalled, so encourage clients to either record the dream or write it down before getting out of bed. Clients will also find it helpful to bring the dream into therapy to discuss. Suggest that they might want to consider the dream as another side of everyday life, much like the story of the servant, and ask themselves, what is the dream trying to communicate?

Just Standing

Three friends went walking in the country. They happened to see a man standing on a hill. One of them said, "I guess he is standing on a hill to search for lost cattle."

"No," the second said, "I think he is trying to find a friend who has wandered off somewhere."

Whereas the third said, "No, he is simply enjoying the summer breeze."

As there was no definite conclusion, they went up the hill and asked him, "Are you searching for strayed cattle?"

"No," he replied.

"Are you looking for your friend?"

"No," he replied again.

"Are you enjoying the cool breeze?"

"No," he replied again.

"Then why are you standing on the hill?"

"I am just standing," was the answer.

(paraphrased from Yanagi, 1981, p. 123).

Often people who suffer from anxiety are out of touch. When they are doing one thing, they are thinking about what they will do later; and then later, they worry about what they did before. They live one step ahead or one step behind themselves. A gap develops between seeking and being. Anxiety rushes in to fill the gap. Gestalt therapist Fritz Perls thought of anxiety as tension between now and later (Perls, 1969). Meditation's quiet offers a way to reunite means and ends, to bring everything together again. In the unified moment, found by pausing, we reconnect. And in those moments, there is no anxiety.

"JUST STANDING" MEDITATION

Take a moment out of the day to pause and stand still. The arms can rest comfortably at the sides. In this moment, there is nothing else but two feet on the ground and an upright body. Allow a natural alignment with gravity where standing is effortless (review Chapter 4 exercises in standing). Don't think about anything: just stand. If thoughts race ahead or behind, bring them back gently to standing. Sense the quality of this experience and let it sink in. When possible, return to the just standing meditation.

This meditation can be performed in many ways, with different body positions such as just sitting, just walking, and also using varied meditation methods such as just breathing, or just chanting. Be open to other possible ways and turn to them often.

17

Overcoming Addictions and Impulse Problems

> When ignorance has been got rid of and knowledge has arisen, one does
> not grasp after sense-pleasures, speculative views, rites and customs, the
> theory of self.
>
> (Majjhima-nikdya I, 67, quoted in Conze, 1995, p. 75)

Addictions and impulse control problems are commonly treated in the therapist's office. There are a number of seemingly contradictory theories, with research to back up the claims. Each of the theories leads to different treatments. Whether the therapist believes the problem has its roots in cognitive beliefs, the physiology of the brain, or problematic behaviors, meditation has been shown to bring about changes at any and all of these levels. Thus, meditation can be a helpful tool for treatments, to be integrated into varied treatment approaches.

Definitions of Addiction

Addiction has been characterized as a compulsion to seek and take drugs, accompanied by loss of control in limiting intake, with corresponding feelings of depression, anxiety, and irritability when access to the drug is prevented. *The Diagnostic and Statistical Manual of Mental Disorders* (DSM-IV-TR, American Psychiatric Association, 2000) has two different sets of criteria: abuse and dependence. Abuse is voluntary and conscious, whereas dependence is pathological and unintended.

Three other factors are involved in understanding drug addiction: tolerance, sensitization, and withdrawal. Tolerance is the loss of the drug's effect with continued use. Building up a tolerance occurs sometimes, but not always. Sensitization is the increased response to a drug from repeated use. Withdrawal is observed when symptoms associated with chronic drug use occur if the drug intake is stopped (Koob & Le Moal, 2001).

Definitions of Impulse Disorders

Impulse control disorders share similar tendencies to addictions. Impulse control disorders are characterized by a repetitive behavior and impaired inhibition (Grant, 2008). People with impulse control problems have an urge to engage in a behavior with negative consequences, just as those with substance dependence do. They experience increasing tension unless the action is taken, and tend to repeat the process after a short time (hours, days, or weeks). The negative syndrome is strengthened by positive reinforcement at the early stages and later, negative reinforcement from the discomfort of stopping. These features are shared with addiction and have led some to propose that impulse control disorders are a form of behavioral addiction (Grant, 2008). Others believe that addictions are a form of compulsion (Koob, 2003). Thus, the therapist may find that similar methods, with appropriate adaptations, are helpful for both addictions and compulsive disorders.

Theories of Addiction

There are a number of theories about addiction, including brain theories, opponent-process theory, compulsive behavior theory, choice theory, natural drive theory, and Buddhist theory.

Brain Theories

The brain theories of addiction are based on the idea that a neurological modification occurs from drug use. These theories combine social/psychological and neurological factors involving reinforcement theory, opponent–process theory, brain reward pathways, and brain-stress pathways (Squire et al., 2003).

Proponents of these theories believe that dependency is not a matter of loose morals, bad choices, or ethnic background. Dependency is a brain chemistry disease. The shift from substance abuse to dependence is a direct result of a change in hard-wiring of the brain (Erickson, 2007). The disease is treatable, and so people who suffer from addictions and impulse disorders should seek treatment (Koob & Moyers, 1998).

HOW DRUGS AFFECT THE BRAIN

Drug dependence begins with positive reinforcement from the pleasure associated with using the substance. According to this theory, there is a brain reward pathway. It begins in the midbrain, projects to the forebrain, and then goes back to the midbrain. This pathway is responsible for driving the normal feelings of pleasure for behaviors that are necessary for survival such as eating, drinking, and sex. When the cortex receives and processes a rewarding sensory stimulus, such as a favorite food, it sends a signal activating a part of the midbrain known as the ventral tegmental area (VTA). The VTA then releases dopamine (DA) to the nucleus accumbens (NA), the septum, the amygdala (AMG), and the prefrontal cortex (PFC). The NA activates the motor functions while the PFC focuses the attention. The dopamine (DA) transmits the sensation of pleasure, the reward for eating the tasty food.

The endocrine and the autonomic nervous systems interact via the hypothalamus and the pituitary to modulate the reward pathway. There is a certain individual level of how much pleasure and vitality each person has, much like Jung's concept of libido and Daoism's idea of Qi. The body tends to self-regulate (Squire et al., 2003).

But when an addict abuses a drug, he or she expends all the pleasure at once. The drug inhibits the release of GABA, which is like taking the foot off the brake, thereby releasing more dopamine. Thus, the drug reward pathway is a complex combination involving the natural reward pathway but in a compromised way. The midbrain, forebrain, and neurotransmitter systems activate the positive sensation that results from taking the drug. The drug dramatically alters the action of the synapses, stimulating the reward pathway in a novel way that links the drug effect all the way down to the neurons.

Figure 17.1. Natural
reward pathway.

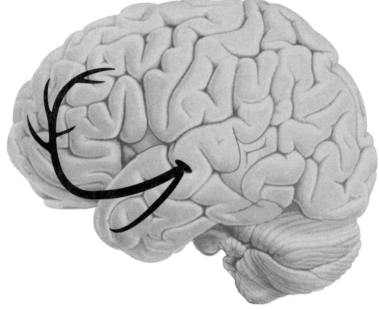

The brain adapts to the continued used of the drug with sensitization. The presence of the drug becomes part of the body's attempt to normalize toward homeostasis, which Koob calls allostasis: the process of obtaining stability through change (Koob & Le Moal, 2001). More quantities of the drug are required for a similar effect and tolerance builds (Squire et al., 2003). The problem with the allostatic balance is that it is a rigid, fixed system. There is no bending like the willow for the drug addict, no natural response to the everyday pleasures of life.

Withdrawal feelings that occur when the user has not used the drug for some time give an opposite experience that includes negative affect, anxiety, and strong physical discomfort. The marked and long-lasting change in dopamine (D) and serotonin (5-HT) levels is opposite to the effect when the drug is taken, leaving the addict feeling depleted. Anxiety and stress are common elements of dependence and withdrawal. The homeostatic balance has been altered by the challenge to body, mind, and brain. This alteration is highly stressful and activates a stress response, as was described in Chapter 15.

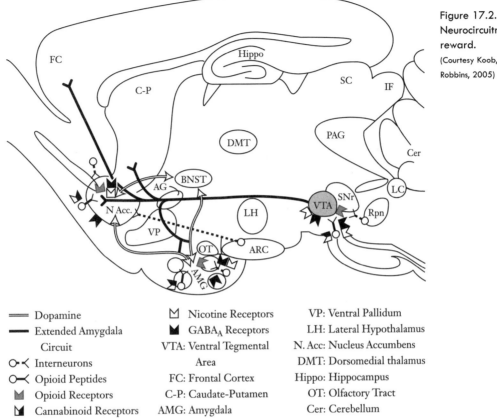

Figure 17.2.
Neurocircuitry of drug
reward.
(Courtesy Koob, Everitt, &
Robbins, 2005)

=== Dopamine

— Extended Amygdala
    Circuit

O—< Interneurons

O—< Opioid Peptides

⊌ Opioid Receptors

⊌ Cannabinoid Receptors

⊔ Nicotine Receptors

⊌ GABA$_A$ Receptors

VTA: Ventral Tegmental
    Area

FC: Frontal Cortex

C-P: Caudate-Putamen

AMG: Amygdala

VP: Ventral Pallidum

LH: Lateral Hypothalamus

N. Acc: Nucleus Accumbens

DMT: Dorsomedial thalamus

Hippo: Hippocampus

OT: Olfactory Tract

Cer: Cerebellum

OPPONENT-PROCESS THEORY

The opponent-process theory helps to explain why people continue to use the drug
even when it becomes unpleasant. Two processes are involved. First comes the pleasure
from using the drug (process A). Along with this pleasure comes a discomfort from
not using the drug (process B). Continued use of the drug leads to tolerance: Pleasure
from process A diminishes while discomfort from Process B increases. The decrease in
natural reward pathway neurotransmitters and increase in stress pathway neurotransmitters are responsible for the shift.

This neurological situation is expressed as avoidance of the discomfort from withdrawal. Addicts feel compelled to continue to indulge in drug use, even though they wish they could stop. But research has shown that avoidance does not relieve suffering; it just perpetuates it (Domjan, 1998; Solomon, 1980). In this way, the dependency cycle continues.

ADDICTION AS A FORM OF COMPULSIVE BEHAVIOR

Koob (2003) believes that drug addiction is both an impulse-control disorder involving tension or arousal preceding an impulsive act, and a compulsive disorder involving anxiety and stress preceding a compulsive repetitive behavior. The shift from pleasurable positive reinforcement to negative reinforcement pushes the user from an impulse difficulty to a compulsive problem. Koob delineates a spiraling distress and addiction cycle. First comes preoccupation and anticipation, followed by binge intoxication, and finally withdrawal with its negative affect. This cycle brings about a physiological change in the biochemistry of the reward pathway and the stress pathway. Localized in what is hypothesized as an extended amygdala, the changes lead away from a normal homeostatic balance to an allostatic one.

Choice Theory

> To deny people's regularly demonstrated ability to reduce or cease self-debilitating behaviors, no matter how powerfully embedded in their lives, is to minimize the opportunity and the fact of change in smoking, drinking, drug use and so on, even for those reckoned to be addicted by diagnostic tools. That people retain tremendous discretion in attacking addictions is critical for our public health and treatment efforts, which should both recognize and support—indeed, treatment should build on—such self-efficacy.
>
> (Peele, 2003, p. 11)

The choice theory states that addiction is not simply a disease or malfunction of the brain. The brain conception of addiction is felt to be mistaken because it characterizes addiction as a disease. Such a view has a serious consequence for

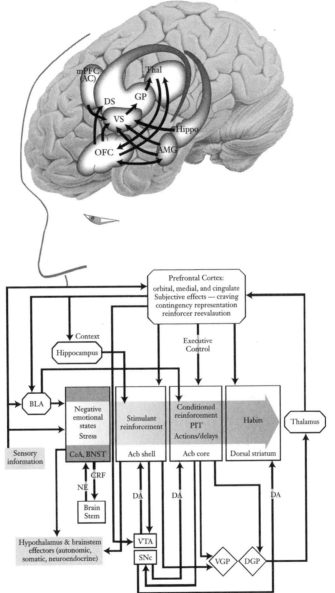

Figure 17.3. Key elements of the neurocircuitry of addiction.

(Courtesy of Koob, 2008)

treatment: It imposes a helpless, hopeless role upon the user. Recovery would seem unlikely (Peele, 2007).

But research indicates that a substantial percentage of people do succeed at recovering from substance dependency. And they often accomplish it with either minimal or no treatment. Recovery is possible. For example, a large National Institute on Alcohol Abuse and Alcoholism (NIAAA) study with 4,422 alcoholic dependent adults, found only one quarter of those satisfying the DSM-IV-TR criteria of alcohol dependent participants received treatment. Furthermore, 28% of treated alcoholics continued to be alcoholic as compared to 24% of those untreated. Although a higher percent of treated alcoholics (35%) were abstinent as compared to 12% of the untreated group, the study found that 64% of the untreated group could drink without dependence as opposed to 36% of the treated sample (Dawson et al., 2005).

These studies show that although some people are not successful in giving up addiction, many are. The power to regulate drug use lies in the deliberate efforts of the user. Change is possible, even under the most severe circumstances, such as brain changes and dependency. Better coping is imperative. When people learn to make healthy choices, they can regain control of themselves and their drug use. One of the primary concerns is to create a climate where addicts can reclaim their own capacities and abilities to overcome dependency naturally. Some of the most effective treatments, such as the 12-step programs, empower people to develop self-control.

Learning to handle substances such as alcohol without dependency is more important than just trying to bring about total abstinence. International comparative studies indicate that cultures such as Italy, with a more permissive conception of alcohol use as part of acceptable social rituals, have a lower incidence of alcohol abuse (Peele, 1987). According to this view, change in public opinion about responsible use of alcohol can help.

One study found that alcoholism relapse could be predicted based on two factors: when coping skills were lacking and when subjects believed in the disease model (Miller, Westerberg, Harris, & Tonigan, 1996). The two key elements for successful therapy are to teach people to take responsibility for their behavior and to reject the definition of substance dependence as a disease.

Natural Drive Theory

Andrew Weil's theory offers an alternative perspective, seeing addiction as a universal problem motivated by an innate drive to feel better. Weil believes experiences that people have when they take mind-altering substances do not really come from the substance itself. The enjoyment the user feels actually comes from within his or her body chemistry. The substance merely releases the elements in the individual's own nervous system. The experience of the substance action is the activation of the brain's own mechanisms.

Drugs and alcohol are an inadequate way to fulfill this natural drive. By relying on something external to do it for us, we cannot feel better; we alienate our own resources. Weil believes that everyone is addicted in one way or another, be it to drugs, exercise, or even to love. Addiction runs deep: to the very core of our existential being that must look to the self to answer such questions as: Who am I? What is the nature of the world? Trying to stop addiction runs contrary to human nature. Weil suggests positive things to be addicted to instead, such as a recovery program rather than alcohol (Weil, 2004).

Buddhist Theory

Buddhism takes another view: Addiction should be looked at more broadly as a universal problem that stands in the way of enlightened consciousness. Addiction as it is usually defined is the craving people feel when they seek after a certain substance. But this seeking for the substance is part of a far more pervasive general problem that is found in every area of life: the problem of craving in general, or more fundamentally, the problem of desire.

The real solution to addiction is to root out all pervasive desire at its source: the endless cycle of seeking pleasure and avoiding pain. This cycle relies on allowing anything to give us pleasure or pain. We give up our capacity to be in control of our own lives and instead put the power beyond our control. This will never lead to happiness, only to suffering, because all things, even the pleasurable ones, are impermanent. People can live free of addiction by first developing a middle way found in meditation.

Meditation develops skills with inner control, mental flexibility, and insightful wisdom. From the calm, meditative center a new kind of happiness develops.

With the direct experience of happiness in meditation comes a natural inclination to stop seeking transitory pleasure and to stop avoiding pain. Satisfaction is no longer sought outside of the calm, centered mind. Attunement, awareness, and harmony emerge naturally from the feelings of calm happiness. Then, there is no craving, no addiction. The exercises in this chapter will reveal the features of this meditational approach to living free of addiction.

Research on Meditation for Addictions

Meditation has been widely researched for addictions. Alexander, Robinson, and Rainforth (1994) performed a statistical meta-analysis of 198 independent treatment outcomes for tobacco, alcohol, and illicit drug use. This meta-analysis controlled for strength of study design and included both heavy and casual users. Results showed that meditation was as effective or more effective than either standard substance abuse treatments (including counseling, pharmacological treatments, relaxation training, and 12-step programs) or prevention programs (such as programs to counteract peer pressure and promote personal development). Additionally, the effects of conventional programs typically decreased sharply after three months, but the effects of meditation on total abstinence ranged from 50 to 89% over an 18- to 22-month follow-up.

Benson also did extensive studies of meditation for drug abuse and found it to be an effective treatment (Benson & Wallace, 1972). Relapse prevention was also investigated using mindfulness-based treatment. Preliminary data supported mindfulness meditation as viable a treatment for addictive behavior (Witkiewitz, Marlatt, & Walker, 2005). Transcendental meditation has also been studied and found to be helpful in rehabilitation from drug abuse (Marcus, 1974; Sykes, 1973).

Pain is often involved in addiction: either avoidance of pain or pain during withdrawal. Studies have shown that meditators tolerated pain better than nonmeditators. In one study, the meditators were able to tolerate pain twice as long as other groups after only two weeks of regular meditation (Wachholtz & Pargament, 2005).

Meditation has also been studied with compulsive gamblers. The researchers found mindfulness meditation to be helpful. Gamblers tend to be resistant to cognitive restructuring used in cognitive behavior therapy. The researchers theorized that meditation, which is nonjudgmental and accepting of all mental states, does not tend to challenge or restructure cognition. In this way, it can help people who have difficulty modifying their thinking (Toneatto, Vettese, & Nguyen, 2007).

Meditation's Approach to Addictions and Compulsions

Research indicates that cognitive and neurological components affect substance dependency and impulse problems. Meditation works directly with the cognitive level and key brain areas to help restore a more normal balance and better adjustment. But it does so in a different way from traditional therapies and without the potentially harmful side effects of pharmacological treatments.

Moderating Impulses: Beyond Pleasure and Pain

Users may think they are gaining great pleasure from indulging in their habit, but the pleasure is always transitory, leading to the pain of withdrawal, followed by another indulgence, and the pleasure and pain cycle continues. Rather than trying to extinguish a craving by not feeling discomfort or challenging the false cognitions, first address the issue of pleasure and pain itself.

Face Suffering to End Suffering

Mindfulness offers a way to face suffering, as an alternative to simply enduring it or changing the cognitions about it, as the next series of exercises reveal. In this way, mindfulness is an alternative to active control techniques that may inadvertently increase rumination. Mindfulness can be performed as its own treatment or in conjunction with other forms of treatment.

A combination of brief insight therapy, hypnosis, and meditation was used to help a man in his late 30s with alcoholism and cocaine abuse. When we first saw him for

treatment, he was part of an eight-week brief therapy research project we were doing. He said that his problem was motivation, but otherwise everything in his life was going well. Following the dynamic insight therapy from the research, he admitted that he had a bigger problem and now had the confidence to tackle it: a long-time cocaine and alcohol addiction. He told us that he and his wife shared many happy experiences using drugs together, and that she did not want to change. He didn't want to give up his closeness with her, but felt that the chemical use was hurting him physically and psychologically. Therefore, he hoped to give up cocaine entirely and become an occasional, social drinker, which he eventually succeeded in doing.

He learned mindfulness and applied it in many settings to become aware of what he really felt. He and his friends typically played golf and drank heavily. He decided to try playing golf without drinking and instead to turn his attention mindfully to his experience. His strokes became accurate, and he played well. Meanwhile, his friends who were drinking as usual played poorly. He realized that he didn't need to drink to enjoy their company and was quite surprised to discover how much he liked playing golf! He also discovered that he didn't want to spoil his enjoyment by drinking while he played. By being mindful in all sorts of settings, he found that he could give up the chemical use and be just as happy.

Building Skills: Mindfulness

The first step is to simply observe, without judgment or change, when feeling comfortable and relaxed. Practice is easier when tensions are lower. Then as the skills develop, mindfulness becomes a resource that can be called upon when needed. Begin to develop mindfulness skills by focusing attention during the therapy session. Be mindful of sensations, feelings, thoughts, and objects of thoughts.

On a concrete level, keep simply noticing the momentary experience as it occurs. If an evaluation is added as to whether this experiencing is good or bad, liked or disliked, notice that too. As the ability to sustain mindfulness improves and some confidence is felt, apply it to the problem.

Building Skills: Practicing Nonattachment

The ability to be nonattached when needed is helpful for controlling addiction. Facing discomfort free of disliking it gives the opportunity to gain control.

Nonattachment can be practiced, at first on small likes and dislikes such as eating a food that you feel neutral about. When chewing, pay close attention to the taste, texture, and aroma. Note the qualities of the taste, without like or dislike. Simply be aware of the sensations and accept them as they are. Repeat the experiment with a slightly disliked food. Accept the taste, texture, and aroma and be sure to notice each element. Do the same experiment with a favorite food. The development of an accepting but disengaged attitude takes practice.

Extend the range of objects for this meditation to bring about a less strong reaction to pleasure or discomfort. A middle way of personal satisfaction develops which leads to a more accommodating feeling about everyday preferences. Others may notice and appreciate the cooperative attitude to set in motion a supportive atmosphere.

Building Skills: Easing Tensions

Relaxing and calming may help in the practice of nonattachment. Developing calm will offer some relief if tensions arise, as well as adding the confidence needed to stay with the process. Use a meditation for relaxation of body or mind. Shift between relaxing for a brief period and then returning to nonattachment.

Harm Reduction

As part of the process, therapists can help abusers to minimize the harm that comes from their addiction. The Buddha was a pragmatist, believing that it is best to start the change process from where people are. Thus, he often individualized his sermons for the audience he was addressing. With users, you may need to begin to intervene by helping them moderate by using less harmful practices such as participating in needle exchange programs, drinking smaller quantities, or drinking in a more controlled manner.

If the client is unwilling or feels incapable of stopping the harmful behavior, work on enhancing coping skills. Encourage regular meditation to help build confidence and mental flexibility. Just learning to meditate can give an experience of mastery. With experiences of mastery, the client builds confidence as a foundation for better choices in the future.

Mindful Disengagement from Craving

The next series of exercises offer the therapist some ways to present mindfulness meditation that works directly on the addiction or compulsion. These exercises can be used with clients, or clients can follow the instructions themselves. Therapists may want to individualize the instructions to fit the unique needs of each client.

When craving occurs, advise the client to sit down and focus attention on it. Notice the sensations with each passing moment. If you start to label them as negative, notice that. Keep returning to the fullness of the experience without being drawn away from the moment-to-moment experiencing. Let the breathing settle and the muscles relax while sitting quietly. Turn attention to breathing as well. While observing, allow any unnecessary tensions to ease. If the thoughts move away from the moment, gently bring them back. Continue to breathe as comfortably as possible while observing. Usually the craving feeling will alter in various ways. Notice the changes as they occur. After a time, the sensations may even ease down or diminish.

Differentiating the Features of Cravings

Closely observing the general craving experience mindfully, you may notice that the craving is not just one overwhelming experience: it has various contributing parts. If this has not been noticed, try to distinguish the parts. Differentiate the ongoing sensations. Are sensations felt in one part of the body as well as in another? What is the quality of breathing? Are breaths long or short? Are there emotions occurring right now? If so, notice what they are. Refine the quality of each feeling, such as, "Now I feel sadness and I also feel fatigue." And what are the types of thoughts? Maintain that meditative awareness, calm and steady.

Extend mindfulness into other settings. Notice the places where the craving is stimulated, people who are associated with it, and personal behaviors and thoughts that accompany it. This will require stopping to observe mindfully at many times through the day and evening. Then, when some of these parts have been distinguished, how might they be interconnected in the momentary experiencing? For example, do thoughts turn to another person and then the craving increases? Or perhaps a memory of a place where drugs were used occurs and then a craving feeling follows. Notice any cues that might signal and elicit the response.

Maintain Nonattachment

Use the skills developed from practicing nonattachment in the earlier exercise with feelings of pleasure and pain that might emerge. Remember, "craving" is only a sensation, not really who you are. Pleasure and pain are transitory, so seek the middle way between, and become calm and centered in meditation.

Choosing Renunciation

As skills in awareness and detachment develop, clients gain more insight into what they are doing and how the involvement in the substance or impulse is actually affecting life in adverse ways. They may begin to feel motivated to give up the harmful substance or behavior that is having a destructive effect. It is helpful to be supportive of the client's capacity to choose. The dependency may seem entrenched. But from the meditational perspective, it is created by the mind–body interaction and because it has been created, it can be dismantled. Meditation may help restore homeostatic balance.

Caution: When withdrawing from substance abuse, the client usually requires medical care to monitor the process. The therapist can offer guidance, in choosing a hospital or medical facility that will ensure a safe and healthy withdrawal.

When ready to take the steps, the client should forgo taking the substance or indulging in the behavior. Prompt the client to notice the tensions and other feelings mindfully. Mindfulness and nonattachment help the client to face the discomfort and accept it is as it occurs, then calm down anyway. Then the client can follow these instructions:

Whatever you have been before, might be tomorrow, or are even feeling right now can all be part of the mindful moment, filled with empty potential. Notice any doubts or worries, but don't let them distract from what is occurring in this moment now. For example, if thinking a thought such as, "I might not ever get over this problem," or "I've always had troubles," consider it just part of the flow in this moment when fully aware. Such thoughts are accepted as part of the mindful flow.

Revising the Sense of Self

The personal self, as usually construed, is an illusion according to Buddhist theory. This idea can be helpful to those who are trying to overcome compulsions and cravings. Often the sense of self is distorted and this distortion may interfere with therapeutic progress. Meditation can bring a grasp of a more unbiased and flexible sense of self. The enduring, fixed self is experienced in meditation as a flow that evolves and changes. To understand this idea, look at a picture of yourself taken when you were a very young child and then view a recent picture of yourself. Of course, there is the core human being who endures through the years, but the two pictures are very different. The self is like a series of snapshots, changing day-by-day, moment-by-moment. Trying to make a fixed identity out of the self is like trying to capture a whole lifespan in a single photograph. Stay in tune with the ongoing development of yourself and you are more in touch with your dynamic nature.

Meditation on Impermanence

Begin with a familiar mindful meditation on breathing to notice how each breath is new, a different breath. Sense how the surrounding circumstances change with each passing moment. Perhaps there is a breeze now, and then it stops. Or maybe there is a sound of a passing car, then silence. Gradually shift the focus of meditation to include the sense of yourself right now. Notice how you might be thinking about yourself in this moment while sitting on this seat now. Pay close attention to whatever is noticed. Perform this meditation again at a later time or on a different day. You might have new thoughts or feelings about yourself. Become aware of all the ways that each moment is a unique combination of thoughts, feelings, and sensations, including the personal sense of self.

Meditation on The Larger Self

No one is the center of the universe. Yet, everyone is the center, intimately enmeshed in the world, not different from it. The center is everywhere and nowhere. So, caring about the personal self must involve a larger perspective.

Contemplate these ideas as a koan. Alternatively, adapt the mandala and mantra meditations. For example, look at a mandala that represents the life cycle, and expand from the personal situation being faced right now, out toward the future. Stepping into the mandala opens the way for a different experience of oneself, immersed in a larger context. Boundaries can broaden to include others, opening new perspectives from which to make better choices.

Nurturing the Positive

The brain, with its quality of plasticity, can readjust back to a healthy balance. Beneficial motivations are part of the whole but are often overlooked as the addiction syndrome takes over conscious awareness. Addicts will usually claim that they began drug use in search for happiness, social acceptance, or fulfillment. There is nothing inherently harmful about wanting to be happy, accepted, or fulfilled, but using drugs to achieve such objectives prevents the development of constructive qualities. Impulsive behaviors can be viewed similarly: The wish to alleviate and live free of discomfort cannot develop properly because the behavior used to bring this about is such a daunting problem. Through mindful awareness, positive qualities that are potentially part of consciousness can be noticed and then developed and integrated into the lifestyle.

A 30-year-old male client came in for therapy for help giving up methamphetamine. He was a long-time user. He decided to seek treatment after hearing from his doctor that he had the heart of a 70-year-old man. "Whatever you are doing, stop it, because it's going to kill you soon," his doctor advised him. The client did not want to die. But on the other hand, he found that methamphetamine helped him to accomplish things. He worked as a waiter and enjoyed being able to move quickly and serve his customers well. He felt that the drug helped him do more, to be cheerful, and to be funny. People liked him when he was on the drug.

We helped him to notice the positive motivations that were also part of his daily experiencing. He wanted to do his job well, to be happy, and to relate to people with warmth and humor. Using meditation, he gained skills in focusing his attention when needed. He learned to relax his body so that he could move smoothly and uninhibitedly, as he did on the stimulants. In noticing these qualities, he became more comfortable with himself and could allow his natural personality to be expressed. He practiced holding his positive motivations in mindful awareness while also being aware that methamphetamine was really hurting him. With the help of this dual awareness, he found himself feeling more inclined to find better ways to be these positive qualities without the drug. Without the deleterious effects on his body and mind, he began to feel better when he was not using the drug. Incorporating regular meditation along with the care of his family doctor, he did give up the methamphetamine. Eventually, the condition of his heart also improved.

In Tune with Life

Shadows grow longer
On life's battlefield
Yet still we stand

(C. Alexander Simpkins)

The life of dependency or impulsive behavior is a constant struggle. The drug use or the impulsive behavior is foremost in mind, taking up a great deal of time and effort. Attention is turned away from real engagement in the world. The problem interferes with awake, aware response. As the addiction or impulse begins to recede, the client becomes interested in turning attention back toward the world. This is an important step for a happy, fulfilled lifestyle without relapse.

A part of the recovery process involves detachment, but contrary to how it may seem, detachment does not mean insensitivity. The other side of mindful detachment is sensitivity, which can be developed to help the client reclaim involvement and engagement.

The samurai of feudal Japan were known for their ability to be detached, even in the face of battle. But they were also extremely sensitive: "The bravest are the tenderest, the loving are the daring" (Nitobe, 1973, p. 32). The samurai were expected to be fearless but also sensitive and wise at every moment. Passion and sensitivity were expressed often (even in the midst of battle) through songs and poetry. It was customary for a samurai to compose a poem under any circumstance. The farewell poem of the samurai Nyudo, spoken just before he died expresses this unique combination of qualities:

> Holding forth this sword,
> I cut vacuity in twain;
> In the midst of the great fire,
> A stream of refreshing breeze!
>
> (Nyudo, Quoted in Suzuki, 1973, p. 84)

For a full recovery, the client needs the strength of character to overcome the addiction or impulse problem while at the same time having the ability to be sensitive, even passionate. Haiku can be used to express such a seemingly incongruous combination of qualities: detachment and engagement. Because of its simplicity and directness, haiku arouses the deepest awareness of everyday life.

Composing Poetry

Writing poetry, especially haiku, can be helpful for regaining sensitivity and attunement. The nature of this form of poetry puts the writer into the center of the moment, which is expressed in very few words. So, even clients who may not be highly verbal can write haiku. Use the instructions from Chapter 13 and encourage clients to compose a poem in various circumstances.

Attuning with Meditation

Enhance sensitive engagement by getting the client to clear his or her mind at this phase of treatment. This practice allows time to be free of past suffering, just present and open to new possibilities. The quality of a clear mind leads to direct experiencing of the world. With regular practice, attunement in the moment grows.

Qi Gong for Balance

Often the recovering addict feels fatigue and discomfort. As some of the addiction theories hypothesize, the addict may be out of balance. Returning to natural homeostasis can be facilitated with Qi Gong exercises.

Raise Energy by Focus on Dandien

Stand with feet shoulder-width apart and palms resting on the lower abdomen, dandien area. Focus all the attention there and visualize warming the dandien as in the warming the dandien exercise. Then as the area develops sensations, such as warmth or tingling, allow the sensations to spread outward as in the extending Qi exercise. Breathe comfortably as the sensations move outward with each breath out. Finally, visualize the circulating Qi by performing the small circulation meditation. Combining these exercises in a sequence as a regular practice may help to raise energy while encouraging a healthy balance to return.

Substitute One Action for Another

Sometimes people who get involved in drugs or have impulse problems feel their lives are worthless and so why shouldn't they indulge themselves in a harmful habit. They may become lost, not knowing what to do with their lives. But even the person who regards him- or herself as worthless can be devoted to helping someone else. By giving to another, a life previously regarded by the individual as being worthless takes on meaning. Devotion to others can be a surprising source for self-cure.

> It is almost impossible to exaggerate the value of an increase in social feeling. The mind improves, for intelligence is a communal function. The feeling of worth and value is heightened, giving courage and an optimistic view. The individual feels at home in life and feels his existence to be worthwhile. . . . All failures . . . are failures because they are lacking in social interest.
>
> (Adler & Deutsch, 1959, p. 42)

Encourage clients to try helping someone else, get involved in a benevolent project or volunteer work. People often find the positive effects of compassionate action transformational.

18

Loving Relationships: Couples and Families

I think that empathy is important not only as a means of enhancing compassion, but I think that generally speaking, when dealing with others on any level, if you're having some difficulties, it's extremely helpful to be able to try to put yourself in the other person's place and see how you would react to the situation.

(Dalai Lama & Cutler, 1998)

Relationships are one of the central concerns of treatment. Half of all people who undergo therapy for varied reasons report having problems with their primary relationship (Good & Beitman, 2000). There is no life without relationship. We are always in relationship, part of the whole. As Heidegger stated, "Being-in-the-world is a structure which is primordially and constantly whole" (Heidegger, 1962, p. 225). So, living in harmonious relationships is at the heart of inner peace and happiness. Integrating meditational methods into the many tried and true Western approaches will offer new resources for positive shared experiences to facilitate the process.

Western Approaches

Psychotherapy has evolved effective methods for treating couples and families. Here is a brief overview of some of the currently popular therapeutic methods. If viewed with the open mind of a meditational perspective, these Western models take on new dimensions that can be helpful for guiding couples and families back to the happy, healthy relationships that are always potentially possible.

Analytically-Based Models

Several effective modern methods have evolved out of traditional psychoanalytic theory. Emotion-focused therapy (EFT) works with the attachments of interpersonal relationships. This view draws upon object relations theory and looks at how a primary past relationship such as that of parent and child, gets transferred to current relationships, having a powerful effect on all future relationships (Bowlby, 1988; Kernberg, 1976).

Contemporary EFT develops this idea, that loving contact is a fundamental need, hardwired into the human being and essential for survival. Love had previously been construed as impossible to define. Sue Johnson (2008), a contemporary proponent, argues that love can and must be understood. People handle life better and are happier and healthier when they can extend and receive love. Paradoxically, the more people can rely on a partner, the more independent they become. It is more important to develop a genuinely close and loving relationship than to just focus on resolving specific conflicts or arguments.

Attachment organization begins in infancy, forming brain function as people develop. Arousal, induced in the primary relationship of the family, stimulates the autonomic nervous system, forming a stable pattern of tendencies. This pattern of arousal generalizes, and can inappropriately influence later relationships such as couples and marriages. Since attachment has such potential to go awry, early Buddhist doctrine conceived of all attachment as negative. But modern Buddhist doctrine encourages embracing the positive by considering others as oneself. So, in this sense, if we hurt others, we hurt ourselves.

Insight-oriented marriage and family therapy is another analytically based approach. This theory works on resolving emotional conflicts that exist either within one or all of the people involved. This approach examines the problems comprehensively by addressing issues at many levels and from multiple perspectives. Individual, interpersonal, family, developmental interactions, expectancies, and irrational roles with maladaptive relationship rules are all considered. The process clarifies, uncovers, and works through theories, feelings, beliefs, and expectations coming from both conscious and unconscious levels (Snyder & Wills, 1989).

Similarly, meditation offers many ways to become aware of the cognitive-emotional experiences that evolve through life and disentangle from the negative ones while attending to the present relationship with a clear, mindful openness.

Active-Strategic Approaches

Treatment of families as a unit was not originally used in Western therapy. Early pioneers back in the 1950s and 1960s such as Don Jackson (Ray, 2005) and Jay Haley (Haley & Richeport-Haley, 2007) boldly stepped away from the psychoanalytic climate of the time to focus on interpersonal relationships and family systems instead. From the Eastern perspective, the oneness should not be ignored. Thus, looking at the person as part of a larger unity will be helpful for understanding the deeper nature of the problem.

Once the concept of family-centered treatment took hold, a number of theories for working interpersonally emerged. Analyzing families as a system allowed for importing dynamics from fields like engineering. Homeostasis of the system and positive and negative feedback were analyzed. Communications, not inner dynamics, became the means for how the system maintained itself. Couples and families form a system with its own dynamics and rules. Symptoms are the expression of a conflict of rules. Sometimes the symptoms are metaphors, trying to communicate something to the family system. People can be empowered to make changes by the therapist's skillful directives, given directly or indirectly. Strategic forms of family therapy emerged that construed problems within the family context, with solutions that required the whole family to work together toward a solution. This approach resembles finding balance through patterns, a mandala, revealing other qualities that may be missed from a more linear perspective.

Milton H. Erickson's hypnotic methods help families and couples rediscover their natural capacities to relate normally and well. Erickson believed that people go through normal developmental cycles, but that they develop conscious limits that get in the way. In hypnosis, people respond directly from the unconscious, and can thereby learn to activate the motivations and behaviors that lead to a healthier adjustment (Rossi, Erickson-Klein, & Rossi, 2006; Simpkins & Simpkins, 2001b).

Behavioral and cognitive-behavioral therapies evolved to help couples and families to gain relationship skills that will improve communications and problem-solving abilities. Therapists intervene to help address problematic behavior patterns. Cognitive-behavioral approaches add cognitive interventions such as through uncovering destructive thought patterns (Jacobson & Margolin, 1979). These cognitive and behavioral approaches are integrated into many of the strategic therapy methods.

Narrative Approaches

Narrative therapy offers a different approach to relationship therapy. Based in a postmodern perspective, many conventional assumptions are questioned. The postmodern view has been compared to Buddhist philosophy (Huntington, 1989) in which no position concerning the ultimate truth or validity of a theory is taken, and so any position can be used therapeutically with equal justification. For example, the definition of what a healthy couple is can be viewed broadly. Typical couples therapy methods such as improving communications to resolve problems are rejected. And the humanistic assumption that the therapist's role should to guide people to relate authentically is also denied. Michael White, one of the founders of this school of therapy, believed that the postmodern view opens potentials for greater success in relationship therapy. According to White, we don't have a fixed inner nature to be discovered. Rather, we are continually constructing new identities for ourselves and for our relationships. White believed that "all expressions of life are units of meaning and experience" (White, 2004 p. 49). The role of the therapist is to help people create more positive, workable meanings and identities.

Meditative Approaches to Relationships

We cannot avoid being in relationship to others and to the world. Each relationship interacts in some way with other relationships, so that each is reflected in and reflects others. The important issue is the quality of the relationship. By the time couples and families come into the office, their relationship has become quite unhappy and disturbed. Their natural interconnections are under attack or being denied. Therapy can help people rediscover the best qualities of their relationship, removing the obstacles. Then the best qualities of relationship can unfold as they will.

Freud believed that conflict was fundamental to human nature. When the situation offers a manageable dilemma, conflict is not bad. From the meditational perspective, conflict can be turned into a positive. When approached with an open inclusive attitude, a negative situation may be seen in a new way. The Dalai Lama has often said that we can learn from every situation, even the conflicted, difficult ones (Simpkins & Simpkins, 2001a). Clients can discover another way to incorporate both sides of the conflict in a new synthesis, not just a choice between alternatives. The conflict can be a source of a new perspective that is the product of the synthesis. As a result, the new perspective can be unique and original.

We learn and grow from discovering our limitations and deficiencies in coping with the world, not just our strengths. Through the process of conflict resolution, helpful strengths and mental skills develop. By practicing awareness, a harmonious balance with the greater whole can be found. "Meditation is not an escape from the world; it is not an isolating, self-enclosing activity, but rather the comprehension of the world and its ways" (Krishnamurti 1970, p. 9).

Neuroscience of the Interpersonal: Mirror Neurons

The recent neuroscience discovery of mirror neurons may explain how the feelings of empathy and rapport that we have for others are part of our anatomy. As therapists, we develop empathy and rapport with clients, feeling along with them. Through this process, we offer new perspectives and possibilities.

Mirror neurons are a neural system that allows for direct understanding of actions and emotions of others by stimulating the brain areas typically involved in performing such actions. This theory posits that the activation happens directly on the motor movement level, without higher-order conceptual processing. These neurons could be the neural correlate for empathy.

The discovery first came as a result of research in another area. Researchers in Parma, Italy (Gallese, Fadiga, Fogassi, & Rizzolatti, 1996) had an ongoing study of monkeys to monitor the planning and carrying out of movements. They implanted electrodes into the motor area of a monkey's brain. Whenever the monkey reached for, grasped, and moved an object, certain cells in the region of the ventral premotor cortex (F5) would fire, setting off an alarm sound to alert the experimenter. Returning from lunch holding an ice cream cone, a graduate student entered the lab where the monkey sat quietly waiting. As the student raised the cone to take a lick, the monkey's alarm monitor went off. The monkey had the same neuronal response from watching this movement as he had when doing such a movement. This began a barrage of studies on what has now become known as the mirror system. Rizolotti and his lab also found other mirror neuron systems in areas for vision, sound, and touch (Gallese, Keysers, & Rizzolatti, 2004).

Humans have a more sophisticated mirror neuron system than monkeys. The mirror neuron cells map three things: movement, watching movement, and imagining movement. The main difference in brain response between watching an action and actually doing it seems to be in the pattern of how the cells fire, not which cells fire. When people observe the actions done by others, a complex network is formed that makes up the core of the human mirror neuron system. The areas involved are the parietal and premotor areas that are also activated when performing similar actions.

Even though single neurons cannot be measured in humans as they are with monkeys, many studies have measured the mirror neuron system in humans indirectly using EEG and neural imaging technologies. One way that mirror neurons have been researched is by observing mu rhythms. The mu rhythms may be EEG indices for mirror neurons (Pineda, Allison, & Vankov, 2000). Mu rhythms are an 8 to 13 Hz window of activity, recorded by EEG primarily anterior to the central sulcus. If a motion is performed, viewed, or imagined, the mu rhythms collapse. As soon as the input is stopped, the mu rhythms resume their patterned 8 to 13 Hz firing. Mu rhythms have been shown to be present in all adults. A concrete application of the empathic use of these neurons has been tested using neurofeedback of the mu rhythms. Subjects learn to move a cursor on a computer by imagining the movement. In one study, the learning took place even more quickly when subjects had a high level of active engagement (Pineda, Silverman, Vankov, & Hestenes, 2003).

Emotions also have a mirror neuron mechanism. The basal ganglia, insula, and anterior cingulated cortex (ACC) are activated when we feel disgust. These regions are also activated when viewing disgusted facial expressions. These neural systems create a bridge of emotional empathy between one person and another. Thus, we can literally feel for and with others through our brain activations.

Further research has revealed other properties of the mirror system. Humans respond, not only to seeing action as targeted movements, but also to implications of action such as non-targeted gestures and intentions of actions (Iacoboni et al., 2005).

A mirror system may also be involved in pain. Singer et al. (2004) found that the anterior insula and ACC involved when experiencing pain are also activated in empathy for pain, similar to the areas activated by disgust. From this study it seemed that empathy for pain may involve affective, but not sensory components. But another study (Singer & Frith, 2005) found that the mental attitude seemed to affect whether the sensory component was involved or not. More research is bringing further refinements of these and other interesting areas.

Mirror neuron theory offers the possibility that empathy is a bottom-up process. Since the capacity for empathy may be hard-wired, it makes sense to use bottom-up methods from meditation to access it.

Research on Meditation with Relationships

Researchers have found that feelings of empathy are associated with more meaningful relationships (Kerem, Fishman, & Josselson, 2001). Recent research has revealed that meditation may increase empathy and benevolence so meditation may be helpful for relationship therapy.

Researchers hypothesized that the concern for others that is cultivated during meditation practice would enhance emotional processing. In this study using fMRI they measured how experienced and novice meditators would respond to sounds that typically provoke an empathic response such as the sound of a laughing baby and a woman calling out in distress. The subjects also heard neutral sounds of background noise at a restaurant. In the areas that have been linked to empathy, the insula and cingulate cortices of the limbic region, both groups showed greater brain activation during meditation than when not meditating. During meditation, the activation in the insula was higher in experts when negative sounds were presented than when positive sounds were presented. These subjects also reported a deepening of their meditation when they heard the negative sounds. This study also made comparisons between meditation and rest states between experts and novices. Here they found increased activation in the empathic centers of the brain to all sounds. These findings suggest that expert meditators are more capable of detecting emotional sounds than novices and that activation is higher while meditating than not (Lutz, Brefczynski-Lewis, Johnstone, & Davidson, 2008).

The scope of research on meditation is enlarging to include interpersonal relationships. A study of a mindfulness-based Kriya meditation technique for couples therapy enhancement found that meditation favorably affected couples' satisfaction in their relationship, autonomy, relatedness, closeness, acceptance of one another, and relationship distress. Following treatment, the couples felt more optimism, spirituality, relaxation, and less psychological distress. They maintained the benefits after a three-month follow-up (Carson, Carson, Gil, & Baucom, 2004). Shannahoff-Khalsa has performed Yoga meditation for couples therapy. The intent of these techniques is to "help heal and bring a greater depth, dimension and growth to a committed relationship" (Shannahoff-Khalsa, 2006, p. 294).

Opening the Session

Since relationships to the world and others are so well integrated into our physical and emotional nature, facilitating better interpersonal interactions will inevitably lead to happier, healthier living. Meditational approaches can be used at every phase of treatment, beginning with the very first session.

Often, a family enters the office brimming with intense hostility. The atmosphere can be so tense that people feel unable to address the issues. Diffusing the situation may allow everyone to working on the problems more easily. This legendary martial arts story suggests possibilities to break through the tension and elicit a more congenial atmosphere.

A wise Okinawan martial arts master taught his students that karate was to smile in any situation. The students left the class mystified. What did the instructor mean? On his way home one of the students came upon a group of American servicemen who were drunk and looking for a fight. They saw the student and started slinging derogatory insults at him. The annoyed student immediately felt like teaching them a lesson. Eager to show off his fighting skills, he rolled up his sleeves to get ready. But just as the student was about to attack, the instructor appeared. He strode over to the servicemen with a warm smile and a friendly hand extended as he said, "Hello! Welcome to Okinawa!" He offered his hand to each of the surprised Americans who couldn't help but shake his hand and return the smile. Within a few minutes, they were all laughing and talking together. The instructor invited the servicemen out to dinner and they soon became friends. When the servicemen learned that the instructor taught martial arts, some wanted to study with him. Now the student understood the master's lesson.

Where is the Conflict?

The conflict of longing and loathing
This is the disease of the mind.

(Blyth, 1960, p. 59)

Many conflicts are illusions. Conflict resolves by recognizing that each choice is part of the whole. Thus, the choices we make, the sides we take, are different aspects of the same thing. Zhuangzi called this idea, "three in the morning." What does this mean? A monkey trainer was giving out acorns. He told the monkeys, "I will give you three in the morning and four in the evening." The monkeys became angry. So the monkey trainer said, "Then you get four in the morning and three in the evening." The monkeys were delighted! (Paraphrased from Watson, 1968, p. 41). From a more mature perspective, differences often dissolve into unity. In the mysterious oneness of the universe, none is better, none is worse.

To learn how to let go of duality within, begin by recognizing the internal component of interpersonal problems. Often people are at odds with their own thoughts: the thinker vs. the thought, the ideal self vs. the real self, subject vs. object.

Meditation offers a way to dissolve the duality. Thinker and thought must become one: The thinker, at this moment of thinking, is part of everything and everyone. And everything is interrelated in this single moment, in an intimate communion. Then the next moment is created anew with its unique interrelationships. The temporary unity is truly there, to be sincerely experienced. The beautiful and famous Buddhist sutra, the Avatamsaka or Flower Garland Sutra, encourages contemplating this oneness with all things. The meditations that follow are a springboard to this deeply felt sense of embodiment in the moment.

INTERDEPENDENCE OF ALL THINGS

Fazang (643–712) was a Buddhist monk who taught the sutra's principle of interconnected oneness using the following demonstration. Imagine this demonstration as if it is being created now. Fazang arranged 10 mirrors, eight in an octagon, and one above and one below. He placed a statue of the Buddha in the middle as the focal point. Then he lit a candle to illumine the statue, producing an endless web of reflected light crisscrossed with an infinite series of images within images, each containing the entire Buddha. This demonstration was a dynamic presentation of the inexhaustible interconnectedness of the universe.

MEDITATIVE ONENESS AND CARING FOR THE ENVIRONMENT

Sit on a chair and quiet the thoughts for a few minutes. Then, sense the body position, wherever you are seated. Feel the sensations of sitting on the chair. Pay attention to the relationship with the seat. Note how you push down as the chair pushes back with an equal and opposite force to keep you supported. Let awareness range out further to the chair sitting on the floor, then out to the walls that are supported by the floor, and the structure that supports these walls, outward to the ground outside. Explore the interrelationship with the air, how each breath in and out interacts with the air in the room. This air, in turn is exchanged with the air outdoors and in other structures. Sense this interrelationship with the greater environment. Extend feelings of caring for the environment: Since the environment is not separate from the self, caring for the environment is caring for the self. Together, all are enhanced.

MEDITATIVE ONENESS AND COMPASSION FOR OTHERS

As the inner dualities are beginning to dissolve and resolve, oneness with others can be explored. The meditation above can be sensed interpersonally as well. Begin by sensing the body, breathing in and out, and sitting quietly. Then extend the awareness to those who are closest, such as family members, or house mates. Feel the presence of the others with feelings of love and compassion for them. Next, range out further to people in the neighborhood. Sense their being, and feel the connection to them. Search for feelings of compassion for others by caring about their concerns and their struggles. Intend good will and kindness toward them as in the natural instinct to care about a child in distress. Keep extending outward, with feelings of good will to the city, the state, the country, and the world. Become aware of the many ways of interdependence. There are other meditations in this book to help explore the inter-relationships with the greater whole. Experiment with different meditations to work on developing this skill further.

What a Thing Is and What It Is Not

We should not worry

About that which is not

Nor be too concerned about

What we have or have not got

Conflict's resolution

Is to awaken from illusion

(C. Alexander Simpkins)

Oneness is always there, but conflicts and problems often obscure the awareness of it. Sorting out difficulties requires a clear perception of the difference between what is and what is not there. Then the true nature of the problem is revealed. Sometimes the client is disturbed by his or her own perceptions, rather than an objective problem itself. The wise response is to discern whether the disturbance is what truly is, or is just what seems to be.

The yin-yang predicts that sometimes one can best understand what a thing is, by perceiving it in terms of what it is not. This paradoxical way of considering a situation allows for new possibilities, especially when people are stuck in redundant patterns. The figure (what a thing is) and background (what a thing is not) are both important in defining its perceived reality. Sometimes it is best to consider what it "*is*," to solve a conflict. Other times it is better to understand what it "*is not*," for conflict resolution, creating alternatives for meaningful constructs. Either not-knowing or knowing can be a beginning for truly knowing, which emerges from both. The meditation instructions that follow are possibilities to be presented to the client. Working together, therapist and client will have ideas that pertain more specifically to the situation, so please feel free to fill in with relevant details.

CONTEMPLATION ON WHAT IT IS AND WHAT IT IS NOT

Sit in meditation for several minutes, clearing the mind of all thoughts. Then think of the situation that is being worked on in therapy. Begin with the concept of the situation, of what it is. What is the complaint? Characterize it clearly with a description that depicts the complaint in factual terms, as a concept. Then, in a sense, put the concept of the complaint in brackets. Try to think about what it is not. If considering a relationship, what is the other person not doing? For example, perhaps he is not affectionate enough, or she is unwilling to disclose herself. After considering what the situation is not, reconsider what the other person is actually doing now. Returning to the examples, the unaffectionate man does not interfere and bother the other; the nondisclosing woman responds shyly with reserve. Although he does not do enough, perhaps he does help on weekends. Now consider whether the situation is based on what the other person is doing, or is it based on what the other is not doing. Be sincere. Is there an intention for a positive contribution to the relationship being made? Is the disturbance based on what is, or on what is not? Is the real disturbance because things are a certain way, or because of a wish that they would be different? After these issues are sorted out, the basis for better balance can be found.

The Roots of Conflict

> There must be an awareness which is not of thought. To be aware without condemnation or justification, of the activities of the self—just to be aware is sufficient.
>
> (Krishnamurti, 1968, p. 113)

To resolve conflict, it may be necessary to follow actions to their roots, to understand the source. Often conflict is viewed as simply a problem in conduct, requiring the strong arm of discipline—strict control of behavior is used to solve the problem. But this approach is only a superficial solution, temporary in its effects. What can be done instead? Therapists often look for the underlying roots of the conflict. These roots must be accepted and addressed, not just the outer surface manifestation. For example, when an adolescent misbehaves, the therapist will ask, what is she expressing? Is she getting attention by breaking the law? Much misconduct comes from a deeper source. What does he really want or need? What are his deeper concerns? Or in couples work, ask what is the real nature of this relationship? Was it originally based in love and commitment or was there another foundation? Therapists are trained to look beyond the obvious to the true nature of the problem. But meditation goes one step further, to thinking itself. The primary root of conflict is the thoughts beneath. By looking directly, without thought, awareness can be direct, preconceptual and intuitive.

MEDITATION WITHOUT THOUGHT

Clear the mind of thoughts. Then, with nothing in mind, observe the conflict. Come to it as if for the first time, with no preconceptions, no animosity. Just observe, with a clear awareness. Then a resolution can be revealed.

Flexible Action

Sometimes even after many attempts, the conflict does not get resolved. Somehow, one or the other cannot come to an acceptable agreement. When there seems to be no possible solution, all those involved may have become entangled in spirit. The water technique can help.

EARTH—WATER MEDITATION

Instead of continuing with the same approach, withdraw for a moment. Clear the mind of the difficulty as in the exercise above. Then, try to change the directional strategy of coping. For example, if strongly insisting on a straight-on encounter, what would a more circular approach be like? Consider how to implement a new alternative. Meditate by clearing the mind and breathing calmly. When the mood has altered, reengage the efforts, but from the new perspective. Better ways to resolve the conflict may emerge. Just stopping for a while opens the windows for the fresh air of possibility.

If no creative alternatives come to mind, withdraw from the frustrated efforts by meditating again. Then, instead of repeating the same thing without success, consider doing the opposite. For example, if seeking a solution by reasoning things out, try drawing on intuition instead. If passionately engaged, step back, calm down, and then try again using logic. If calm, cool logic is not helping, draw upon the emotions. If unable to advance, try retreating; if in retreat, try engaging. Then something new might be able to happen. Even if the opposite isn't completely correct, new associations will occur. Yin follows yang, yang follows yin, neutralizing imbalances, offering new potential for change.

Qi-sao for Change

The organism of man does not confront the world but is in the world.

(Watts, 1957, p. 70)

No one is separate from the world; everyone is always part of it, interacting. The world and others must be taken into account. Others matter, more than one may want to admit. Change is part of the dynamic flow of life. People need to learn how to allow it. The noncontending response is to conform to the demands of the problematic situation by staying with it, decisively flexible yet fluid, springy and yielding. But to do so requires sensitivity, which can be enhanced with this traditional martial arts training exercise, *Qi-sao*. It can be a metaphor for sensitively interacting with others. Through Qi-sao practice one develops a way of perceiving as if listening with the skin. Each senses the other in a new way. Partners often find that they can stay attuned without contending. This experience opens a new potential for harmonious interaction.

QI-SAO EXERCISE

This exercise can be performed by the therapist and client and then with the partners of a couple or two family members. Let one partner be the guide, and the other follow, sensitively. Stand a few feet apart, facing each other. The partner raises one

Figure 18.1. Qi-sao.

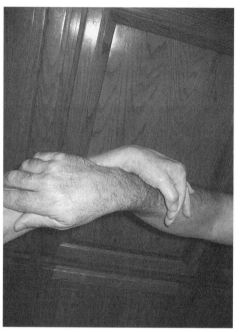

arm, bent at the elbow, extending the hand forward. Raise and place your hand lightly over the wrist of the other and close the eyes. The partner moves his or her semirelaxed arm around slowly, extending back and forth, up and down. Stay with the partner's hand, lightly moving in unison. Sense the force of movement without adding any force of your own. After several minutes, switch roles. You lead, and the partner follows. Repeat the exercise with the other hand as well. Both people should remain as relaxed as possible.

This exercise gives a definite experience of noncontending while staying in touch with what is happening. Following carefully, without changing the course of things, permits change to take place if it happens. This response does not require complete withdrawal or pulling back in retreat when obstructed or blocked. Stay with the flow of events and wait for the appropriate moment to respond, often when the opposing force has spent itself somewhat. Every force contains the seeds of its counterforce. When awareness has been correctly focused, the arms may feel tingling from the raised Qi energy in that area.

RELATIONSHIP QI-SAO

Sometimes people communicate unsuccessfully because they are so intent on winning the argument or persuading the other of their point of view that the victory is a costly one. They win the battle but lose the war. Apply Qi-sao as an alternative by attuning to the other person's communications, much like attuning to the other's movements in Qi-sao. Listen carefully to what the other person is saying. Stay with his or her logic, thoughts, and feelings. But also maintain self-awareness of feelings and thoughts without letting the other's perspective engulf you. Shift back to the other. Sense the other's point of view and infer the likely perceptions; as real to the other as yours are to you. Often when the other person is truly experienced, not just listened to, he or she will be more open as well. Communication can flow, back and forth in harmonious Qi-sao. Differences may resolve naturally, by working together to restore balance for both. Sometimes one, even both, must seem to lose, so that both may win.

Developing Love and Empathy

Empathy is one of the most delicate and powerful ways we have of using ourselves.

(Carl Rogers quoted in Simpkins & Simpkins, 2001b, p. 75)

Learn to engage in situations in ways that are more complex than either-or, or black and white. The whole is greater than the sum of its parts. So, to truly empathize with the other, and search benevolently for what is in common, the big issues lead to a wider perspective. That perspective includes both the other's point of view and yours, together as one. Find the dynamic balance point, beyond conflict. Together you will uncover the way out of conflict that leads to a deepening of love. As neuroscience has revealed, empathy is natural to the brain, so why not allow nature to take its course by enhancing this ability to care and feel the love for the other.

Empathy can have a powerfully positive effect and is an important quality for compassionate living in relationship. Psychologists learn how to become more empathic in order to help their clients. Use mindfulness skills to direct awareness toward the world. Increasing the empathic sensitivities makes it possible to develop compassion and extend caring, kindness, trust, and love towards others in ways that naturally reach beyond personal ego. Loving feelings can be fostered and nurtured in this way. Then a positive world of meaning can be shared. The next meditation script will help develop these feelings.

MINDFUL OBSERVATION

Use the skills from mindfulness exercises to foster understanding, empathy, and love for the significant other in an important relationship. Begin by noticing such things as how the other is dressed—the style, color of clothes. Observe how this person stands, sits, or walks. Try listening to voice tones, footsteps, the rhythms and patterns of sound. Imagine the world of experience of the other. Vividly recreate imaginatively what it would be like to be walking, sitting, talking as that person, with their concerns. Is it possible to feel a resonance with the emotions of the other in the mirror of the imaginative recreation? Allow this to occur. Understanding and compassion may follow.

Meditate Together

Sharing meditation can be an excellent way to break down barriers and build positive experiences together. We have often had families and couples take time each day to share in meditation for several minutes or longer. People find the experience interesting and enjoyable. It initiates shared time that is conflict free. It also forms a basis for better times together, something to look forward to, and a solid basis for a positive future.

Pick a meditation method for the family or couple to perform together. For those who have never meditated, use one of the early meditations such as, think of a color or attention to breathing. For more advanced meditators, use clearing the mind or mindful in the moment, or focus on a symbol or sound. Ask everyone to find a comfortable position, either on the couch, chairs, or floor. Sit together and invite the group to perform the meditation for several minutes. When finished, ask them to stretch a bit if they would like. People often smile and feel refreshed. Share what the color was or what the experience was like for each participant.

One way to follow shared meditation is to create a group Renga. See the instructions in Chapter 13. A good time to create a Renga is just after the family or couple has come to a positive moment of mutual meditative feeling or understanding. The Renga will help everyone to recognize the experience more fully.

If you use "homework" between sessions, assign regular meditation together during the week. If homework is not used, suggest that the couple/family make time during the week to meditate together, even if only for a short time. The effects are nonspecific and far-reaching.

GROUP THERAPY MEDITATION

For the therapist who holds group therapy, consider adding meditation into the sessions. Meditation as a group can be a source for strength and positive progress. The group carries a certain momentum, and people will enjoy sharing in the experience. We have often found that group meditation brings the members together in a unique manner. The quality of the group work will be enhanced. Utilize the different meditation methods in Part II to give people the opportunity to find the ways that work best, together.

19

Enlightened Therapy: Facilitating the Meditative Process

We weave the cloth
Of our every day
By what we do and give
The fabric of our destiny
Is made of how we live.

(C. Alexander Simpkins)

Clients may begin the therapeutic process by seeking release from suffering, but effective therapy, especially when it includes meditation, helps a broader perspective develop. Life-goals shift from an egocentric search for relief to a larger purpose. The work that is done to overcome difficulties can easily become the foundation for clear perception, wisdom, and insight, leading to happiness, not just for the individual self, but in a fulfilling life that includes compassionate caring for others.

Research on Meditation and Well-Being

Researchers have characterized the enlightened aspect of meditation as well-being. Studies of many different forms of meditation have found that the practice improves the quality of life. For example, Yoga studies have concluded that meditation can improve functioning in general on a number of measures, including better memory and productivity, reduced anxiety, improvements in hypertension and sleeplessness, as

Figure 19.1. Strolling in the valley by the stream. (Junbi Huang, Chinese, 1989–1991. Ink on paper, 1959. 52–1/4" x 26–3/4." Gift of Ambassador and Mrs. Everett F. Drumright, 1987: 126. San Diego Museum of Art.)

well as converting loneliness into solitude (Dhar, 2002). Mindfulness has also been shown to play a role in psychological well-being (Brown & Ryan, 2003). Kabat-Zinn (1993) has found that meditation is a way to apply the mind for well-being, finding many health benefits from mindfulness practice. Wallace, another experienced meditation researcher, believes that building bridges between psychology and Buddhism can help in the quest for mental balance and well-being (Wallace & Shapiro, 2006). These and many other studies are encouraging about the ability to influence one's level of happiness and health by engaging in regular meditation (Bonadonna, 2003).

Begin Therapy with Wholehearted Sincerity

Hold faithfulness and sincerity as first principles.
(*Confucian Analects* 1–8-2, quoted in Legge, 1971, p. 141)

Sincerity comes first. The therapist can begin by working with the client's ability to be open to the process even if the problems are complex or challenging. Sincerity means engaged involvement. Thus, the client can be encouraged to do more than care about therapy for one hour a week during the session and then never think about it the rest of the week. Meditative engagement in the therapeutic process involves quality attention during the week between sessions. And meditation methods offer tangible ways to do so.

Sincere engagement brings satisfactions that come with being fully immersed in the process, satisfactions that tend to generalize. Clients may find themselves participating wholeheartedly in other facets of life; whether in school, with friends, living as part of a family, or working at a job. Therapeutic change will continue to unfold in its ever-changing cycles. Then the Dao of therapy will inevitably have its effects on those who walk its path.

Meditation for Confidence

Clients sometimes prevent themselves from making a sincere effort because they believe that they cannot. Building confidence may be a needed first step. When regular meditation is practiced in each session, it facilitates a process that builds confidence.

Begin with quiet clearing of the mind, the focus on one thing such as breathing, or a comforting visualization. As the client begins to feel calmness and comfort develop, the therapist may help the client to notice the change. Often those who lack confidence do not notice their positive achievements, even the small ones. With regular practice of the skills, for example quieting thoughts, focusing attention, attending mindfully, and allowing the free flow of attention, the client can begin to experience mastery, and thereby gain confidence. Many also experience the moments of meditation as a calm resource within that can be relied upon when needed.

The Yin and Yang of Responsibility and Guilt

As has been discussed in many of the chapters, everyone lives as part of the greater whole. But recognizing harmony with the whole is a matter of choice. At any given moment one can choose to live in balance or not. Meditation trains us to become aware of the forces affecting the whole, which helps to clarify the best choices for the situation.

Rather than recognizing their abilities, clients often blame the outside world for preventing them from realizing their potential. They deny their part, and in so doing, lose touch with the whole. Rather than blaming the target for being hard to hit, the archer who misses the mark should look at his or her own technique. Then the archer can make the necessary corrections to help improve. Similarly, rather than blaming others, clients will be more successful with therapy when willing to view themselves as the source for making changes.

All people make mistakes, but having the humility to admit fault and correct the action may be painful. A heroin addict began therapy with the intention of giving up the habit. He had led his life on the edge. His father and uncle were both in jail, and he saw no better future for himself. He doubted his inner integrity and honor, from all that he had done and been. But we saw the great inner integrity and honor that he had, though he had not perceived it nor expressed it yet. Through meditation and hypnosis, he changed. He began to feel strong enough to withdraw completely from drugs and change his life. We recommended that he check into a hospital to withdraw safely. While on the ward of the drug treatment program, he encountered a fellow user from his past. They had gotten into a serious fight years ago and our client remembered carving his initials into the other man's stomach. The client felt tremendous guilt and sadness about what he had done. He faced his mistake, the suffering it brought, and apologized. In time, our client made a complete recovery. As his lifestyle changed, so did his circle of friends. Eventually he met a woman who had never been involved in drugs or crime. They fell in love and married and he became a respected and responsible administrator at a company. He even forgave his father. But in order to do so, he had to face that he made bad choices and had caused pain in himself and others. After tolerating the discomfort of feeling his own suffering, he could empathize with others' suffering as well, and then made better, wiser choices. Facing suffering is an essential step in the process.

To face what one has done, alone in the emptiness of being, takes inner strength and honesty. No one else can actually force this by discipline, nor provide correction. Meditation can be part of building the inner strength and spiritual discipline needed to face even the darkest past, experience the suffering, and change.

Redemption is part of meditation traditions. Some of the great ancient meditational leaders transformed from an evil life to a good one. One prime example was one of the greatest Buddhist kings of India, King Asoka (274–236 BC). Early in his kingship, he had been a cruel killer, maintaining his power with bloody violence. But a Buddhist monk helped him recognize a better way, and Asoka not only converted to Buddhism but also became one of the most benevolent and wise kings in India's history. His story is an inspiration, especially to people who have made serious mistakes in the past. Change is possible for anyone who sincerely faces him- or herself and decides to change. The therapist can guide the client to use meditational skills that help to face even the most traumatic and painful mistakes.

Tolerating Uncomfortable Feelings Meditatively

Sit quietly and allow the feeling to emerge. Stay aware of each moment's sensations, relax and accept the feeling. Gently keep focusing on simply noticing each moment, and let change come. Don't evaluate the experience. Simply feel the emotion as it is, trusting that a more positive feeling can emerge from the larger whole. When embraced in this way, the feeling may gradually become manageable, opening an opportunity to learn from the experience and transcend its meaning.

The Mindful Teacher Within

Each feeling and thought can be a guide to deeper understandings. As the Daoist master Zhuangzi explains:

> If a man follows the mind given him and makes it his teacher, then who can be without a teacher? Why must you comprehend the process of change and form your mind on that basis before you can have a teacher? Even an idiot has his teacher. But to fail to abide by this mind and still insist upon your rights and wrongs—this is like saying that you set off for Yueh today and got there yesterday.
>
> (Quoted in Watson, 1968, p. 39)

A feeling or attitude that may seem to be a problem is often an incomplete attempt to communicate something. If only one side of the unity is accepted, understanding becomes distorted or inaccurate. In Eastern medicine, problems are often a situation of too much yin or too much yang. With a more inclusive understanding, emotional disturbance finds its natural balance, and better choices can be made.

One client was troubled by nightmares of monsters chasing her. She disliked feeling certain emotions, especially anger. She tended to be quiet, somewhat shy, and pleasant. She worked on unblocking her energy and began to experience her feelings more fully. As she did so, she was encouraged to take a broader perspective that was accepting of all her emotions. She learned to trust herself and to be able to recognize how her emotions could help her know herself better. Eventually she became capable of expressing more of her feelings with others. Her boyfriend appreciated knowing what she felt, even if she sometimes expressed annoyance, and they worked out a better relationship. She could see that the monsters were exaggerations of her own blocked emotions, trying to find expression as part of a normal life. The frightening dreams stopped.

Sustaining awareness may be difficult at times of challenge, but when challenges are faced with awareness, the true nature of the situation can become clear. With the clarity gained, clients can take control of their destiny and make better choices.

Clients will often want to reject parts of themselves: "I hate the way I lose my temper," or "I wish I wasn't so impatient." Don't judge a feeling or thought too quickly. There is always more there than is immediately apparent. Follow the flow of what comes up, and then choose a more positive reaction in accord with the situation.

Use the focusing exercises to turn attention to the mind and emotions. Follow the Eightfold Path and mindfulness methods to explore what is noticed and felt. Use the instructions for working with emotional reactions. Individualize for the client's tendencies and reactions in relationship to the exercise, rather than imposing technique.

Embracing Emptiness

If you want to know who this one is, dive down into the depths of your being where no intellection is possible to reach; and when you know it you know that there is a place where neither birth nor death can touch.

(Zen monk Ta-hui [1089–1163] quoted in Suzuki, 1994, p. 7)

When clients have difficulties, their habitual avoidances lead to gaps in awareness and perception. By facing the gaps with trusting awareness, clear vision lights a new way, guiding through the darkness. Even if difficult or challenging, keep the focus on the gaps and trust that solutions will appear. In the emptiness, inner change can happen. Here the therapist can guide the process with support and pacing to fit the client's needs.

A point comes in therapy after the client becomes aware of his or her habitual patterned reactions. The old patterns begin to feel inadequate, incomplete, and no longer satisfying, empty of meaning. The client recognizes the emptiness, and there is no going back. But nothing new has emerged, and so there seems to be no going forward either. The client must enter the void, with its uncomfortable emptiness. As has been discussed, emptiness is not just negative, that something is missing and should be there. Nor is emptiness something to be feared. It is not a thing, and neither good nor bad. Emptiness is openness, the fertile ground for becoming. With realization of emptiness, change becomes possible. "The feared empty space is a fertile void. Exploring it is a turning point towards therapeutic change" (Van Dusen quoted in Stevens, 1975, p. 90). Eventually, new alternatives emerge. Meditation methods foster the transformation. Free from the fetters of the past, limited conceptions can be relinquished so new potentials can emerge.

Contemplation of the Empty Self

> Realization of egolessness is not something negative like losing one's self-identity, but rather is positive in that through this realization one overcomes one's ego-centredness and awakens to Reality.
>
> (Abe, 1985, p. 213)

In the emptiness, people sometimes feel and fear a loss of self. The familiar way of being is no longer comfortable. "Without my problems, who am I?" asked one of our clients who was at this critical point in treatment. Often, what is being felt is the loss of an ego-centered life. And even though it may have been inadequate and troubling, it is familiar, and in a way, there is comfort in the familiar. And so, a feeling of loss was there. A psychotic patient, who had reached this point and faced release, complained sadly to us, "Yesterday I was Jesus Christ. Today I'm nobody." But letting go of this false identity allowed for the discovery of a true one. Then he could go forward.

Centering Exercise: Empty Standing

Some people may find it easier to experience the empty center more concretely through physical balance. Specific instructions are given in Chapter 4, in the section

"Finding Balance and Attuning to Standing." Notice that exact center point, perfectly aligned with gravity, when the body is most at ease and comfortable. Stand quietly, allowing relaxation, empty of effort. The empty center is always there to be experienced from within. Seek the balance point.

Return to the center and work out a solution from there, no longer trapped by what has been, nor projecting limitations into the future. Try to stay in the center and let go of commitment to any particular perspective. From the foundation of the neutral center, a new adjustment can be built. Then change is possible.

Improving the Quality of Life

The Way of meditation is to go about everyday life, but with a difference. Every activity, every situation is an opportunity to live an enlightened life. "When you are concentrated on the quality of your being, you are prepared for the activity." (S. Suzuki, 1979, p. 105) Then the quality of awareness is the activity itself. And every activity is performed fully, immersed in the moment without conflict, just doing it. This quality of activity brings a profound integration between mind and action, in harmony with the world. Every aspect of existence can be lived in this way, lighting every corner of life. Any moment can bring enjoyment. Pleasure can be found in the smallest things. Feel the quiet breeze, hear a bird singing in a nearby tree, or see a cloud drift by in the sky. Even in the midst of the most difficult times, small miracles are also happening.

The Meditative Moment

Sit quietly, eyes half-open, half-closed. Mindful in the moment, relax the thoughts and allow the unconscious mind to flow. Don't think about anything in particular while relaxing very deeply. Feel oneness with the surroundings, part of the flow of life. Sense from within, without thought, in this moment, free and at peace. The winds of Qi are stirring. The currents are within. Stay centered in the meditative moment and find the enjoyment that is everywhere and always there.

Making the Needed Changes

The foolish believe that their own interests will suffer if they put the benefit of others first. They are wrong, however. Benevolence is all-encompassing, equally benefiting oneself and others.

(Zen Master Dogen, quoted in Yokoi, 1990, p. 62)

Therapeutic insight can bring a happy state, but insight alone is not enough: It is important to make real changes. Integrating change into everyday life begins deliberately at first, in small ways. Over time, the happiness one feels from living well and doing well becomes natural and instinctive.

Awareness applied appropriately can help develop better qualities. For example, when feeling impatient with someone, notice the feeling. Then address it by stepping back to quiet the breath and meditate for a few moments. More patience toward the other person may develop. Empathy may follow.

Begin with small challenges and keep mindful of the process. Working out a muscle makes it stronger. Similarly, exercising the Bodhisattva qualities will help them grow and develop. The brain changes as well. Regular meditation helps to persevere and stay committed.

INITIATING COMPASSIONATE AND BENEVOLENT ACTION

A healthy and happy adjustment often generalizes into a feeling for others as well. Compassion will grow when planted in the fertile soil of health. Compassion for others is an inherent trait in the healthy personality. East met West when Alfred Adler said, "Empathy and understanding are facts of social feeling, of harmony with the universe" (Adler & Deutschur, 1959, p. 43). And East and West continue to be unified as meditational therapy is practiced around the world!

References

Abe, M. (1985). *Zen and western thought.* Honolulu, University of Hawaii Press.

Abe, M. (1995). *Buddhism and interfaith dialogue.* Honolulu, University of Hawaii Press.

Abou Nader, T. M., Alexander, C. N., & Davies, J. L. (1990). The Maharishi technology of the unified field and reduction of armed conflict: A comparative longitudinal study of Lebanese villages. In R. A. Chalmers, C. Clements, H. Schenkluhn, & M. Weinless (Eds.), *Scientific research in the transcendental meditation and TM-Sidhi program: Collected papers* (Vol. 4). Vlodrop, Netherlands: Maharishi Vedic University Press.

Adler, K. A., & Deutsch, D. (Eds.). (1959). *Essays in individual psychology: Contemporary applications of Alfred Adler's theories.* New York: Grove Press.

Adolphs, R., Tranel, D., & Damasio, A. R. (1998). The human amygdala in social judgment. *Nature, 393*, 470–474.

Aftanas, L., & Golosheykn, S. (2005). Impact of regular meditation practice on EEG activity at rest and during evoked negative emotions. *International Journal of Neuroscience, 115*(6), 893–909.

Alexander, C. N., Rainforth, M., & Gelderloos, P. (1991). Transcendental meditation, self-actualization, and psychological health: A conceptual overview and statistical meta-analysis. *Journal of Social Behavior and Personality, 6*(5), 189–248.

Alexander, C. N., Robinson, P., & Rainforth, M. (1994). Treating and preventing alcohol, nicotine, and drug abuse through Transcendental Meditation: A review and statistical meta-analysis. *Alcoholism Treatment Quarterly, 11*(1–2), 13–87.

Alexander, C. N., Swanson, G. C., Rainforth, M. V., & Carlisle, T. W. (1993). Effects of the transcendental meditation program on stress reduction, health, and employee development: A prospective study in two occupational settings. *Stress and Coping International Journal, 6*, 245–262.

American Psychiatric Association. (2000). *Diagnostic and Statistical Manual of Mental Disorders* (4th ed. Rev.). Washington, DC: Author.

Anand, B. K., & Chhina, G. S. (1961). Investigations on yogis claiming to stop their heart beats. *Indian Journal of Medical Research, 49*, 90–94.

Anand, B. K., & Chhina, G. S. (1961b). Some aspects of EEG studies in yogis. *Electroencephalography and Clinical Neurophysiology, 13*, 452–456.

Antonuccio, D. O. Danton, W. G., & DeNelsky, G. Y. (1995). Psychotherapy versus medication for depression: Challenging the conventional wisdom with data. *Professional Psychology: Research and Practice, 26*(6), 574–585.

Arana, D. (2006). The practice of mindfulness meditation to alleviate the symptoms of chronic shyness and social anxiety. *Dissertation Abstracts International: Section B: The Sciences and Engineering,* 67(5-B), 2822.

Arnheim, R. (1966). *Toward a psychology of art: Collected essays.* Berkeley: University of California Press.

Badawi, K., Wallace, R. K, Orme-Johnson, D., & Rouzere, A. M. (1984). Electrophysiologic characteristics of reparatory suspension periods occurring during the practice of the transcendental meditation program. *Psychosomatic Medicine, 46*(3), 267–276.

Bard, A. P. (1928). The neuro-humoral basis of emotional reactions. In C. A. Munchison, (Ed.), Foundations of experimental psychology (449–487). Worcester, MA: Clark University Press.

Barlow, D. H., Chorpita, B. F., & Turovsky, J. (1996). Fear, panic, anxiety and disorders of emotion. In D. A. Hope (Ed.), *Nebraska symposium of motivation: Vol. 43. Perspectives on anxiety, panic, and fear* (pp. 251–328). Lincoln: University of Nebraska Press.

Batchelor, S. (1990). *The faith to doubt: Glimpses of buddhist uncertainty.* Berkeley, CA: Parallax Press.

Bechera, A., Tranel, D., Hanna, D., Adolphs, R., Rockland, C., & Damasio, A. R. (1995). Double dissociation of conditioning and declarative knowledge relative to the amygdala and hippocampus in humans. *Science, 269,* 1115–1118.

Behanan, K. (1937). *Yoga as scientific study.* New Haven, CT: Yale University Press.

Benson, H. (1975). *The relaxation response.* New York: William Morrow.

Benson, H. (1978). Treatment of anxiety: A comparison of the usefulness of self-hypnosis and a meditational relaxation technique: An overview. *Psychotherapy and Psychosomatics, 30,* 229–242.

Benson, H., Lehmann, J. W., Malhotra, M. S., Goldman, R. F., Hopkins, J., & Epstein, M. D. (1982). Body temperature changes during the practice of g Tum-mo yoga. *Nature, 295,* 234–236.

Benson, H., Malvea, B. P. & Graham, J. R. (1973). Physiologic correlates of meditation and their clinical effects in headache: An ongoing investigation. *Headache, 13,* 23–24.

Benson, H., Marzetta, B. R., & Klenchuck, H. M. (1974). Decreased blood pressure in borderline hypertensive subjects who practiced meditation. *Journal of Chronic Diseases, 7852,* 289–291.

Benson, H., & Wallace, R. (1972). Decreased drug abuse with transcendental meditation: A study of (1862) subjects. In C. J. Zarafonetis (Ed.), *Drug abuse: Proceedings of the International Conference.* Philadelphia: Lea & Febiger.

Bernard, C. (1957). *An introduction to the study of experimental medicine.* New York: Dover Publications. (Original work published 1865).

Bhatia, M., Kumar, A., Kumar, N., Pandey, R. M., & Kochupilla, V. 2003. Electrophysiologic evaluation of Sudarshan Kriya: An EEG, BAER and P300 study. *Indian Journal of Pharmacology 47,* 157–163.

Blofeld, J. (1994). *The Zen teaching of Huang-Po: On the transmission of mind.* Boston: Shambhala.

Blyth, R. H. (1960). *Zen and Zen classics* (Vol. 1). San Francisco: Hokuseido Press.

Boaz, F. (1911). *Handbook of Northern American Indians, Parts I & II.* Washington, DC: Smithsonian Publications.

Bokenkamp, S. R. (1999). *Early Daoist scriptures.* Berkeley, CA: University of California Press.

Bonadonna, R. (2003). Meditation's impact on chronic illness. *Holistic Nurse Practitioner, 17*(6), 309–319.

Bowen, M. (1978). *Family therapy in clinical practice.* New York: Aronson.

Bowen, S., Witkiewitz, K., Dillworth, T., Chawla, N., Simplson, T., Ostafin, B., et al. (2006). Mindfulness meditation and substance use in an incarcerated population. *Psychology of Addictive Behaviors, 20*(3), 342–347.

Bowlby, J. (1988). *A secure base: Parent-child attachment and healthy human development.* New York: Basic Books.

Brosse, T. (1946). A psychophysiological study. *Main Currents in Modern Thought, 4*, 77–84.

Brown, D., Forte, & Dysart, M. (1984a). Visual sensitivity and mindfulness meditation. *Perceptual and Motor Skills, 58*(3), 775–784.

Brown, D., Forte, M., & Dysart, M. (1984b). Differences in visual sensitivity among mindfulness meditators and non-meditators. *Perceptual and Motor Skills, 58*(3), 727–733.

Brown, K. W., & Ryan, R. M. (2003). The benefits of being present: Mindfulness and its role in psychological well-being. *Journal of Personality and Social Psychology. 84*(4), 822–848.

Brown, R. P., & Gerbarg, P. I. (2005). Sudarshan Kriya yogic breathing in the treatment of stress, anxiety, and depression: Part II-clinical applications and guidelines. *Journal of Alternative and Complementary Medicine, 11*(4), 711–717.

Buswell, R. E. (1991). *Tracing back the radiance: Chinul's Korean way of Zen.* Honolulu: University of Hawaii Press.

Cahn, R. B., & Polich, J. (2006). Meditation states and traits: EEG, ERP, and neuroimaging studies. *Psychological Bulletin, 132*(2), 180–211.

Cannon, W. B. (1927). The James–Lange theory of emotion: A critical examination and an alternative theory. *American Journal of Psychology, 39*, 10–24.

Cannon, W. B (1932). *The wisdom of the body.* New York: Norton.

Carson, J. W., Carson, K. M., Gil, K. M., & Bauccom, D. H. (2004). Mindfulness-based relationship enhancement. *Behavior Therapy, 35*(3), 471–494.

Chan, W. T. (1963). *A sourcebook in Chinese philosophy.* Princeton, NJ: Princeton University Press.

Churchland, P. M. (1988). *Matter and consciousness* (2nd ed.). Cambridge, MA: MIT Press.

Cleary, T. (1991). *Vitality, energy, spirit: A Taoist sourcebook.* Boston: Shambala.

Cleary, T. (Trans.). (2000a). *Taoism meditation: Methods for cultivating a healthy mind and body.* Boston: Shambhala.

Cleary, T. (Trans.). (2000b). *The Taoist classics: The collected translations of Thomas Cleary.* (Vol. 4). Boston: Shambhala.

Conze, E. (1995). *Buddhist texts through the ages.* Oxford: Oneworld.

Cook, V. J., & Newson, M. (2007). *Chomsky's universal grammar: An introduction* (3rd ed.) New York: Wiley-Blackwell.

Cranson, R. W, Orme-Johnson, D. W, Gackenbach, J, Dillbeck, M. C., Jones, CH and Alexander, C. N. (1991). Transcendental meditation and improved performance on intelligence-related measures: A longitudinal study. *Personality and Individual Differences, 12*(10), 1105–1116.

Creswell, D. J., Baldwin, M. W., Eisenberger, N. I., & Lieberman, M. D. (2007). Neural correlates of dispositional mindfulness during affect labeling. *Psychomatic Medicine, 69*, 560–565.

Dalai Lama, & Cutler, H. (1998). *The art of happiness.* New York: Riverhead.

Damasio, A. R. 1994. *Descartes's error.* New York: Putnam's.

Das, N., & Gastaut, H. (1955). Variations in the electrical activity of the brain, heart, and skeletal muscles during yogic meditation and trance. *Electroencephalography and Clinical Neurophysiology (Suppl., 6)*, 211–219.

Davidson, R., Goleman, D., & Schwartz, G. (1976). Attentional and affective concomitants of meditation: A cross-sectional study. *Journal of Abnormal Psychology, 85*, 235–308.

Davidson, R. J., Kabat-Zinn, J., Schumacher, J., Rosenkranz, M., Miller, D., Santorelli, S. F., et al. (2003). Alterations in brain and immune function produced by mindfulness meditation. *Psychosomatic Medicine, 65*, 564–570.

Davies, J. L., & Alexander, C. N. (1989). *Alleviating political violence through reduction of collective stress: Impact assessment analysis of the Lebanon war.* Paper presented at the annual meeting of the American Political Science Association, Atlanta.

Dawson, D. A., Grant, B. F., Stinson, F. S., Chou, P.S., Huang, B., & Ruan, W. J. (2005). Recovery from DSM-IV alcohol dependence, United States, 2001–2002. *Addiction, 100*, 281–292.

DeBerry, S. (1982). The effects of meditation-relaxation on anxiety and depression in a geriatric population. *Psychotherapy: Theory, Research, and Practice, 19*(4), 512–521.

Deikman, A. J. (1963). Experimental meditation, *Journal of Nervous and Mental Disease, 136*, 329–343.

Desikachar, T. K. V. (1995). *The heart of Yoga: Developing a personal practice.* Rochester, VT: Inner Traditions International.

de Silva, L. A. (1975). *The problem of self in Buddhism and Christianity.* London: Macmillan.

Deutsch, E. (Trans.) (1968). *The Bhagavad Gita.* New York: Holt, Rinehart & Winston.

Dhar H. L. (2002). Meditation, health, intelligence and performance. *Medicine update APICON, 202*, 1376–1379.

Dillbeck, M. C. (1980). Test of a field theory of consciousness and social change: Time series analysis of participation in the TM-Sidhi program and reduction of violent death in the U.S. *Social Indicators Research, 22*(4), 399–418.

Dillbeck, M. C. (1982). Meditation and flexibility of visual perception and verbal problem solving. *Memory & Cognition, 10*(3), 207–215.

Dillbeck, M. C., Assimakis, P. D., Raimondi, D., & Orme-Johnson, D. W. (1986). Longitudinal effects of the transcendental meditation and TM-Sidhi program on cognitive ability and cognitive style. *Perceptual and Motor Skills. 62*(3), 731–738.

Dillbeck, M. C., Cavanaugh, K. L., Glenn, T., Orme-Johnson, D. W., & Mittlefehldt, V. (1987). Consciousness as a field: The transcendental meditation and TM Sidhi program and changes in social indicators. *Journal of Mind and Behavior, 8*, 67–104.

Dillbeck, M. C., Orme-Johnson, D. W. (1987). Physiological differences between transcendental meditation and rest. *American Psychologist. 42*(9), 879–881.

Dohrenwend, B., & Dohrenwend, B., (1981). *Stressful life events and their concepts.* Brunswick, NJ: Rutgers University Press.

Domjan, M. (1998). *The principles of learning and behavior* (4th ed.). Pacific Grove, CA: Brooks/Cole.

Dube, S. N. (1980). *Cross currents in early Buddhism.* New Delhi, India: Monohar.

Dumoulin, H. (1988). *Zen Buddhism: A history: India and China.* New York: Macmillan.

Dumoulin, H. (1990). *Zen Buddhism: A history: Japan.* New York: Macmillan.

Durant, W. (1968). *The story of philosophy.* New York: Washington Square Press.

Duyvendak, J. J. L. (1992). *Tae te ching: The book of the way and its virtue.* Boston: Tuttle.

Dweck, C. S. (2006). *Mindset.* New York: Random House.

Elkin, I., Shea, M. T., Watkins, J. T., Imber, S. D., Sotsky, S. M., Collins, J. F., et al. (1989). National Institute Of Mental Health treatment of depression collaborative research program: General effectiveness of Treatments. *Archives of General Psychiatry, 46*(11), 971–982.

Elkins, G., Marcus, J., Rajab, H., & Durgam, S. (2005). Complementary and alternative therapy use by psychotherapy clients. *Psychotherapy: Theory, Research, Practice, Training., 42*(2), 232–235.

Erickson, C. K. (2007). *The science of addiction: From neurobiology to treatment.* New York: Norton.

Erickson, M. H. (1978, July). Workshop, Phoenix, Arizona.

Esch, T., & Stefano, G. B. (2005). Love promotes health. *Neuroendocrinology Letters, 26*(3), 264–267.

Evans-Wentz, W. Y. (1954). *The Tibetan book of the great liberation.* London: Oxford University Press.

Evans-Wentz, W. Y. (1960). *The Tibetan book of the dead.* London: Oxford University Press.

Evans-Wentz, W. Y. (1967). *Tibetan Yoga and secret doctrines.* London: Oxford University Press.

Fontein, J., & Hickman, M. L. (1970). *Zen painting and calligraphy.* Boston: Museum of Fine Arts.

Frank, J. D., & Frank, J. (1991). *Persuasion and healing.* Baltimore: Johns Hopkins University Press.

Frank, J. D., Hoehn-Saric, R., Imber, S., Liberman, B., & Stone, A. (1978). *Effective ingredients of successful psychotherapy.* New York: Brunner/Mazel.

Gallese, V., Fadiga, L., Fogassi, L., & Rizzolatti, G. (1996). Action recognition in the premotor cortex. *Brain, 119,* 593–609.

Gallese, V. Keysers, C., & Rizzolatti, G. (2004). A unifying view of the basis of social cognition. *Trends in Cognitive Sciences, 8*(9), 396–403.

Gasgoigne, S. (1997). *The Chinese way to health: A self-help guide to traditional Chinese medicine.* Boston: Tuttle.

Goleman, D. & Goleman, T. B. (2001). The emotionally intelligent workplace. In D. P. Goleman, C. Chermiss, & W. G., *The emotionally intelligent workplace: How to select for, measure, and improve emotional intelligence in individuals, groups, and organizations.* New York: Jossey-Bass, Inc.

Goleman J. & Schwartz, G. E. (1976). Meditation as an intervention in stress reactivity. *Journal of Consulting and Clinical Psychology, 44*(3), 456–466.

Good, G. E., & Beitman, B. D. (2000). *Counseling and psychotherapy essentials: Integrating theories, skills, and practices.* New York: Norton.

Govinda, L. A. (1960). *Foundations of Tibetan mysticism.* New York: Samuel Weiser.

Grant, J. E. (2008). *Impulse control disorders.* New York: Norton.

Green, E. E., Green, A. M., & Walters, E. D. (1970). Voluntary control of internal states: Psychological and physiological. *Journal of Transpersonal Psychology, 2*(1), 1–26.

Greenwald, H. (1975). *Direct decision therapy.* San Diego, CA: Edits.

Grepmair, L., Mitterlehner, F., Loew, T., Bachler, E., Rother, W., & Nickel, M. (2007). Promoting mindfulness in psychotherapists in training influences the treatment results of their patients: A randomized, double-blind, controlled study. *Psychotherapy and Psychosomatics, 76,* 332–338.

Grigg, R. (1995). *The new Lao Tzu: A contemporary tao te ching.* Boston: Tuttle.

Gyatso, (1995). *The world of Tibetan Buddhism: An overview of its philosophy and practice.* Boston: Wisdom.

Hagelin, J. S., Rainforth, M. V., Cavanaugh, K., Alexander, C. N. , Shatkin, S. F., Davies, J. L., et al. (1999). Effects of group practice of the transcendental meditation program on preventing violent crime in Washington, DC: Results of the national demonstration project, June–July *Social Indicators Research, 47*(2), 153–201.

Haley, J., & Richeport-Haley, M. (2007). *Directive family therapy.* New York: Haworth.

Hanh, T. N. (1992). *The diamond that cuts through illusion.* Berkeley, CA: Parallax.

Hankey, A. (2006). Studies of advanced stages of meditation in the Tibetan Buddhist and Vedic traditions. I: A comparison of general changes. *Evidence-based Complementary and Alternative Medicine, 3*(4), 513–521.

Haywood, J. W., & Francisco, J. V. (1992). *Gentle bridges: Conversations with the Dalai Lama on the sciences of mind.* Boston: Shambhala.

Heidegger, M. (1962), *Being and time.* San Francisco: Harper San Francisco.

Henderson, H. G. (1977). *Haiku in English.* Rutland, VT: Tuttle.

Herrigel, E. (1960). *Zen in the art of archery.* New York: Vintage.

Herrigel, E. (1971). *The method of Zen.* New York: Vintage Books.

Herrigel, G. (1958). *Zen in the art of flower arrangement.* London: Arkana.

Hinkle, L. E. (1973). The concept of stress in the biological and social sciences. *Science, Medicine, and Man, 1,* 31–48.

Holmes, S. W., & Horioka, C. (1973). *Zen art for meditation.* Rutland, VT: Tuttle.

Huntington, C. W. (1989). *The emptiness of emptiness: An introduction to early Indian madhyamika.* Honolulu: University of Hawaii Press.

Iacoboni, M. (2001). Cortical mechanisms of human imitation. *Science, 286,* 2526–2528.

Iacoboni M., Molnar-Szakacs I., Gallese V., Buccino G., Mazziotta J. C., Rizzolatti G. (2005). Grasping the intentions of others with one's own mirror neuron system. *PLoS Biology, 3*(3), e79.

Isen, A. M., Shalker, T. E., Clark, M., & Karp, L. (1978). Resources required in the construction and reconstruction of conversation, *Journal of Personality and Social Psychology, 36,* 1–12.

Jacobson, N. S., & Margolin, G. (1979). *Marital therapy: Strategies based on social learning and behavior exchange principles.* New York: Brunner/Mazel.

James, W. (1896). *The principles of psychology* (Vols. 1 & 2). New York: Henry Holt.

James, W. (1902). *The varieties of religious experience: A study in human nature.* New York: Modern Library.

James, W. (1918). *Selected papers on philosophy by William James.* London: J. M. Dent.

Janis, I. (1971). *Stress and frustration.* New York: Harcourt Brace Jovanovich.

Johnson, S. (2008). *Hold Me Tight.* New York: Little Brown & Co.

Jung, C. G. (1977). *The archetypes and the collective unconscious.* Princeton, NJ: Princeton University Press. (Original work published 1934–1954).

Jung, C. G. (1981). *The Structure & Dynamics of the Psyche,* Princeton, NJ: Princeton University press.

Kabat-Zinn, J. (1993). Mindfulness meditation: Health benefits of an ancient Buddhist practice. In D. Goleman & J. Gurin (Eds.), *Mind, body medicine: How to use your mind for better health* (pp. 259–275). Yonkers, NY: Consumer Reports.

Kabat-Zinn, J. (2003). Mindfulness-based interventions in context: Past, present, and future. *Clinical Psychology: Science and Practice, 10*(3), 144–156.

Kaptchuk, T. J. (1983). *The web that has no weaver: Understanding Chinese medicine.* New York: Congdon & Weed.

Kasamatsu, A., & Hirai, T. (1966). An electroencephalographic study of the Zen meditation. *Folia Psychiatrica et Neurologia Japonica, 20*, 315–336.

Kasamatsu, A., & Hirai, T. (1969). An electroencephalographic study of the Zen meditation (Zazen). *Psychologia, 12*, 205–225.

Katz, R., & McGuffin, P. (1993). The genetics of affective disorders. *Progress in Experimental Personality & Psychopathology Research, 16*, 200–221.

Keene, B. (1979). *Sensing, letting yourself live.* San Francisco: Harper & Row.

Kennedy, J. F. (1955). *Profiles of courage.* New York: Harper Academic.

Kerem, E., Fishman, N., & Josselson, R. (2001). The experience of empathy in everyday relationships: Cognitive and affective elements. *Journal of Social and Personal Relationships, 18*(5), 709–729.

Kernberg, O. (1976). *Object-relations theory and clinical psychoanalysis.* New York: Jason Aronson.

Kohr, R. I. (1977). Dimensionality in the meditative experience. *Journal of Transpersonal Psychology, 9*(2), 193–203.

Komito, D. R. (1983). Tibetan Buddhism and psychotherapy: A conversation with the Dalai Lama. *The Journal of Transpersonal Psychology, 15*(1), 1–13.

Koob G. F. (2005). The neurocircuitry of addiction: Implications for treatment. *Clinical Neuroscience, 5*, 89–101.

Koob, G. F. (2003). Neuroadaptive mechanisms of addiction: Studies on the extended amygdala. *European Neuropsychopharmacology, 13*(6), 442–452.

Koob, G. F., Everitt, B. J., & Robbins, T. W. (2008). Reward, motivation, & addiction. In L. G. Squire, D. Berg, F. E. Bloom, S. Du Lac, A. Ghosh, & N. Spitzer (Eds.), *Fundamental Neuroscience, Third Edition* (pp. 349 987–1016). Amsterdam: Academic press.

Koob, G. F., & Le Moal, M. (2001). Drug addiction, dysregulation of reward, and allostasis. *Neuropsychopharmacology, 24*, 97–129.

Koob, G. F., & Moyers, B. (1998). Interview on KPBS, March 29.

Krishnamurti, J. (1968). *The first and last freedom.* Wheaton, II: Theosophical.

Krishnamurti, J. (1970). *The only revolution.* New York: Harper & Row.

Kronsick, J. A., & Petty R. E. (1995). Attitude strength: An overview. In R. E. Petty & J. A. Krosnick (Eds.), *Attitude strength: Antecedents and consequences.* (pp. 1–24). Mahwah, N. J.: Erlbaum.

Kubose, S. K. (1976). An experimental investigation of psychological aspects of meditation. "Psychologia" 19, 1, 1–10.

Kushner, K. (2000). *One arrow, one life: Zen, archery, enlightenment.* Boston: Tuttle.

LaFleur, W. R. (1985). *Dogen studies.* Honolulu: University of Hawaii Press.

Lambert, M. J., Shapiro, D. A., & Bergin, A. E. (1986). The effectiveness of psychotherapy. In S. L. Garfield & A. E. Bergin (Eds.), *Handbook of psychotherapy and behavior change* (3rd ed., pp. 157–211). New York: Wiley.

Langer, E. J. (1989). *Mindfulness.* Cambridge, MA: Da Capo.

Lazar, S. W., Kerr, C. E., Wasserman, R. H., Gray, J. R. Greve, M., Treadway, T., et al. (2005). Meditation experience is associated with increased cortical thickness. *NeuroReport, 16*(17), 1893–1897.

Lazarus, A. (1989). *The practice of multimodal therapy: Systematic, comprehensive, and effective psychotherapy.* Baltimore: Johns Hopkins University Press.

Lazarus, R. S. (1991). *Emotion and adaptation.* New York: Oxford University Press.

Lazarus, R. S., & Folkman. S. (1984). *Stress, appraisal, and coping.* New York: Springer.

LeDoux, J. E. (1992). Brain mechanisms of emotion and emotional learning. *Current Opinions of Neurobiology, 2,* 191–197.

Lee, S. H., Ahn, S. C., Lee, Y. J., Choi, T. K, Yook, K. H., & Suh, S. Y. (2007). Effectiveness of a meditation-based stress management program as an adjunct to pharmacotherapy in patients with anxiety disorder. *Journal of Psychosomatic Research, 62*(2), 189–195.

Legge, J. (1962). *The texts of taoism* (2 vols.), New York: Dover.

Legge, J. (1971). *Confucius.* New York: Dover.

Lesh, T. V. (1970). Zen meditation and the development of empathy in counselors. *Journal of Humanistic Psychology, 10,* 39–74.

Leung, Y., & Singhal, A. (2004). An examination of the relationship between Qigong meditation and personality. *Social Behavior and Personality: An International Journal, 32*(4), 313–320.

Lieberman, M. D., Gilbert, D. T., Gaunt, R., & Trope, Y. (2008). Reflection and reflexion: A social cognitive neuroscience approach to attributional inference. *Advances in Experimental Social Psychology,* In Press.

Liu, D, (1986). T'ai Chi Ch'uan and meditation. New York: Schocken Books.

Loori, J. D. (1994). *Two arrows meeting in mid air: The Zen koan.* Boston: Tuttle.

Low, A. (1995). *The world, a gateway: Commentaries on the mumonkan.* Rutland, VT: Tuttle.

Lutz, A., Brefczynski-Lewis, J., Johnstone, T., & Davidson, R. J. (2008). Regulation of the neural circuitry of emotion by compassion meditation: Effects of meditative expertise. Retrieved July 12, 2008, from www.PubmedCentral.nih.gov/articlerender.fedl?artid=2267490.

Lutz, A. Gretschar, L. L., Rawlings, N., Ricard, M., & Davidson, R. J. (2004). Long-term meditators self-induce high-amplitude gamma synchrony during mental practice. *Neuroscience, 101*(46), 16369–16373.

Ma, H. S., & Teasdale, J. D. (2004). Mindfulness-based cognitive therapy for depression replication and exploration of differential relapse prevention effects. *Journal of Consulting and Clinical Psychology, 72*(1), 31–40.

Mann, F. (1973). *Acupuncture: The ancient art of healing and how it works scientifically.* New York: Vintage.

Marcus, J. B. (1974). Transcendental meditation: A new method of reducing drug abuse. *Drug Forum, 3*(2), 113–136.

Mayer, M. (1999). Qigong and hypertension: A critique of research. *Journal of Alternative and Complementary Medicine, 5*(4), 371–382.

McDonald, R. J., & White, N. M. (1993). A triple dissociation of memory systems: Hippocampus, amygdala, and dorsal striatum. *Behavioral Neuroscience, 107,* 3–22.

McEwen, B. S. (1998). Protective and damaging effects of stress mediators. *New England Journal of Medicine, 338,* 171–179.

McEwen, B. S., & Magarinos, A. M. (1997). Stress effects on morphology and function of the hippocampus. *Annals of the New York Academy of Sciences, 821,* 271–284.

McGuire, E. A., Gadian, D. G., Johnsrude, I. S., Good, C. D., Ashburner, J., Frackowiak, R. S. J., et al. (2000). Navigation-related structural change in the hippocampi of taxi drivers. *Proceedings of the National Academy of Sciences, 97*(81), 4398–4403.

Miller, J. J., Fletcher, K., & Kabat-Zinn, J. (1995). Three-year follow up and clinical implications of a mindfulness meditation-based stress reduction intervention in the treatment of anxiety disorders. *General Hospital Psychiatry, 17,* 192–200.

Miller, W. R., Westerberg, V. S., Harris, R. J., & Tonigan, J. S. (1996). What predicts relapse? Prospective testing of antecedent models. *Addiction* (Suppl.), *91* 155–171.

Ming, Z. (Trans.) (2001). *The medical classic of the yellow emperor.* Beijing: Foreign Languages Press.

Miura, I., & Sasaki, R. F. (1965). *The Zen koan.* San Diego, CA: Harcourt, Brace Jovanovich.

Mizuno, K. (1995). *Buddhist sutras: Origin, development, transmission.* Tokyo, Japan: Kosei.

Murata, T., Takahashi, T, Hamada, T, Omori, M., Kosaka, H., Yoshida, H. et al. (2004). Individual trait anxiety levels characterizing the properties of Zen meditation. *Neuropsychobiology, 50*(2), 189–194.

Murphey, M. & Donovan, S. (1997). *The physical and psychological effects of meditation.* (2nd ed.). Sausalito, CA: Noetic Sciences.

Newberg, A. B., & Iversen, J. (2005). The neural basis of the complex mental task of meditation: Neurotransmitter and neurochemical considerations. *Medical Hypotheses, 65*(3), 625–626.

Nielsen, L., & Kasznlak, A., (2006). Awareness of subtle emotional feelings: A comparison of long-term meditators and nonmeditators. *Emotion, 6*(3), 392–405.

Nitobe, J. (1973). *Bushido: The soul of Japan.* Boston: Tuttle.

Okakura, K. (1989). *The book of tea.* New York: Kodansha.

Okakura, K., (1989). *The book of tea.* Tokyo: Kodansha.

Oman, D., Hedberg, J., & Thoresen, C. (2006). Passage meditation reduces perceived stress in health professionals: A randomized, controlled trial. *Journal of Consulting and Clinical Psychology, 74*(4), 714–719.

Osis, K., Bokert, E., & Carlson. M. L. (1973). Dimensions of the meditative experience. *Journal of Transpersonal Psychology, 5*(1), 109–135.

Panjwani, U., Selvamurthy, W., Singh, S. H., Gupta, H. L., Mukhopadhyay, S., & Thakur, L. (2000). Effect of sahaja yoga meditation on auditory evoked potentials (AEP) and visual contrast sensitivity (VCS) in epileptics. *Applied Psychophysiology and Biofeedback, 25*(1), 1–12.

Panikkar, R. (2001). *The Vedic experience mantramanjari: An anthology of the vedas for modern man and contemporary celebration.* Delhi: Motilal Banarsidass.

Peele, S. (1987). Why do controlled–drinking outcomes vary by country, era, and investigator?: Cultural conceptions of relapse and remission in alcoholism. *Drug and Alcohol Dependence. 20,* 173–201.

Peele, S. (2003). Addiction—Choice or disease. *Psychiatric Times, 2,* 11–12.

Peele, S. (2007). Addiction as disease policy, epidemiology, and treatment consequences of a bad idea. In J. Henningfield, W. Bickel, & P. Santora (Eds.), *Addiction treatment in the 21st century: Science and policy issues* (pp. 153–163). Baltimore: John Hopkins Press.

Perkins, F. (2004). *Leibnitz and China: A commerce of light.* Cambridge, UK: Cambridge University Press.

Perls, F. (1969). *In and out of the garbage pail.* Lafayette, CA: Real People Press.

Pine, R. (1989). *The Zen teaching of Bodhidharma.* San Francisco: North Point Press.

Pineda, J. A., Allison, B. Z., & Vankov, A. (2000). The effects of selfmovement, observation, and imagination on mu rhythms and readiness potentials (RP's): Toward a brain–computer interface (BCI). *IEEE Transactions on Rehabilitation Engineering, 8*(2), 219–222.

Pineda, J. A., Silverman, D. S., Vankov, A., & Hestenes, J. (2003). Learning to control brain rhythms: Making a brain-computer interface possible. *IEEE Transactions on Neural Systems and Rehabilitation. Engineering, 11*(2), 181–184.

Piver, S. (2008). The surprising self-healing benefits of meditation. *Weil Lifestyle.* http://www .drweil.com/drw/u/ART02791/self-healing

Place, U. T. (1956). Is consciousness a brain process? *British Journal of Psychology, 47*, 44–50.

Price, A. F., & Mou-lam, W. (1990). *The diamond sutra and the sutra of Hui-Neng.* Boston: Shambala.

Putnam, H. (1988). *Representation and reality.* Cambridge, MA: MIT Press.

Radhakrishnan. (1923). *Indian philosophy* (Vols. 1 & 2). London: George Allen & Unwin.

Rauch, S. L., Jenike, M. A., Alpert, N. M., Baer, L., Breiter, H. C., Savage, C. R., et al. (1995). Regional cerebral blood flow measured during symptom provocation in obsessive-compulsive disorder using O-15-labelled CO_2 and positron emission tomography. *Archives of General Psychiatry, 51*, 62–70.

Rauch S. L., Savage, C. R., Alpert, N. M. (1995). A positron emission tomographic study of simple phobic symptom provocation. *Archives of General Psychiatry, 52*, 20–28.

Rauch S.L. van der Kolk, B. A., Fisler, R. E., Alpert, N. M., Orr, S. P., Savage, C. R., et al. (1996). A symptom provocation study of posttraumatic stress disorder using positron emission tomography and script driven imagery. *Archives of General Psychiatry, 53*, 380–387.

Rausch, S., Gramling, S., & Auerbach, S. (2006). Effects of a single session of large-group meditation and progressive muscle relaxation training on stress reduction, reactivity, and recovery. *International Journal of Stress Management, 13*(3), 273–290.

Ray, W. (2005). *Don D. Jackson: Selected essays at the dawn of an era.* Phoenix, AZ: Zeig, Tucker & Theisen.

Reik, T. (1951). *Listening with the third ear.* Garden City, NY: Doubleday.

Reps, P. (1980). *Zen flesh, Zen bones.* Rutland, VT: Tuttle.

Rizzolatti, G. (1996). Premotor cortex and the recognition of motor actions. *Cognitive Brain Research, 3*, 131–141.

Rosenthal, R., & Jacobson, L. (1968). *Pygmalion in the classroom.* New York: Holt, Rinehart & Winston.

Rossi, E. L. Erickson-Klein, R., & Rossi, K. L. (2006). *The neuroscience edition: The collected papers of Milton H. Erickson, M.D: On hypnosis, psychotherapy, and rehabilitation.* Phoenix, AZ: Milton H. Erickson Foundation Press.

Rush, A. J., Stewart, R. S., Garver, D. L., & Waller, D. A. (1998). Neurobiological bases for psychiatric disorders. In R. N. Rosenberb & D. E. Pleasure (Eds.), *Comprehensive neurology* (2nd ed., pp. 555–603). New York: Wiley.

Sadler, A. L. (1963). *Cha-No-Yu. The Japanese tea ceremony.* Rutland, VT: Tuttle.

Samuels, M., & Samuels, N. (1973). *Seeing with the mind's eye.* New York: Random House.

Sancier, K. M., & Holman, D. (2004). Multifaceted health benefits of medical qigong. *Journal of Alternative and Complementary Medicine, 10*(1), 163–165.

Sarma, D. S. (1989). *The Upanishads: An anthology.* Delhi: Bharatiya Vidya Bhavan.

Sasaki, R. F., (Trans.). 1975. *Recorded sayings of Ch'an master Lin-chi.* Kyoto: Institute for Zen Studies.

Sasaki, S. (2002). *Chado: The way of tea.* Boston: Tuttle.

Schachter, S., & Singer, J. (1962). Cognitive, social, and physiological determinants of emotional state. *Psychological Review, 69*, 379–399.

Schneider, A. M., & Tarshis, B. (1986). *An introduction to physiological psychology.* New York: Random House.

Sekida, K. (Trans). (1977). *Two Zen classics: Mumonkan & hekiganroku.* New York: Weatherhill.

Seligman, M. E. P. (1990). *Learned optimism.* New York: Knopf.

Seligman, M. E. P. (1992). *Helplessness: On depression, development, and death.* New York: W. H. Freeman.

Seligman, M. E. P. (2002). *Authentic happiness: Using the new positive psychology to realize your potential for lasting fulfillment.* New York: Free Press.

Selye, H. (1974). *Stress without distress.* New York: Signet.

Seyle, H. (1976). *The stress of life,* New York: McGraw Hill.

Shannahoff-Khalsa, D. (2003). Kundalini Yoga meditation techniques for the treatment of obsessive-compulsive and OC spectrum disorders. *Brief Treatment and Crisis Intervention, 3*(3), 369–382.

Shannahoff-Khalsa, D. (2006). *Kundalini Yoga meditation: Techniques specific for psychiatric disorders, couples therapy, and personal growth.* New York: Norton.

Shapiro, D. H. (1980a). *Meditation self-regulation strategy and altered states of consciousness.* New York: Aldine Press.

Shapiro, D. H. (1983). Meditation as an altered state of consciousness: Empirical contributions of Western behavioral science. *Journal of Transpersonal Psychology, 15*(1), 61–81.

Shapiro, D. H., & Giber, D. (1978). Meditation and psychotherapeutic effects: Self-regulation strategy and altered state of consciousness. *Archives of General Psychiatry, 35*(3), 294–302.

Shapiro, D. H., & Walsh, R. N. (1984). *Meditation: Classic and contemporary perspectives.* New York: Aldine.

Shapiro, S., Astin, J., Bishop, S., & Cordova, M. (2005). Mindfulness-based stress reduction for health care professionals: Results from a randomized trial. *International Journal of Stress Management, 12*(2), 164–176.

Shapiro, S., Brown, K. W., & Biegel, B. M., (2007). Teaching self-care to caregivers: Effects of mindfulness-based stress reduction on the mental health of therapists in training. *Training and Education in Professional Psychology, 1*(2), 105–115.

Shapiro, S., Schwartz, G. E., & Bonner, G. (1998). Effects of mindfulness-based stress reduction on medical and premedical students. *Journal of Behavioral Medicine, 21*(6), 581–599.

Shaw, M. (1994). *Passionate enlightenment: Women in tantric Buddhism.* Princeton, NJ: Princeton University Press.

Shiki, M. (1998). *Songs from a bamboo village.* Rutland, VT: Tuttle.

Siegel, D. (2007). *The mindful brain.* New York: Norton.

Silberer, H. (1909). Report on a method of eliciting and observing certain symbolic hallucination phenomena. In D. Rapaport (Ed.), *The organization and pathology of thought.* New York: Columbia University Press. p. 195–233.

Simpkins, C. A., & Simpkins, A. M. (1996). *Principles of meditation: Eastern wisdom for the western mind.* Boston: Tuttle.

Simpkins, C. A., & Simpkins, A. M. (1997a). *Living meditation: From principle to practice.* Boston: Tuttle.

Simpkins, C. A., & Simpkins, A. M. (1997b). *Zen around the world: A 2500-year journey from the Buddha to you.* Boston: Tuttle.

Simpkins, C. A., & Simpkins, A. M. (1999a). *Simple Taoism: A guide to living in balance.* Boston: Tuttle.

Simpkins, C. A., & Simpkins, A. M. (1999b). *Simple Zen: A guide to living day by day.* Boston: Tuttle.

Simpkins, C. A., & Simpkins, A. M. (2000). *Simple Buddhism: A guide to enlightened living.* Boston: Tuttle.

Simpkins, C. A., & Simpkins, A. M. (2001a). *Simple Tibetan Buddhism: A guide to tantric living.* Boston: Tuttle.

Simpkins, C. A., & Simpkins, A. M. (2001b). *Timeless teachings from the therapy masters.* San Diego, CA: Radiant Dolphin Press.

Simpkins, C. A., & Simpkins, A. M. (2002). *Tao in ten: Easy lessons for spiritual growth.* Boston: Tuttle.

Simpkins, C. A., & Simpkins, A. M. (2003a). *Yoga basics.* Boston: Tuttle.

Simpkins, C. A., & Simpkins, A. M. (2003b). *Zen in ten: Easy lessons for spiritual growth.* Boston: Tuttle.

Simpkins, C. A., & Simpkins, A. M. (2003c). *Buddhism in ten: Easy lessons for spiritual growth.* Boston: Tuttle.

Simpkins, C. A., & Simpkins, A. M. (2004). *Self-hypnosis for women with audio CD.* San Diego, CA: Radiant Dolphin Press.

Simpkins, C. A., & Simpkins, A. M. (2005). *Effective self-hypnosis: Pathways to the unconscious with audio CD.* San Diego, CA: Radiant Dolphin Press.

Simpkins, C. A., & Simpkins, A. M. (2006). *Taekwondo: Building on the basics.* San Diego, CA: Radiant Dolphin Press.

Simpkins, C. A., & Simpkins, A. M. (2007). *Meditation from thought to action with audio CD.* San Diego, CA: Radiant Dolphin Press.

Singer, R., Seymour B., O'Doherty J., Kaube, H., Dolan J. D., & Frith, C. (2004). Empathy for pain involves the affective but not the sensory components of pain. *Science, 303,* 1157–1162.

Singer, T., & Frith, C. (2005). The painful side of empathy. *New & Views. Nature Neuroscience, 8,* 845–846.

Smith, A. D., & Miller, L. H. (1993). *The stress solution.* New York: Pocket Books.

Smith, H. (1991). *The world's religions: Our great wisdom traditions,* Harper San Francisco.

Smith, J. C. (1976). Psychotherapeutic effects of transcendental meditation with controls for expectation of belief and daily sitting. *Journal of Consulting and Clinical Psychology, 44*(4), 630–637.

Snyder, D. K., & Wills, R. M. (1989). Behavioral versus insight-oriented marital therapy: Effects on individual and interpersonal functioning. *Journal of Consulting and Clinical Psychology, 57,* 39–46.

Solomon, R. L. (1980). The opponent-process theory of acquired motivation: The costs of pleasure and the benefits of pain. *American Psychologist, 35*(8), 691–712.

Spiegelberg, H. (1972). *Phenomenology in psychology and psychiatry.* Evanston, IL: Northwestern University Press.

Squire, L., Bloom, F. E., McConnell, S. K., Roberts, J. L., Spitzer, N. C., & Zigmond, M. J. (2003). *Fundamental Neuroscience* (2nd ed.). New York: Academic Press.

Ssu-ma, Ch'ien. (1994). *The grand scribe's records,* (Vol. 1, W. H. Nienhauser, Ed.). Bloomington: Indiana University Press.

Stanislavski, C. (1983). *Creating a role.* New York: Theater Arts Books. (Original work published 1961).

Stevens, J. (1989). *The sword of no-sword.* Boston: Shambhala.

Stevens, J. O. (Ed.) (1975). *Gestalt is.* Moab, Utah: Real People Press.

Stryk, L. (1968). *World of the Buddha reader.* Garden City, NY: Doubleday.

Sugiura, Y. (2004). Detached mindfulness and worry: A meta-cognitive analysis. *Personality and Individual Differences, 37*(1), 169–179.

Sulekha, S., Thennarasu, K., Vedamurthachar, A., Raju, T. R., & Kutty, B. M. (2006). Evaluation of sleep architecture in practitioners of Sudarshan kriya yoga and Vipassana meditation. *Sleep and Biological Rhythms, 4*(3), 207–214.

Suzuki, D. T. (1955). Studies in Zen. New York: Philosophical Library.

Suzuki, D. T. (1960). *Manual of Zen Buddhism.* New York: Grove.

Suzuki, D. T (1969). *The Zen doctrine of no-mind.* York Beach, ME: Samuel Weiser.

Suzuki, D. T. (1973). *Zen and Japanese culture.* Princeton, NJ: Princeton University Press.

Suzuki, D. T. (1994). *The Zen koan as a means of attaining enlightenment.* Boston: Tuttle.

Suzuki, S. (1979). *Zen mind, beginner's mind.* New York: Weatherhill.

Sykes, D. E. (1973). Transcendental meditation as applied to criminal justice reform, drug rehabilitation, and society in general. *The University of Maryland Law Forum, 3,* 2.

Tang, Y. Y., Ma, Y., Wang, J., Fan, Y., Feng, S. Lu, Q., et al. (2007). Short-term meditation training improves attention and self-regulation. *Proceedings of the National Academy of Sciences of the United States of America (PNAS), 104*(43), 17152–17156.

Tart, C. (1975). *Transpersonal psychologies.* New York: Harper & Row.

Toneatto, T., Vettese, L., & Nguyen, L. (2007). The role of mindfulness in the cognitive-behavioral treatment of problem gambling. *Journal of Gambling Issues, 19,* 91–100.

Tory, P. B. (2004). A mindfulness-based stress reduction program for the treatment of anxiety. *Dissertation Abstracts International:* Section B: The Sciences and Engineering, 64, 10-B, 5203.

Twemlow, S. W. (2001). Training psychotherapists in attributes of "mind" from Zen and psychoanalytic perspectives, Part I: Core principles, emptiness, impermanence, and paradox. *American Journal of Psychotherapy, 55*(1), 1–21.

Van Nuys, D. (1973). Meditation, attention, and hypnotic susceptibility. A correlational study. *International Journal of Clinical and Experimental Hypnosis, 21,* 69–69.

Vivekananda, S. (1953). *Vivekananda: The yogas and other works.* New York: Ramakrishna-Vivekananda Center.

Wachholtz, A. B. & Pargament, K.I. (2005). Is spirituality a critical ingredient of meditation? Comparing the effects of spiritual meditation, secular meditation, and relaxation on spiritual, psychological, cardiac, and pain outcomes. *Journal of Behavioral Medicine, 28*(4), 369–384.

Waddell, A. (1894). *The Buddhism of Tibet or lamaism.* Cambridge, UK: W. Heffer.

Waddell, N. (1994). *The unborn: The life and teachings of Zen master Bankei 1622–1693.* San Francisco: North Point Press.

Wallace, R. K., Dillbeck, M. C., Jacobe, E., & Harrington, B. (1982).The effects of the transcendental meditation and TM-sidhi program on the aging process. *International Journal of Neuroscience, 16,* 53–58.

Wallace, B., & Fisher, L. E. (2003). *Consciousness and behavior.* Long Grove, IL: Waveland.

Wallace, B., & Shapiro, S. (2006). Mental balance and well-being: Building bridges between Buddhism and western psychology. *American Psychologist, 61*(7), 690–701.

Walsh, R. (1980). The consciousness disciplines and the behavioral sciences: Questions of comparison and assessment. *American Journal of Psychiatry. 137*(6), 663–673.

Walsh, R., Victor, B., & Bitner, R. (2006). Emotional effects of sertraline: Novel findings revealed by meditation. *American Journal of Orthopsychiatry. 76*(1), 134–137.

Walsh, R. (1978). Initial meditative experience: Part II. *Journal of Transpersonal Psychology, 10*(1), 1–28.

Watson, B. (1968). *The complete works of Chuang Tzu.* New York: Columbia University Press.

Watson, B. (1993). *The Zen teachings of master Lin-Chi.* Boston: Shambala.

Watts, A. (1957). *The way of Zen.* New York: Vintage Books.

Webster's Unabridged Dictionary (1998). New York: Random House.

Weil, A. (2004). *The natural mind: A revolutionary approach to the drug problem.* Boston: Mariner.

Weiss, J. M., & Simson, P. G. (1985). Neurochemical basis of stress-induced depression. *Psychopharmacology. Bulletin, 21,* 447–457.

Wenger, M. A., & Bagchi, B. K. (1961). Studies of autonomic functions in practitioners of Yoga in India. *Behavior Science, 6,* 312–323.

Wenger, M. A., Bagchi, B., & Anand, B. K. (1961). Experiments in India on voluntary control of heart and pulse. *Circulation, 24,* 1319–1325.

Wenger, M., Bagchi, A., & Anand, B. (1963). Voluntary heart and pulse control by Yoga methods. *International Journal of Parapsychology, 5,* 25–41.

White, M. (2004). *Narrative practice and exotic lives: Resurrecting diversity in everyday life.* Adelaide, South Australia: Dulwich Center.

Whitehorn, J. C. (1956a). The healthful benefits of stress. *Journal of Chronic Diseases, 4*(6), 644–648.

Whitehorn, J. C. (1956b). Stress and emotional health. *The American Journal of Psychiatry, 112,* 773–781.

Whorf, B. L. (1956). *Language thought and reality.* Cambridge: The MIT Press.

Whorf, B. L. (1940). Science and linguistics. *Technology Review, 42*(6), 229–31.

Wilhelm, R. (1990). *Tao te ching, The book of meaning and life.* London: Arkana.

Wilhelm, H. & Wilhelm, R. (1995). *Understanding the i ching.* Princeton, NJ: Princeton University Press.

Witkiewitz, K., Marlatt, G. A., & Walker, D. (2005). Mindfulness-based relapse prevention for alcohol and substance use disorders. *Journal of Cognitive Psychotherapy, 19*(3), 211–228.

Wolff, H. (1950). *Proceedings of the association for research in nervous and mental disease,* Baltimore, MD: Williams & Wilkins.

Wong, E. (1997). *Harmonizing yin and yang: The dragon-tiger classic.* Boston: Shambala.

Wundt, W. (1932). Wundt's psychology. *American Journal of Psychology, 54*(4), 615–629.

Yampolsky, P. (1971). *The Zen master Hakuin: Selected writings.* New York: Columbia University Press.

Yanagi, S. (1981). *The unknown craftsman: A Japanese insight into beauty.* Tokyo: Kodansha.

Yokoi, H. (1990). *Zen master Dogen.* New York: Weatherhill.

Yutang, L. (Ed.). (1942). *The wisdom of China and India.* New York: Random House.

Index

Abe, M., 297
abuse, 251
action. *See* Right Action
active meditations, 242–43
acupuncture, 30
acute stress, 217
addictions and impulse problems, 251–71
  brain theories, 252–54
  Buddhist theory, 259–60
  choice theory, 256, 258
  definitions of, 251–52
  meditation and, 260–71
  natural drive theory, 259
  neurocircuitry of, *257*
  opponent-process theory, 255–56
  recovery from, 258, 269
  research on meditation for, 260–61
  theories of, 252–60
Adler, Alfred, 299
Adler, K. A., 271
affect labeling, 126
aging, 52–53
alchemy, 25–26, 143
Alexander, C. N., 260
allostasis, 254
American Psychological Association, 217
Amida Buddhism, 23
amygdala, 195, 235, 238
Anand, B. K., 56
anxiety. *See* fear and anxiety
archery, 169
Aristotle, 232–33
Arnheim, R., 152

arts
  poetry, 173–79
  Qi and, 147–48
  tea ceremony, 170–73
  therapeutic use of, 64, 185
  Zen Buddhism and, 39–40, 169–79
asanas, 22
Asoka, King, 294
Assimakis, P. D., 222
attachment, 273. *See also* nonattachment
attention, 75–81
  to breathing, 98
  concentration and, 103
  inner and outer, 78–79
  observation and, 77–78
  Right Effort and, 119–20
  seeing and, 75–77
  spontaneous vs. deliberate, 79–81
  withdrawal of, 99–102
attitudes, 110–11, 122–25
auditory visualization exercise, 82
autonomic nervous system, 218
Avatamsaka, 153, 281
awareness
  of breathing, 92–94
  withdrawal and, 99–102
ayama, 90

Bagchi, B. K., 48
balance, 70–71, 212–13, 229–30, 270, 293–96.
    See also homeostasis; yin-yang
bamboo flute music, 169
Bankei, 38, 200–201

Bard, Philip, 189–90
Basho, 174–75
Behanan, Kovoor, 48
behavior, attending to, 116
behavioral learning, 189
behavioral therapy, 233–34, 275
Benson, Herbert, 221, 222, 260
Bergson, Henri, 31
Bernard, Claude, 213
Bhagavad-Gita, 20, *21*, 99
Bhakti Yoga, 23
bipolar disorder, 193
Blyth, R. H., 47, 280
Boaz, Franz, 65
Bodhidharma, *36*, 36, 75
Bodhisattva, *32*, 117, 230–31
body
    emotion and, 189–90
    homeostasis of, 213
    mindfulness of, 123–24
    parts of, 124
    positioning of, 69–72, *72–74*
    relaxation of, 223–24
    temperature of, 106–7
Bokert, E., 49
brain. *See also* neuroscience
    addictions and, 252–54
    emotions and, 195, *196*, *198*
    meditation research on, 51–52, 55–57
    reward pathway in, 253, *254*, *255*
brain stem, 195
breathing, 90–98
    alternate nostril, *96*, 96
    anxiety and, 247
    attention to, 98
    awareness of, 92–94
    the complete breath, 94–95
    concentration on, 105
    control of, 91
    counting breaths while, 93
    direct methods of, 91–92
    emotions and, 203–4
    indirect methods of, 91–92, 97
    listening to, 93–94
    mindful, 124–25
    postures integrated with, 98
    significance of, 90
    stages of, 91
    visualization and, 96–97
    Zen, 97–98

brief meditation, 239–42
Brosse, Thérèse, 48
Brown, D., 53
Buddha. *See* Gautama, Siddhartha
Buddhism, 32–36. *See also* Buddhist meditation;
        Zen Buddhism
    addiction theory in, 259–60
    breathing in, 91
    Eightfold Path of, 33, 108–20
    emotional theories in, 191–92
    and emptiness, 35, 162
    evolution of, 34
    Five Precepts of, 116
    Four Noble Truths of, 33, 108
    Middle Way of, 33
    types of, 34
Buddhist meditation. *See also* Zen Buddhist meditation
    characteristics of, 17, 184
    therapeutic use of, 184
    wisdom attained through, 35–36

calligraphy, 169
Cannon-Bard theory of emotion, 189–90, 213
Cannon, Walter, 189–90, 213
Carlson, M. L., 49
Carus, Paul, 45
catharsis, 232–33
central nervous system, *220*, 220
Cha-no-yu. *See* tea ceremony
Chan, W. T., 23
change, 28–29, 299
Chao-chao, 210
Chao-chou, 37
Chevreul pendulum, *88*, 88–89
Chhina, G. S., 56
Chinul, 2
choice theory, 256, 258
Chomsky, Noam, 158
chronic stress, 217
cleansing breaths, 96
clear mind. *See* empty mind
clients
    meditation benefits for, 4, 57–58
    meditation types suited for, 64, 184–85
cognitive appraisal theory of emotion, 191, 216–17
cognitive-behavioral therapy, 194, 234, 275
cognitive research, 50–53
color, focusing on, 163–64
compassion, 282, 299
compulsive behavior, 256

concentration, 102–7, 207
  attention and, 103
  on body warming, 106–7
  on breathing, 105
  on inner image, 104
  on motion, 106
  on one thing, 103–4
  on process of concentration, 103–4
  on sound, 104–5
Conception Vessel, *135*
confidence, 292–93
conflict, 280–84
Confucian Analects, 292
Confucianism, 19, 36
coping, 215–17
cortex, 52
corticotrophin-releasing hormone (CRH), *220*, 220–21
couples. *See* relationships
cravings, 264–65
creativity, 147–48. *See also* arts
crime, 55–56

Da Vinci, Leonardo, 84–85
daily life. *See* everyday life
Dalai Lama. *See* Gyatso, Tenzin
dandien, *145*, 145–47, 208, 270
Dao, 27
Dao De Jing, 16, 24, 132, 206, 227, 237
Dao-hsin, 37
Daoism, 23–31. *See also* Daoist meditation
  alchemy and, 25–26, 143
  breath in, 90–91, 94, 96
  and change, 28–29
  and the Dao, 27
  and dreams, 247–48
  emotional theories in, 192–93
  and emptiness, 27, 162
  evolution of, 24–25
  mandalas in, 153
  and nonaction, 29–30
  and Qi, 30–31
  religious, 26–27
  and simplicity, 29
  yin and yang in, 27–28
  Zen Buddhism and, 36
Daoist meditation
  attention in, 80
  characteristics of, 17, 185
  healing of illness through, 42

scientific research on, 57–58
  therapeutic use of, 185
Daruma (Bodhidharma) (Hakuin Ekaku), *36*
Dawa-Samdup, Kazi, 47
daydreams, guided, 81
decisions, 111
Deikman, A. J., 49
dependence, 251
depression, 193, 194
desensitization, 234
detachment, 269
Deutsch, D., 271
devotion to others, 270–71
Dhammapada, 32, 108
dharana, 22
dhyana, 22
The Diagnostic and Statistical Manual of Mental Disorders, 251
Diamond Sutra, 35, 38
Dillbeck, M. C., 222
Direct Decision Therapy, 111
Dogen, 39, 166, 299
Dohrenwend, B., 216
Dohrenwend, B., 216
Donovan, S., 59
dopamine, 253, 254
dreams, 247–49
drugs. *See* addictions and impulse problems
Dysart, M., 53

Eastern traditions. *See also specific traditions*
  early Western interest in, 42–44
  emotions in, 191–93
  fear and anxiety in, 237–38
  Western introduction of, 44–46
  Western spokesmen for, 46–47
EEG research, 51–52, 56–57, 239, 277
effort. *See* Right Effort
Eight Pieces of Brocade, 136–38, *138–44*, 208, 243
Eightfold Path, 33, 108–20, 207–8
Emerson, Ralph Waldo, 43
emotion-focused therapy, 273
emotions. *See also* feelings
  acceptance of, 199–200
  brain structures involved in, 195, *196*, *198*
  breathing and, 203–4
  Cannon-Bard theory, 189–90, 213
  cognitive appraisal theory, 191, 216–17
  defined, 188
  Eastern theories, 191–93

emotions (*continued*)
  James-Lange theory, 189
  meditation and, 195–204
  moods vs., 193
  neuroscience of, 195
  nonattachment to, 201–3
  preferences and, 201
  theories of, 188–93
  two-factor theory, 190–91
empathy, 272, 276–79, 287–88, 299. *See also* others,
  caring for
emptiness. *See also* empty mind
  Buddhism and, 35, 162
  Daoism and, 27, 162
  embracing, 296–98
The Empty Cup (Simpkins and Simpkins), *15, 162*
empty mind, 15–17, 161–68
  anxiety and, 241
  emotions and, 203
  focusing on color, 163–64
  indirect methods of, 167–68
  koans, 166
  visualization, 164–65
  zazen, 165–66
energy, 30–31. *See also* Qi
energy ball, *146,* 146–47
environment, caring for, 281
epinephrine, 218
episodic stress, 217
Erickson, Milton, 3, 85, 274
Ericksonian hypnosis, 80, 149, 274
eustress, 215
Evans-Wentz, Walter Y., 46–47
everyday life, 37–38, 225, 228–29, 298
existentialism, 233
exposure, 234
eye positions, 71–72
eye swing exercise, 76
Eysenck Personality Inventory (EPI), 57

families. *See* relationships
family systems theory, 190
Fazang, 281
fear and anxiety
  behaviorist theories, 233–34
  cognitive theories, 234
  deconstructing, 243–45
  dynamic theories, 233
  Eastern theories, 237–38
  existential theories, 233
  hypnosis and, 234

  indirect treatments of, 245–50
  meditation for, 238–50
  neuroscience of, 235–37
  research on meditation for, 238–50
  two pathways of, 235–37, *236*
  Western theories, 232–34
feelings. *See also* emotions
  acceptance of, 199–200
  mindfulness of, 126–27
Feng Shui, 30
Five Element theory, *25,* 25
Five Precepts, 116
Fletcher, K., 222
flexibility, 284–85
flight or fight response, 218
flower arranging, 169
Flower Ornament (Flower Garland Sutra),
  153, 281
Focus (Simpkins and Simpkins), *104*
Forte, M., 53
Four Noble Truths, 33, 108, 207
Freud, Sigmund, 276

GABA, 253
gardening, 169
Gaunt, R., 186
Gautama, Siddhartha (Buddha), 32, 119, 120, 263
General Adaptation Syndrome, 214
Gestalt theory, 190
Gilbert, D. T., 186
Gnani Yoga, 23
Goleman, Daniel, 222
Governor Vessel, *136*
Govinda, L. A., 157
Greenwald, Harold, 111
group therapy meditation, 288–89
gTum-mo, 106
guided daydreams, 81
guilt, 293–96
Gyatso, Tenzin (Dalai Lama), 1, 33, 34, 46, 159, 202,
  208–9, 272, 276

haibun, 174
haiga, 174, 177, 179
haiku, 169, 174–77, 269
Hakuin, 40–41
Haley, Jay, 274
hand positions, 72, *73, 74*
Hankey, A., 51
harmony, 157, 160
Hatha Yoga, 22–23

health
  Daoism and, 26, 30
  meditation and, 55
  Qi and, 132–33
Heart Sutra, 163
Heidegger, M., 204, 272
Hemingway, Ernest, 230
Henderson, H. G., 177
Herrigel, Eugene, 47
Herrigel, G., 47
Hinkle, L. E., 216
hippocampus, 235–37
Hippocrates, 213
homeostasis, 190, 213, 218, 223, 254
HPA axis. *See* hypothalamus-pituitary-adrenal
    (HPA) axis
Huang-Po, 38
Hui-neng, 38
humor, 210–11
hypnagogic imagery, 84
hypnagogic states, 83–84
hypnosis, 80, 81, 86, 149, 234, 274
hypothalamus, 195, 218, 220
hypothalamus-pituitary-adrenal (HPA) axis, 218, *219*,
    220, 235

I Jing, The Book of Changes, 28–29, 43, 149, 153
ideomotor response, 87–89
Ikebana, 169
impermanence, 266–67
impulse problems. *See* addictions and impulse
    problems
incense, 169
Indra's Net meditation, 155–56
ink painting, 169
insight-oriented marriage and family therapy, 273
insights, in therapy, 38
integrative body-mind training (IBMR), 222
intelligence, 54
intent. *See* Right Intent
interdependence of all things, 281
interpersonal relationships. *See* relationships
Inuit, 65
invision, 82–83, 155
is and is not, 282–83
Isen, A. M., 208–9
Issa, 175–76

Jackson, Don, 274
James-Lange theory of emotion, 189
James, William, 45, 67, 75, 80, 119, 189

Janis, I., 216, 225
jobs, 117–18
Johnson, Sue, 273
Jung, Carl Gustav, 149, 152, 188, 253

Kabat-Zinn, J., 222, 292
Karma Yoga, 23
Katz, R., 193
Keene, B., 69
Kekule, F. August, 84
Kikaku, 242
koans, 40–41, 166, 174
Koob, G. F., 254, 256
Koto, 169
Krishnamurti, 283
Kriya meditation, 279
Kubose, S. K., 49
Kundalini Yoga, 23, 58, 238
Kyudo, 169

Lane, Beatrice Erskine, 45
Lange, Carl, 189
language, 66, 113–15, 176
Laozi, *24*, 24, 26, 228
Lazarus, Richard S., 191, 216–17, 225
learned helplessness, 194
Leibniz, Gottfried Wilhelm, 43
Leihzi, 24
letting go. *See* nonaction; nonattachment
Lieberman, M. D., 186
life stress, 214
limbic system, 195, *197*
Lin Chi, 124, 163
listening
  to breathing, 93–94
  obstacles to, 114
livelihood. *See* Right Livelihood
Lotus (Daqian Zhang), *178*
love, 197, 273, 287. *See also* relationships

Mahabharata, 20
Mahamudra, 93
Mahayana Buddhism, 34
Majjhima-nikdya I, 121, 251
mandalas, 84, 149, 152–57, 267
  Jung and, 152
  meditations using, 155–57
  representation of reality through, 151
  as symbols, 152–53
  types of, 153–55
Mantra Yoga, 23

mantras, 157–60
    concentration on, 105
    concentration using, 157
Marlatt, G. A., 58
martial arts, 169
mathematics, 150–51
matter, 30–31
Mazi, 227
McGuffin, P., 193
medication
    effectiveness of, 194
    neurochemical theory and, 193
meditation
    attention in, 18
    benefits for clients, 4
    benefits for therapists, 2–3
    body positioning for, 69–72, 72–74
    cognitive and neuroscience research on, 50–53
    conceptions of, 16
    experiential nature of, 16–17
    group, 68–69, 288–89
    language and, 66
    mandalas and, 155–57
    mental and physical control through, 42, 47–56
    physiological research on, 47–49
    place for, 68–69
    practical considerations, 67–69
    properties of, scientific research on, 49–50
    psychological research on, 53–56
    scientific study of, 42, 47–59
    selection of, for therapy, 63–66, 183–86
    shared, 68–69, 288
    stories as means of teaching, 14–15
    time for, 69
    types of, 17, 56–57, 63–66, 183–86
    Western introduction of, 44–46
memory, 54
Menninger Foundation, Topeka, Kansas, 48
method acting, 103
Middle Way, 33
Miller, J. J., 222
mind. See also unconscious
    defined, 17
    emptying, 15–17, 161–68
    filling, 17
    levels of functioning, 2
    mental functioning associated with, 2, 4
    mindfulness of, 128–30, 225
    relaxation of, 224
mindfulness, 121–31. See also mindfulness meditation
    addictions and, 261–62
    anxiety and, 238, 241

body, 123–24
breathing, 124–25
Eightfold Path and, 109
feelings, 126–27
mind, 128–30, 225
in the moment, 130–31, 226–27
nonjudgmental attitude, 122–25
research on treatment using, 58
suffering and, 261
mindfulness meditation
    addictions/compulsions and, 260–61
    fear/anxiety and, 234
    stress and, 222, 226
Ming, Z., 212
minute meditations, 240–42
mirror neurons, 276–78
monkey mind, 163
moods
    awareness of, 206–7
    biological theories, 193
    cognitive theories, 194
    defined, 204
    effects of, 208–9
    emotions vs., 193
    meditation and, 204–10
    neuroscience of, 195
    reinterpretation of, 207–8
motion, concentration on, 106
motivation, 67–74, 112–13
Mumon, 13, 119
Mumonkan, 166
Murphey, M., 59

narrative therapy, 275
natural drive theory, 259
Nei Dan, 134, 143, 145–47
    dandien, 145, 145–47
    energy ball, 146
    extending Qi, 146
    fear/anxiety and, 246
    small circulation meditation, 147
nervous system response to stress, 218
neuroendocrine system, 218
neuroplasticity, 235–36
neuroscience. See also brain
    of emotions, 195
    of fear and anxiety, 235–37
    meditation research based on, 50–53
    mindfulness and, 122
    of moods, 195
    of relationships, 276–78
    therapeutic value of, 186–87

neurotransmitters, 220–21, 235
niyamas, 22
Noh drama, 169
nonaction, 29–30, 227–29
nonattachment, 201–3, 263, 265
nonjudgmental attitude, 122–25
nonspecific factors, 11–12, 187
norepinephrine, 193, 218
not-doing, 100–102
nucleus accumbens, 253
numbers, 150–51
Nyudo, 269

observation, 77–78
obsessive-compulsive disorder (OCD), 238
occupations, 117–18
Okakura, K., 169, 170
Om, 105, 153, 158
Om Mani Padme Hum, 158–60, *159*
opponent-process theory, 255–56
Orme-Johnson, D. W., 222
Osis, K., 49
Osler, William, 214
others, caring for, 270–71, 282, 299. *See also*
    empathy

pacing, 120
Pagua, 149, *150*
pain, 260
palming, 76, 76–77
parasympathetic nervous system, 218
Patanjali, 20–22, 90, 100
Peele, S., 256
perception, 53–54, 129, 130, 149–50
Perls, Fritz, 249
physical control and feats, 22, 42, 48, 106–7
place for meditation, 68–69
poetry, 173–79. *See also* haiku
    early development of, 174–75
    haiga, 177, *178*, 179
    haiku, 174–77
    renga, 179
    sensitivity and attunement through, 269
    types of, 174
positions. *See* body positioning
postmodernism, 275
posttraumatic stress disorder (PTSD), 236, 238
prana, 22, 90
pranayama, 22, 90–91
pratyahara, 22, 100–102, 207
preferences, letting go of, 201
prefrontal cortex, 122, 238–39, 253

progressive relaxation, 234
Pythagoras, 150–51

Qi. *See also* Qi Gong
    balance and, 213
    breath and, 91
    exercises for, 134–38, *138–44*, 140, 143
    health and, 132–33
    individual vitality and, 253
    as matter and energy, 30–31
Qi Gong, 57–58, 91, 133–48, 208, 270
    Nei Dan, 134, 143, *145–46*, 145–47
    Wei Dan, 134–38, *138–44*, 140, 143
    wholeness contemplation, 147
Qi-sao, 285–87

Radhakrishnan, Sarvepalli, 18, 45
Raimondi, D., 222
Rainforth, M., 260
Raja Yoga, 23
Rama, Swami, 48
Rasa Mandala, 154–55, *155*
Rasa Mandala meditations, 156–57
recognition, 128
redemption, 294
reinterpretation, 191, 207–8
relationships, 272–89
    active-strategic approaches to, 274–75
    analytically-based models of, 273–74
    compassion in, 282
    conflict in, 280–84
    interdependence in, 281
    meditation and, 275–89
    narrative approaches to, 275
    neuroscience of, 276–78
    Qi-sao exercise for, 285–87
    research on meditation with, 278–79
    tension in, 279
    Western approaches to, 272–75
relaxation
    addictions and, 263
    fear/anxiety and, 234, 247
    scientific research on, 50–51
    stress and, 223–25
relaxation response, 221
renga, 174, 179, 287
resistance, to withdrawal of attention, 102
responsibility, 293–96
reward pathway, 253, *254, 255*
Rig Veda, 20
Right Action, 115–17
Right Attitudes, 110–11

Right Effort, 119–20
Right Intent, 111–13
Right Livelihood, 117–18
Right Meditation, 109
Right Speech, 113–15
Right Views, 109–11
Rikyu, 171
Rinzai Zen, 40, 163
rituals, 64, 185, 224. *See also* tea ceremony
Robinson, P., 260
Rogers, Carl, 287
Role Induction Interview, 109
role playing, 189

samadhi, 22
Samuels, M., 81
Samuels, N., 81
samurai, 269
savasana pose, 100, *101*
Schachter, Stanley, 190–91
science. *See also* neuroscience
    cognitive and neuroscience research on meditation,
        50–53
    early interest in Eastern philosophy, 42–44
    meditation as subject of study for, 42, 47–59
    physiological research on meditation, 47–50
    psychological research on meditation, 53–56
    treatment research, 57–58
    types of meditation, 56–57
seeing, 75–77, 128–29
self-actualization, 54–55
self-hypnosis, 87
self, sense of, 266–67, 281, 297
self-worth, 270–71
Seligman, M. E. P., 194
Selye, Hans, 214, 215
senryu, 174
sense of self. *See* self, sense of
sensitivity, 269
sensitization, 252, 254
sensory visualization exercise, 82
septum, 253
serotonin, 193, 254
Shaku Soen, 45
Shakuhachi, 169
Shannahoff-Khalsa, D., 58, 279
Shapiro, D. H., 59
Shapiro, S., 42
shared meditation, 68–69, 288
Shaw, M., 188
Shiki Masaoka, 174, 176

Shin Buddhism, 23
Shri Yantra, 153, *154*
Shri Yantra meditation, 156
Siegel, D., 122
Silberer, Hans, 83–84
Simpkins, C. Alexander, 9, 122, 268, 282, 290
simplicity, 29
sincerity, 292
Singer, Jerome, 190–91
Singer, R., 278
sitting, 71, *72*
somatic marker hypothesis, 122
Soto Zen, 39
sound
    concentration on, 106, 158–60
    significance of, 157–58
specific factors, 12
speech. *See* Right Speech
Squire, L., 212
Ssu Ma Ch'ien, 24
standing, 71, 249–50, 297–98
Stanislavski, Constantin, 103
strategic therapy, 191
stress, 212–31
    acute, 217
    Bodhisattva approach to, 230–31
    chronic, 217
    coping with, 215–17
    early concepts of, 213–15
    episodic, 217
    etymology of, 214
    meditation for reduction of, 221–31
    neuroscience of, 218, *219–20*, 220–21
    pleasure and, 215
    research on meditation for, 221–22
    syndrome of, 214
Strolling in the valley by the stream (Junbi Huang), *291*
Sudarshan Kriya Yoga (SKY), 53
suffering, 261
suggestion, 87–88
Sumi-e, 169
Suzuki, D. T., 45–46, 112
Suzuki, S., 4, 167, 298
Symbolic Alchemy, 26
symbols, 149–60
    hypnagogic imagery and, 84
    representation of reality through, 150–51
    therapeutic use of, 64, 185

Ta-hui, 296
Taiji Quan (Tai Chi Chuan), 133

Tantric Yoga, 81
Tart, Charles, 50
tea ceremony, 68, 169–73, 224
temper, taming, 200–201
Tesshu, 199
therapists
    experiential understanding gained by, 16–17, 39
    meditation benefits for, 2–3, 58, 222
    scientific research on meditation for, 58
    stress reduction for, 222
therapy
    direct and indirect methods, 92
    enlightened, 290–99
    insights in, 38
    meditation types suited for, 63–66, 183–86
    nonspecific factors in, 11–12
    scientific research on meditation for, 57–58
Theravada Buddhism, 34
thought, mindfulness of, 128–30
Tibetan Book of the Dead, 47
Tibetan Buddhism
    development of, 34
    mandalas in, 84, 153, 155
    mantras in, 158–60
    physical feats of, 42, 106
    research on meditation in, 51–52
    Western introduction of, 44, 46–47
time
    effects of meditation over, 239–42
    for meditation, 69
tolerance, 252, 254, 255
trait anxiety, 239
Transcendental Meditation (TM), 23, 55, 56, 222, 260
treatment. *See* therapy
Trope, Y., 186
Twenty-four warriors of Koyo (Tosa Mitsunori), *40*
two-factor theory of emotion, 190–91
Two people, one step. Laozi and the gatekeeper leave the city
    (Kasumi), *24*

unconscious, 85–89
    attending to, 85
    conscious mind vs., 86
    ideomotor response and, 87–89
    unconscious response exercise, 87
    visualization and, 87–88
unity, 18, 43, 280–83
Upanishads, 20

Vedanta, 20–21
Vedas, 20

Vedic meditation, 51
ventral tegmental area, 253
violence, 55–56
Vipassana meditation, 53
visual agnosia, 128–29
visualization, 81–85
    auditory visualization exercise, 82
    breathing and, 96–97
    chanting combined with, 160
    creative invisioning, 83
    Da Vinci's exercise, 84–85
    emptying the mind through, 164–65
    hypnogogic imagery exercise, 84
    intent and, 112–13
    invision and, 82–83
    object invisioning, 83
    passive imagery exercise, 83–84
    pattern reorganization exercises, 85
    preliminary exercise, 81–82
    sensory visualization exercise, 82
    unconscious, 87–88
Vivekananda, 21, 44, 91
voluntary nervous system, 218

Waddell, L. Austine, 43–44
Walker, D., 58
walking, meditative, 106, 224–25
Wallace, B., 42, 292
Walsh, R. N., 59
Watts, A., 285
Wei Dan
    developing awareness of Qi, 134–35
    fear/anxiety and, 246
    moving, 136–38, *138–44*
    recognizing feeling of Qi, 134
    stationary, 140, 143
Weil, Andrew, 237, 259
well-being, 4, 12, 196, 290, 292
Wenger, M. A., 48
wheel of dharma, *109*
Wheel of Existence, 153
White, Michael, 275
Whitehorn, John C., 215
Whorf, B. L., 65–66
willpower, 80
withdrawal, addiction and, 252, 254, 265
withdrawal of attention, 99–102
Witkiewitz, K., 58
Wolff, H., 214
work, 117–18
World Parliament of Religions (Chicago, 1893), 44

Wu Chi Tai Chi Diagram, 29, *30*
wu-wei. *See* nonaction
Wundt, Wilhelm, 79, 80

yamas, 22
Yantra of Creation, 153, *154*
Yantras, 153
Yellow Emperor, 26, 27, 132–33
yin-yang, 18, 27–28. *See also* balance
The Yin-Yang (Simpkins and Simpkins), *28*
Yoga, 20–23. *See also* Yoga meditation
    breath in, 90, 94, 96, 238
    emotional theories in, 192
    limbs (stages) of, 21–22
    mental and physical control through, 22
    Om as mantra in, 105
    types of, 22–23
Yoga meditation
    characteristics of, 17, 23, 184
    physical feats of, 42
    scientific research on, 56, 58
    therapeutic use of, 184
Yoga Sattva, 20
Yoga Sutra of Patanjali, 90
Yoga Sutras, 21–22
Yosa Buson, 173, 175

zazen, 91, 165–66
Zen Buddhism, 36–41. *See also* Zen Buddhist
        meditation
    arts associated with, 39–40, 169–79
    and deconstruction, 38
    and everyday life, 37–38
    gradual cultivation in, 39
    Japanese, 39
    koans in, 40–41, 166, 174
    origins and development of, 36–37
    and poetry, 173–79
    scientific research on, 56–58
    and sudden enlightenment, 38–39
    and tea ceremony, 170–73
    Western introduction of, 47
Zen Buddhist meditation
    breathing in, 91, 97–98
    characteristics of, 184–85
    emptying the mind in, 165–66
    enlightenment through, 37, 39
    scientific research on, 56–58
    therapeutic use of, 184–85
    and unity, 18
    while walking, 106
Zhuangzi, 24, 94, 161, 181, 183, 228, 246,
        280, 295